The Neglected Majority: Essays in Canadian Women's History

Edited by
Susan Mann Trofimenkoff
and Alison Prentice

McClelland and Stewart

© 1977 by McClelland and Stewart Limited
All Rights Reserved

Reprinted 1978

0-7710-8595-8

The Canadian Publishers
McClelland and Stewart Limited
25 Hollinger Road, Toronto

Printed and bound in Canada

Cover photo credit:
"WCTU Convention, Halifax, 1922."
Ruth James Collection, Lunenburg, Nova Scotia.
Courtesy of the Women's Kit Resource Centre,
Ontario Institute for Studies in Education.

Canadian Cataloguing in Publication Data

Main entry under title:

The Neglected majority: essays in Canadian
women's history

(The Canadian social history series)
Bibliography: p.
ISBN 0-7710-8595-8

1. Women-Canada-History-Addresses, essays, lectures.
I. Trofimenkoff, Susan Mann, 1941-
II. Prentice, Alison L., 1934-   III. Series.

HQ1453.N44   301.41'2'0971   C77-000116-5

Contents

Acknowledgements

Many of the essays in this collection have been presented as papers at conferences. Most have also been published previously. We wish to thank the individuals, organizations and periodicals listed below for their encouragement of Canadian women's history and for permission to reprint.

Isabel Foulché-Delbosc, "Women of Three Rivers, 1651-1663". A longer version of this essay, entitled "Women of New France (Three Rivers: 1651-63)" was published in the *Canadian Historical Review,* XXI (June, 1940) pp. 132-49. Editing for this volume has consisted chiefly of paring down the extensive bibliographical notes which appeared in the earlier version.

Sylvia Van Kirk, "The Impact of White Women on Fur Trade Society". This essay was originally published as "Women and the Fur Trade" in *The Beaver* (Winter, 1972) pp. 4-21.

Alison Prentice, "The Feminization of Teaching". An earlier version, entitled "The Feminization of Teaching in British North America and Canada, 1845-1875," was presented to the Tenth Annual Conference of the Canadian Association for American Studies on "Women in North America," University of Ottawa, October, 1974, and was published in *Social History/Histoire sociale,* VIII (May, 1975) pp. 5-20.

D. Suzanne Cross, "The Neglected Majority: The Changing Role of Women in 19th Century Montreal". Earlier versions were presented to the 52nd Annual Meeting of the Canadian Historical Association, Queen's University, June 1973 and published in *Social History/Histoire sociale,* VI (November, 1973) pp. 202-23.

Veronica Strong-Boag, " 'Setting the Stage': National Organization and the Women's Movement in the Late Nineteenth Century," was presented to the Colloquium on "Canadian Society in the Late Nineteenth Century" at McGill University, January, 1975.

Susan Mann Trofimenkoff, "Henri Bourassa and 'the Woman Question' ". An earlier version of this essay was presented to the Ottawa Historical Association, January, 1975. It was first published in the *Journal of Canadian Studies*, x (November, 1975) pp. 3-11.

Mary Vipond, "The Image of Women in Mass Circulation Magazines in the 1920s". This paper was first presented to the Tenth Annual Conference of the Canadian Association for American Studies, on "Women in North America", University of Ottawa, October, 1974, and was published in *Modernist Studies*, I (1974-75) pp. 5-13.

Ruth Pierson, "Women's Emancipation and the Recruitment of Women into the Labour Force in World War II" was presented to the 55th Annual Meeting of the Canadian Historical Association, Laval University, June, 1976.

Introduction

The history of women no longer needs defending. Partly as a result of a women's movement which has inspired women's studies courses and programmes across the western world, and partly because of new directions in historical writing itself, an intriguing new field has emerged, a field which is at once a challenge and a response to a contemporary scholarship increasingly aware of its own past biases.

Reasons for the earlier neglect of women's history are easy to find. They are even understandable. A profession which, since its nineteenth century beginnings, was dominated by one sex was unlikely to take a great interest in the history of the other. And since men, mostly from the upper middle classes, were in charge, they quite naturally defined the boundaries of history in their own terms. Until very recently these were political and diplomatic. Given the limited suffrage and the limited horizons which these same men usually thought proper for their own womenfolk, it is not surprising that few women are to be found in conventional histories. Then too the university setting of much of the early development of the historical profession tended to preclude women. The students were male, heading for careers in the ministry, the liberal professions, politics and diplomacy, all areas barred to women. No wonder women were never mentioned from the lectern or in the textbook. In such a narrowly defined world, women literally had no place.

Some women of course could find a tiny niche within the hallowed ground. The mothers, wives, daughters, or, for the more racy historians, lovers of the great political actors sometimes aroused a stray historian's interest. But that interest was confined to the influence such women exerted, for better or worse, on the prescribed roles of the great men in their lives.[1] On occasion too the suffragettes crept into the history books, but they rarely stayed long enough for any close analysis. Canadians still have to turn to an American – and a woman – for a scholarly, albeit now somewhat dated, account of the woman suffrage movement in this country.[2] But then the women depart, having been charming dancing partners at Confederation balls or importunate ladies summoning their husbands from more important works of state.[3]

One might expect that the newer breed of economic and social historians would pay more attention to women, but they too have seemed reluctant to discard the blinkers of their predecessors. With few exceptions, the economic or labour historian has considered work in the market place to be the only labour worthy of consideration. And even there, where some women could in fact be found, the preoccupation of historians with organized workers has once again kept the door barred. Businesses and labour unions have rarely been run by or for women. And even where they were, historians have generally ignored them.[4]

That most professional historians have been male and have considered the powerful and the organized the only actors worthy of their attention have perhaps been the chief reasons for the neglect of women's history. But they are not the only reasons. When people did attempt to look at women in Canadian history, a number of obstacles stood in their way. The first was the tendency to model historical writing about women on the "great man" approach to history. The result of this tendency has been that many studies of historical women have suffered from a lack of context. Portrayed as heroines or saints, whose every deed was admirable, the subjects of these works seem isolated, their relationship to their society and to the history of their place and time shadowy at best.

The problem of sources has been another major hurdle in the path of women's history. Where the famous may have had a saintly record, the not so famous have often had no record at all. Either documents were not collected in the first place – and archivists are just awakening to their responsibilities in this field – or, more tragically, papers are neglected, uncatalogued, misplaced or even lost. The wrenching of new information from traditional sources has thus been a difficult task, to say nothing of trying new methods on different types of data.

Recent trends in historical scholarship have made it much harder to ignore the role of women, or to use the problems of sources as excuses for inaction. Indeed, with the rapid expansion of social history as a field of enquiry, only the most myopic of scholars can now avoid discussing women. In the history of social class, social mobility, social reform, social organization, the history of education, marriage, children, and the family, women are everywhere. Canadian women have a past. And contemporary women are demanding that this history be made known. Historians will have to take up the challenge of the contemporary women's movement: they will have to discuss and study, write and teach women's history.

The essays in this book are among the first Canadian responses to the challenge. And they are also part of the challenge itself, since all of the authors are women. They are women who insist on knowing about "their" history and who insist upon teaching it. And with their well ingrained historical skepticism – "there must have been more to it than that" – they demand that Canada's past, from the fur trade to the world wars, be enlarged to include women. Without women, the history of education, of reform movements, of ideas, of work itself, is at best severely limited, at worst makes no sense at all.

As the essays in this volume illustrate, women's history is as varied and complex as any other history. It touches all subject areas of the discipline; it entails a variety of approaches and various methods; and, like all good history, it raises as many questions as it answers.

One approach to the history of women is through the history of ideas. As Susan Trofimenkoff's study of Henri Bourassa demonstrates, Canadian thinkers and propagandists often expressed strong views on the nature and role of women. One may look for such opinions in the writings of one person, as Trofimenkoff has done, or in a variety of sources as Mary Vipond does in her investigation of mass circulation magazines of the 1920s. The essay by Alison Prentice in part deciphers the attitudes of educators in the mid-nineteenth century to the role of women in the common schools. All three essays illustrate the thinking of Canadian image makers in periods when ideas about the nature of women and their role in the family and the labour force were clearly in ferment.

But the opinions described inevitably raise questions. How typical were the attitudes portrayed? How influential were they? Were the statements made by educators about women teachers merely attempts to justify changes that had already occurred or were they ahead of their times? Did Bourassa's diatribes represent a minority position, a last ditch stand against existing social transformations? Or was he typical of French Canadian opinion? And how does the picture of Bourassa painted here alter the one we already have of him? Clearly intellectual history can only take us so far in the history of women. Ideas, whether voiced by a majority or a minority, are an important prescription for social behaviour, but they do not necessarily describe that behaviour. Increasingly, therefore, historians have become interested in examining the individual and collective behaviour of women themselves in the past. Did they conform to the roles that the image-makers prescribed for them?

Most of the articles in this book thus also deal with the actions of women. Isabel Foulché-Delbosc's pioneering essay, written long before historical demography became fashionable, looks at early marriage and family patterns in Three Rivers. While her conclusions must be examined in the light of more recent work on the demographic history of New France, her study remains a useful introduction to many of the themes that continue to preoccupy historical demographers and historians of women. What proportion of women in a given community or period married and what was the average age of marriage? How many were widowed and how many remarried? What was the average number of children born to women in the past and how many of their children grew up to become mothers or fathers themselves? Certainly as Foulché-Delbosc suggests, information on changing patterns of marriage and child rearing must be part of any history of women.

Sylvia Van Kirk's essay looks at marriage and the family from another perspective. Her study of the changing marriage patterns of Hudson's Bay Company traders sheds light on the lives of Indian and white women in the west during the early decades of the nineteenth century. It also demonstrates the vital links between married man and economic man: where would the Hudson's Bay Company have been without the necessary and valued co-operation of the traders' Indian wives? The white wives who followed were not quite of the same calibre, perhaps. Yet without Van Kirk's sympathetic analysis of their position, a whole dimension in the development of class and racial barriers in nineteenth century Western Canada would remain unexplored and unexplained.

Marriage was not the only calling for women in the past. The essay by Alison Prentice examines the transformation of public elementary school teaching from a largely male to an increasingly female occupation, while Suzanne Cross looks at women's work outside the family during the period of early industrialization in Montreal. Ruth Pierson also investigates the involvement of women in the labour force, this time during the Second World War; she describes the ways in which agencies of the federal government attempted to manipulate the female labour pool during and after the war. Taken together, these essays and those dealing with marriage and with images of women demonstrate the number and complexity of the forces which determined the changing economic role and status of women in the past.

From the foregoing one might suspect that the essays in this volume portray women merely as the passive victims of ideological, economic or social forces. Yet this is far from the case. A particularly useful approach to the history of women is the study of the organizations and institutions that women themselves have created in an effort to control and improve their lives. The *salles d'asiles* of the Grey Nuns described by Suzanne Cross are tantalizing reminders that Canada has a long history of organized activity by women. Cross also refers briefly to benevolent societies run by Protestant laywomen in mid-nineteenth century Montreal. Such institutions are only now beginning to get the attention they deserve. In her essay on the organizing work that preceded the formation of the National Council of Women, Veronica Strong-Boag analyzes the concerns of women whose response to their own plight and that of their fellow men and women was to organize women nationally, in order to fight the political and social battles that they felt were the only avenues to genuine social reform. Their notion of reform was of course highly coloured by their class; in this way they were little different from their male counterparts of the same era.

If this collection of essays suggests the variety and scope of the work that is currently being done in the history of women, then it will have fulfilled one of its major goals. But we also hope that the articles will suggest to readers how many questions remain to be explored. The early feminization of teaching in Lower Canada, for example, has yet to be satisfactorily explained. How and why did women teachers become numerically dominant in French-Canadian elementary schools several decades before this happened in the English speaking provinces? The apparent entry of large numbers of married women into the labour force in mid-nineteenth century Montreal also needs further study. Are the numbers of children registered in the *salles d'asiles* sufficient evidence that a good many mothers were working outside their own homes? How big was the turnover of children in these early day care centres? Turning to the twentieth century and the impact of World War II on patterns of women's work, here too there are questions. To what extent were the national patterns described by Pierson duplicated in the provinces? How effective were the efforts of the federal government to promote or curtail the entry of women into various kinds of work? Students of

11

women's work have to look not only at attitudes to the sexual division of labour, but also at the organizations which facilitated and the legislation which governed the entry of women into various occupations and professions, and the ways in which all of these changed over the years.

The essays in this volume represent a variety of possible approaches to the history of women, reveal some of the complexity of that history and raise questions for future study. They also reveal the richness of the sources available to the historian of Canadian women. In some cases she or he must go to the writings of men: the parish priests, fur traders, school superintendents, journalists and government officials who have written, preached and legislated on the subject of women. The anxious passion of church and state to count and record the minute dealings of their people has bequeathed tons of statistics to historians. Marriage registers, parish records, school reports and government documents of all sorts are mines of data. Then there are the records kept by the women themselves. Minutes of the meetings of women's organizations, letters and diaries are of a quantity and quality that is only now beginning to be recognized.[5]

If these articles do in fact increase our knowledge about Canadian women's past, indicate some of the questions historians of women are asking, some of the approaches and methods they are using and some of the sources they have unearthed, they all also omit one thing. None of the authors take sides in the debate that swirls around "the meaning of women's history." Has it been a tale of gradual emancipation from a grim past to an ever brighter future – a kind of feminist whiggery? Or has it been a bleak spectre of perpetual or perhaps even increasing oppression? In either case can women be seen as a class or a caste or a minority group? None of these questions is directly confronted in this book. Some may therefore find it disappointing; there are no theoretical models and there are no teleological explanations.

But the editors, admitting their vested interest in two of the essays, believe that the omission is for the time a necessary one. We do not yet know enough about women's experience in the Canadian past to spin vast explanatory webs. We do not know enough even to know whether models from other fields are particularly apt for women's history. What we do know is that women have been members of different majorities and different minorities; they have belonged to all classes and religions and races. Their experiences have varied accordingly, and have also varied across time and place. Women have only their sex in common.

What commonality that has provided is still largely unknown and some of the evidence suggests that it too might be very little. An Indian woman in the prairie west will have had a life very different from that of an Irish domestic in nineteenth century New Brunswick; a factory worker in Montreal, newly arrived from the farm, may have had little in common with the office "girl" of Toronto in the 1920s, even if she too just came from the country. And the club ladies who worried so much about the health, manners and morals of these women lived in totally different worlds from theirs. On the other hand, the "woman question" of the early twentieth century did assume the existence of common problems and interests among women. Frequently their education, occupations, wages and working conditions or political rights had all too clearly been allocated solely on the basis of sex. If the history of women has been essentially diverse, there have also been important common threads.

The only way to discern both the differences and the common causes and to measure their importance for the women concerned, and ultimately perhaps for ourselves, is through extensive historical research into the lives of women in the past and into the ideologies and events that affected them. We think that such research will, in the end, enlarge our understanding of all history. We hope this book will act as a spark.

Susan Mann Trofimenkoff
Alison Prentice

Chapter 1

Women of Three Rivers: 1651-63

Isabel Foulché-Delbosc

There are available sources for the social historian which have as yet been little used and which serve to throw considerable light upon colonial domestic life. These include the notarial and law-court records of Quebec Province, Montreal, and Three Rivers. The following essay relies principally upon the material relating to Three Rivers for the period 1651-63. There are two reasons for this choice of time and place. The first is documentary. Three Rivers is better supplied with early sources both of a judicial and a legal nature than either Quebec or Montreal.[1] The second reason is representative. Three Rivers, the half-way house between Quebec and Montreal, had something in common with each of these two settlements. Established in 1634, it shared with Quebec the tradition of a relatively well-organized corporative system, and with Montreal the precariousness of the frontier. It is therefore a microcosm in which to study the women of New France at a period before special regional characteristics became pronounced. Almost any general statement could be applied equally well to Quebec or Montreal.

The population of Three Rivers in the year 1653 has been estimated at 203 persons, divided into the following categories: married couples, 38; unmarried men, 13; boys, 38; girls, 26; soldiers, 50.[2] Ten years previously there had been no homes, only a wilderness. In 1634 troops and workmen had arrived at the mouth of the river now called the St. Maurice to make a clearing and build a fort and quarters for the garrison. This spot was already known to the fur traders and they soon began to bring their wives and families and build their own dwellings, becoming, in fact, true settlers. Among the first were the Godefroys and their relatives the Le Neuf brothers and their families. These men were fur traders who worked with two of the trusted agents of the Company of New France, Jacques Hertel and François

Marguerie. The latter had a sister Marie at home in Normandy and evidently Hertel decided that she would make him a good wife. A bargain was struck between the two friends. Marguerie was to send for his sister who would take ship plentifully supplied with clothing, linen, and household utensils all to be paid for by the distant brother. The two men made the marriage contract between them and the bride appended her signature upon arrival.[3] Accordingly Marie Hertel, née Marguerie, became the founder of one of the earliest homes in Three Rivers and the mother of some of the first children born there. Gradually the little settlement grew and by 1666 numbered 455 souls.[4] Apparently in thirteen years the population had more than doubled under the most difficult circumstances of harsh frontier life and constant danger from hostile Indians.[5]

It would seem that for women in Three Rivers as throughout New France at this time, all roads led to matrimony. The scarcity of women, the economic difficulties of existence, the danger, tended to produce the same result: all girls became wives, all widows remarried; so that the study of women becomes a study of the legal and social effects of marriage.[6] To be sure a few girls in subsequent years chose the vocation of nun, particularly some of those who had been boarded with the Ursulines or *Hospitalières* at Quebec, but they must always have been a very small proportion of the feminine population.[7]

The girls who married in Three Rivers before the year 1658 had, of course, been born elsewhere.[8] There were a few Canadian-born among them but most had come from France.[9] A distinction may be made between the girls whose families resided in New France, whether they were born in Canada or not, and those who had immigrated alone to the New World. At this particular period, before any definite effort was made by the home authorities to provide wives for the soldiers and settlers of New France, the unattached girls seem to have been brought out by individual arrangement as *engag*ées to work in the household of one or other of the settlers. They too usually married, but not until their early twenties, an age appreciably older than that customary among the Canadian-born girls.[10] A marriage contract drawn up on February 2, 1651, between Blaise Juliet and Antoinette de Liercourt mentions the fact that the latter was domiciled at the fort. The principal witness to the contract was Jacques Le Neuf "écuyer sieur de La Potterie, gouverneur du fort et habitation des Trois Rivières," and it seems probable that Antoinette had been employed by the Governor's family. In the marriage contracts drawn up by Ameau between 1653 and 1662, three girls are described at different times as living in the house of Pierre Boucher, at that time Commandant of the fort and interim Governor, etc.[11] Another girl was mentioned as residing in the house of Jean Godefroy, Sieur de Lintot, an important fur trader and landowner.[12] These colonists were likely to have had domestic servants and probably the girls were employed in that capacity. Presumably they had completed their contracted period of service as there is no record of any legal difficulties with their employers.

Fortunately for the historian, however, there do exist records of certain disputes which reached the courts and which enable us to reconstruct a few details in the lives of domestic servants of the period. Perhaps the domestic servant problem has never been more acute than it was in New France during the seventeenth century. Marriage was the arch-enemy and employers fought it tooth and nail – or to be more exact, with legal weapons.

Michel Le Neuf, Sieur du Hérisson, the local judge, needed a servant. While on a visit to Quebec he discovered what he sought in the person of Anne Le Sont, a woman of mature years. Evidently sure that he would not repent of his bargain, he induced the willing Anne to sign a contract on November 21, 1655, not for two or three years, but for life. But Michel Le Neuf had not chosen the one kind of contract that would really have bound Anne for life. She had scarcely reached Three Rivers when she was tempted to break her perpetual bond for another. Anne Le Sont changed hands and changed her name. She was now Mme. Jean Desmarais. The disgruntled judge appealed to the court and produced his bond. He tried to prevent the marriage banns, claiming that the bridegroom had left a wife in France; besides (unkindest cut of all!) that the bride was at least sixty. The Jesuit Father Gareau satisfied himself that Jean Desmarais was not a bigamist and performed the ceremony, even dispensing with one of the three banns while the case was still *sub judice*. Desmarais volunteered to indemnify Michel Le Neuf but Anne, whose feelings had been outraged, descended to vituperation against her former employer. The matter was finally settled by Pierre Boucher on May 15, 1656: the bridegroom was to pay the Sieur du Hérisson 24 *livres*, 10 *sols*, which the latter had advanced to Anne Le Sont in Quebec and 50 *livres* to indemnify him for the number of objects lost by her while in his service. Anne was to pay also for the notarial costs in drawing up the perpetual bond. She was to pay the above sums less the 20 pounds due her for her four months of actual service. Finally the Sieur du Hérisson was to restore her personal effects and she was to apologize to him in court for her insulting words.[13]

François Le Maître, called le Picard, a soldier in the garrison of Three Rivers and a master tailor, desiring to set up house and home prevailed upon one Judithe Rigault to marry him. Judithe was an *engagée* in the service of the Governor's wife, Mme Le Neuf de La Poterie, and had bound herself to five years of service at 30 *livres* per year. Of this time there were still two years and five months uncompleted. Mme Le Neuf was particularly incensed at the desertion because as a result of her sea voyage the unfortunate girl had been incapacitated for two months after her arrival, and had required medical attention. Furthermore her services, after her recovery, had been lent to Mme d'Ailleboust of Montreal for a period of nine months; and now her departure coincided with the busy season of the sowing. Mme de La Poterie had spent considerable money on Judithe's behalf: 119 *livres*, 9 *sols*, and 7 *deniers* for clothing and other things needed for the journey to Canada and 30 *livres*, 13 *sols* as an advance on the passage money. The indignant mistress therefore seized Judithe's personal effects and took the matter to the *Lieutenant civil et criminel* at Three Rivers, even asking compensation for the objects broken by Judithe during her service. Judgment was rendered on June 9, 1654. Judithe was not to be paid for the two months of her illness nor for the nine months she had served Mme d'Ailleboust, making it necessary in the latter case for Judithe to claim the money herself. She was to pay Mme de La Poterie for the expenses incurred on her behalf after deducting her wages. Judithe and her husband appealed this decision to the Governor-General in Quebec and Jean de Lauzon pronounced final sentence on July 21, 1654. Strangely enough at Three Rivers both parties seem to have agreed that the bond was for three years. It had been discovered in the meantime and when produced at Quebec proved to be for five years. This raised the assessment for advance on passage money, etc., which seems to have been calculated on the basis of the total amount of wages. It was now assessed at 31 *livres*, 8 *sols*, 4 *deniers*. [14] Judithe was given credit for the time of her illness as well as for the period of her service in Montreal, so that it was now the mistress who would have to seek reimbursement from Mme d'Ailleboust. As Mme de La Poterie had not opposed the banns and as she had witnessed the marriage contract, she was given no indemnity for the unexpired period of the bond, and she was to restore Judithe's personal property. The latter was to repay her former mistress for the clothing and other things advanced to her as well as for the passage money, first deducting 77 *livres*, 10 *sols*, her wages for two years, seven months of service.[15]

How did colonists procure their servants in France? Generally, it would seem, through the good offices of a settler returning to France on business. Such persons would usually have a host of commissions to perform and among them the hiring of a man or maidservant and the advance of the necessary money for clothing, food, and passage. The wages mentioned in the bonds seem to have varied considerably. Mme de La Poterie paid Judithe Rigault at the rate of 30 pounds a year but the same lady paid Jeanne Godin, another *engagée*, at double that amount. Anne Le Sont had been paid 60 pounds a year. Not infrequently we find colonists settling their debts by means of their servants' labour. For instance, if A owed B money he could send him his bond-servant free of charge for a specified period; or if B had no need of a servant and wished to escape his obligation to one already under bond to him, A could promise to take the servant off his hands, thus discharging his debt to B.[16]

If a bond of three or five years tended to provide brides in their twenties, and if the difficulties of the voyage tended to prevent very young French girls from visiting friends or relatives in New France, there was nothing to prevent the marriage of Canadian-born girls at a tender age. Indeed, it was apparently common for the latter to marry at puberty. Most Canadian girls married between the ages of twelve and sixteen, thirteen being the age most frequently chosen. Among the brides of Three Rivers, Marguerite Crevier married Jacques Fournier at the age of twelve; at the time of her second marriage she was sixteen. Her sister Marie married Nicolas Gatineau when she was thirteen. Marie Vien married Jean Lanqueteau at the age of thirteen and was widowed at fifteen. Many other examples could be given.[17] There are even cases of marriage contracts made when the prospective bride was too young for marriage so that the execution of the contract would be held in abeyance for a year or two until the bride had reached the age of twelve or thirteen. This was the case with Madeleine Hertel whose contract was drawn up on June 11, 1657,[18] when she was not quite twelve and who was married October 29, 1658.[19] A proof of the general attitude of the settlers as to the proper age for the marriage of their daughters is to be found in the following item from the marriage contract made in 1653 by Gillette Baune, widow of Marin Chauvin, and Jacques Bertant, relative to the care of her daughter by the first marriage in case she should predecease her new husband: "Ont accordé en outre lesdictes parties que si ladicte Baune vient à décéder avant que ladicte Marie Chauvin, sa fille du premier lict, ayt atteint l'age de douze ans, ledict Bertant sera obligé de la nourrir jusques à l'age de douze ans."[20] At twelve, the marriageable age, her future need give no anxiety.

The poorer the family, the more advantageous an early marriage for the daughters, for the scarcity of women laid the whole burden of support upon the husband, not upon the father. New France was the country of the *douaire* not of the *dot*. In fact, it is possible that this frontier situation sometimes worked to the disadvantage of daughters for the benefit of sons.[21]

One would like to know something of the life of these little girls before they married. Perhaps the Jesuit Fathers who taught them their catechism also gave them the rudiments of letters. Two of them with illiterate mothers were able to sign their names to their marriage contracts at a fairly early age.[22] As they were soon to have the direction of a household, it is permissible to assume that they helped their mothers, who, in their state of recurrent pregnancy, would require help with the cooking, the cleaning, the washing, the care of the animals, and the gardening.

Widows at Three Rivers in the sixteen-fifties were, alas, numerous. But permanent widowhood was almost as unusual in the colony as spinsterhood.[23] Even Pierre Boucher, the patriarch, making his will in 1688, envisaged the possibility of remarriage for his widow who had borne him fifteen children.[24] Of the twenty-three marriage contracts drawn up by Ameau between 1653 and 1662, twelve were those of widows and the same proportion was maintained in the marriage register. Not infrequently women had three husbands and there was at least one case of a woman with four.[25]

In France both law and custom discouraged remarriage, but conditions in Canada and the fact that there was no religious bar seem to have affected not only the custom but the legal practice as well. In order to safeguard the property of minors whose rights might be adversely affected by the remarriage of a parent, Francis II in 1560 issued what was called the *Edit des Secondes Noces*.[26] This edict prevented the second wife or husband from having a larger share in the property of the first marriage than any one of the children of that marriage. As most early Canadian widows had small children, they would come under this edict as well as under the Custom of Paris.

If remarriage is hardly astonishing, we cannot but be impressed with the precipitation attending it. The codified Custom of Paris did not require any specific lapse of time before remarriage as did certain laws in the *pays du droit écrit*. However, under the Custom of Paris it was usual for the widow to spend a year of mourning before marrying again. Otherwise she might endanger her rights in any legal controversy over the inheritance. In Three Rivers during our period, however, it was the rule to marry well within the year. Some widows remarried within three months and others even sooner.[27] No doubt this precipitation was due in large part to the atmosphere of constant danger and the relative helplessness of a young widow with small children to protect herself and her family, cultivate the farm, etc. No woman could do this single-handed.

These were terrible years. Ever since 1642 the Iroquois had been continually on the warpath. In 1648-49 the Hurons were attacked and dispersed, the Jesuits martyred. In 1652 the Governor of Three Rivers and fifteen companions lost their lives in an ambush. In 1653 the town was besieged. Pierre Boucher, the hero of this siege, obtained a truce but one that was not long observed. Enemy bands even went as far as the outskirts of Quebec. In 1656 the Hurons were butchered on the Isle of Orleans. In 1660 Dollard and his companions made their heroic stand at Long Sault. An Iroquois arrow made many a widow.

Marie Denot, wife of Etienne Vien, one of the early landowners of Three Rivers, lost her husband, probably in 1652. She had two daughters, Marie, thirteen years old, and Marie-Madeleine, a baby of two. The elder became the wife of Jean Lanqueteau (or Lanctot) probably only a short time before her mother's second marriage to Mathieu Labat, in the beginning of 1653. Both mother and daughter were soon widowed. Jean Lanqueteau was killed by the Iroquois on November 23, and Mathieu on December 9, 1654. The twice-widowed Marie Denot with two daughters and an imminent grandchild chose a protector and third husband in Louis Ozanne. She also found a husband for her widowed daughter who had recently been delivered of a son, François. On January 26, 1655, there was a double wedding in the parish church: Louis Ozanne became the mother's third husband and Philippe Etienne the second husband of the daughter.[28] Many other such cases may be found in the judicial archives of Three Rivers.

Thus the solution chosen or forced upon the individual with regard to his personal problems when repeated by many is seen to have solved the problem of the community. The problem of New France at this critical moment was one of simple existence; the miracle is that the colony was not wiped out completely. It is astonishing that population could be maintained and increased at a time when there was very little immigration, and probably a high infant mortality.[29] Since 1645, when the Company of New France handed over the trade of the colony to its inhabitants, little emphasis was laid upon the obligation to colonize.[30] Intending settlers were likely to have their ambition cooled by the *Jesuit Relations* with their tales of the Iroquois terror. Population was increased within the colony by a kind of unconscious mobilization of every available woman. The history of the remarried widows shows that the process of child-bearing was little interrupted by exterior catastrophe. The very early marriages in making use of the entire period of fertility had the result of increasing the birthrate.

These second and third marriages created certain interesting problems with respect to the children, and these problems were solved in various ways. When the inheritance was so small that a division of the property between widow and children according to law would have rendered difficult the maintenance of the family, it was usual to let it go in bulk to maintain the new household and allow it to be inherited equally by the children of both marriages. No guardian would be appointed; the second husband would assume responsibility for the welfare of his wife's first family and would administer their property with his own. Thus Laurent Leclerc in his marriage contract with the widow Bourgery declared that: "en considerant que les enfans provenus dudict feu Bourgery n'ont pas de bien sufisamment pour les nourrir et entretenir, il a promis après ledict mariage accompli et consommé prendre soin d'eslever, nourrir et entretenir lesdicts enfans sur le bien qui leur pourra appartenir, quoy que bien petit, et ne soit suffisant pour y subvenir, auquel ils obéiront comme à leur proper père et luy rendront service convenable."[31]

A widow of means, which usually meant one with considerable land, would generally appear before the judge shortly after her husband's death and ask the appointment of a guardian and that an inventory be made of her husband's estate. The judge would summon a meeting of the deceased husband's relatives and friends who would choose a guardian (*tuteur*) and a sub-guardian (*subrogé-tuteur*). As a rule the widow was chosen guardian and some prominent inhabitant sub-guardian. These two were present at the drawing up of the inventory as well as one or two others appointed for the purpose by the assembly of family and friends. The furniture, livestock, etc., were divided equally, half for the widow and half for the children as a group. This division was made either in kind or in some kind of legal tender after an auction. Real estate was also divided into equal parts, sometimes with ludicrous consequences as in the case of little Jeanne

Isabel. Jeanne's guardian and her step-father, the latter representing her mother's interest, drew lots for the partitioning of a house and land, with the result that the south-west side of the house and the north-east side of the land fell to the mother, the daughter inheriting the remaining halves. Consequently each party had to cede a strip of land to the other in order to reach their respective doors.[32] The Custom of Paris forbade a remarried widow to act as guardian of her former husband's children and so upon her remarriage, if she had been guardian, it was necessary to have another family council for the selection of a new guardian, frequently the step-father, some relative of the deceased husband, or some representative settler. The guardian had to look after the children's property and render an account of his administration to them when they had attained their majority or at an earlier period to the family council if so required by that body.

The children usually lived with their mother who was given an allowance out of the estate for their board – usually at this period 120 *livres* a year for each child. If the children were placed elsewhere, the same amount was alloted to the family boarding them.[33]

Naturally many households contained the children of two or more marriages. In one case at least, the situation was considered too complicated. Médard Chouart, Sieur de Groseilliers, the noted pilot, explorer, and fur-trader married Mme Véron de Grandmesnil, a widow with two small boys. Their step-father, who seems to have been a man of violent temper, disagreed with his wife about their upbringing. The final result was an appeal to the judge who gave the children into the care of their guardian with the stipulation that the latter be paid the usual 120 *livres* a year for each child.[34] Perhaps the boys returned to their mother's care during the Sieur de Groseillier's lengthy absences. At any rate she was living with the children of both marriages in 1667.[35]

In the interests of completeness, something should be said of the category of women who are neither wives nor maids. Apparently they were non-existent in New France at this period. The influence of church and civil authorities, the conditions that made for early marriage, all tended to exclude such women. Every woman sent from France to Canada was a prospective settler's wife and her morals were investigated before she was allowed to sail. Pierre Boucher was categorical upon this point. It was customary to have the friends and relatives of the girls certify as to their moral character before they embarked. If they turned out to be undesirable, they were returned to France. The home authorities applied a different yardstick to the girls, depending upon whether they were destined for Canada or the West Indies.[36] In 1658 d'Argenson wrote to his brother that a merchant from La Rochelle had landed a *fille enceinte* and that her prospective employer had objected; the Governor himself was indignant – Canada was not to be a second St. Kitt's! He ordered the girl to be deported.[37] The *Relation* of 1654 says that in the space of eighteen years the executioner had exercised his office only twice when he had publicly flogged two "bad women" and that these were later banished.[38] Some attempt, too, was made to control or banish morally undesirable men. This was more difficult as the little colony could ill spare any fighters. In Montreal in the middle of the century where the dangers of geographic position made the tension greater and where Maisonneuve established an atmosphere of moral and religious rectitude, we find condemnations of a type not found among the documents at Three Rivers, although there are instances of violent deeds at the neighbouring Cap de la Madeleine and there is one case of adultery.[39] Doubtless the more westerly and dangerous post was likely to harbour the wilder sort of colonist. The records contain condemnations for gambling, bigamy, adultery, and for the solicitation of married women – Mistress Page and Mistress Ford dragging their Falstaff before the tribunal.[40] The fifteen-year-old girl who was publicly whipped at Quebec in 1649 for theft, had her name coupled with that of one of the married citizens of the capital. The man was lodged in prison to await his trial.[41] This girl may have been one of the two mentioned above as being deported at a later date.

But if banishment was a suitable solution for habitual sinners, it could scarcely be applied to the unfortunate or impetuous and inexperienced girl. What happened to these? No doubt they usually married. Marriage was easily accessible, far more so than in France. The practice of granting dispensation of one or two banns, which was done both under the Jesuit administration and later under the bishop, probably forestalled an occasional minor disgrace. In a settlement where warfare was constant, where the difficulty of communication rendered useless the lapse of time required by the banns, the church granted dispensation easily and as matter of policy, and in any case, wisely.[42] The Abbé Ferland in his study of the baptismal records of Notre Dame de Québec from 1621 to 1661 has found only one illegitimate child among 674 births.[43] Generally speaking, any illicit intercourse with women had to take place beyond the bounds of the settlements, that is, among the Indians. There were even a few cases of carousals involving Indian women and settlers, in the houses of the latter.[44] Governor La Poterie had tried to prevent such occurrences by an ordinance of 1662 forbidding the inhabitants under any circumstances to receive the natives in their houses after nightfall.[45]

One might have expected that the hasty marriages of very young persons would have produced many disappointments with subsequent broken homes as a result. This was not the case. There are few known cases of legal separation of husband and wife. Marguerite Crevier who married Jacques Fournier in 1657 returned to the house of her parents in 1660. This marriage was later annulled and both parties remarried.[46]

It is not possible, within the limits of this paper, to discuss in detail the houses within which the colonial women lived and worked. That their dwellings were simple and unadorned we would assume even if precise evidence were lacking. Few had any upper storey. Most contained a stable partitioned from the living quarters and located in a northern corner. Fireplaces were, of course, the only means of heating or cooking. Chimneys were of clay and this fact together with the extreme cold of the winters and the inflammable nature of the thatch or shingle roof caused many fires. Window glass may have been used by the wealthy but apparently oiled paper or thin parchment was sometimes employed as a window covering. Floors and interior walls were made of boards as were the partitions separating the living and sleeping quarters. The absence of beds in the inventories may be accounted for by assuming that the colonists used built-in bunks along the walls. Of course the wealthier families had beds and other fine furniture brought from France. Chairs seem to have been very rare. Evidently long backless benches served instead. Chests of all sizes were used for a variety of storage purposes, as indeed was the case in Europe at this time. Utensils were almost all of metal. Cooking pots were of iron or copper as were the bit spoons and ladles. Spits and hooks were of iron. There was almost no earthenware. Practically everything for the table was made of pewter: forks, spoons, cups, plates, porringers, as well as the measuring cups used in cooking. There is only one mention of silver articles, in connection with the Hertel family, and these consisted of only two goblets, six spoons, and three forks.

Doubtless the poverty and simplicity of house and furnishings reduced the amount of indoor labour required of the women. But their tasks always included gardening and tending the cows, pigs, and chickens. The vegetable gardens evidently always included cabbages, and possibly beans as well as a few root crops such as turnips, onions, and carrots. As yet there were no potatoes.[47] The washing of personal and household linen was women's work. Some earned a little money by doing the laundry of members of the garrison. Very likely the women assembled on the river bank to do their washing as they did in France.

At this period there were no sheep in the colony, no flax, and no hemp. Consequently there were no hand-looms or spinning-wheels. The home industries developed later. Textiles had to be imported from France. From these the women made dresses for themselves and their children as well as shirts and underwear for the men. Men's outer dress – doublets and hose, coats and hats – had to be brought out from France. They were very scarce and costly in the colony. Worn clothing, sold after a man's death, fetched a price which seems excessive in terms of other commodities.[48] The materials used for women's clothing seem to have been chosen for durability rather than colour or beauty. They included: *crézeau* (serge or kersey), *grisette* (cheap gray stuff), *treillis* (sackcloth, buckram), *ras de Châlons* (napless material, shalloon), *toile de Mélis* (sail-cloth).

The scarcity of specie made barter a common practice and there were cases of women exchanging grain or vegetables for manufactured goods which another family had imported. In summer French merchants arrived to trade furs for merchandise but this is probably because furs were legal tender, not because the women were in the fur trade. There was at least one outstanding exception in Jeanne Enard, wife of Christophe Crevier, Sieur de la Meslée, mother of six children and mother-in-law of Pierre Boucher. By her husband's own avowal she was the business head of the family both as regards the fur trade and household management.[49] Another woman, Mathurine Poisson, wife of Jacques Aubuchon, was a recognized merchant and sold imported goods to the colonists. She acted in her own name and had no need for her husband's permission in her dealings.[50]

We can visualize these women going about their daily errands on foot or by boat on the river highway, on snowshoes in the winter, assembling on invitation to witness a marriage contract, turning out in force for baptisms, weddings, and funerals as well as High Mass on Sunday mornings, after which public notices were cried and posted, and auctions held. We can see them gossiping with the neighbours and returning home to cook the mid-day meal – all very much as if they were at home in France instead of in the heart of the Canadian wilderness surrounded by hostile Iroquois. Through all these documents they appear very human. Sometimes litigious to the point of absurdity, they thus reveal the piquant details of their lives and themselves as well. Some of them stand out with startling clearness. Mme Christophe Crevier, estimable wife and mother, was apparently disagreeable in business relations, a termagant. Mme des Groseilliers, the first advocate of women's rights, attains her moments of grandeur. During those troubled times, it was these women (who else?) who nursed the sick and wounded, cooked for the colony's defenders, cared for the children, acted as midwives. It was they who looked after the household and the family business during their husbands' long absences. We must regret that the records are so meagre of these achievements. It was no light accomplishment to have bequeathed to later generations the traditions of the French household, built up of the thousand and one events of ordinary human living.

These traditions were strongly individualistic and included a keen sense of property. Boundaries had to be maintained; goods or produce damaged had to be paid for; slandered reputations atoned for. For them, the family was the first loyalty. The one collective institution which flourished during the period and which has remained to this day – the guardianship of minors – is essentially a family matter. But in the early years of the colony, before families had many ramifications, we find outsiders devoting their time and energy to the interests of little children with praise-worthy zeal.

This essay has attempted to give a general view of women's life and work in Three Rivers during the early critical years when marriage dominated the lives of women and forced all other occupations, except that of the religious life, out of existence. The women of the struggling colony had to fulfil their destiny as wives and mothers during a longer period of their lives than is required of most women of European stock. Often married at twelve or thirteen they continued their careers uninterrupted even by major calamities. Few in number as they were, they assumed successfully the task of populating the colony.

Chapter 2

The Impact of White Women
on Fur Trade Society

Sylvia Van Kirk

During the early period of the fur trade, the white man in pene-
trating the wilds of Western Canada, faced a situation in which,
for practical purposes, the social norms of European civilization
were no longer operable. Since colonization was not envisaged,
no white women accompanied the fur traders. Family units
which would have reflected, in however rough a state, their former domestic life were impossible. Instead, the traders were
forced to come to terms with an alien, nomadic culture; their
livelihood depended upon the very existence of the Indian whose
way of life gave him distinct advantages in coping with the wilderness environment. In this light, the Indian woman played an
important role as a liaison between the two cultures. Trained as
she was in the skills necessary for survival, a native woman,
while filling the role of wife and mother left void by the absence
of white women, was uniquely qualified to help the white trader
adapt to the exigencies of life in Rupert's Land.

The men of the Montreal-based North West Company, who
had inherited the framework and traditions of the French colonial fur trade, had always appreciated the economic advantages
to be gained by forming alliances with Indian women. Besides
helping to secure the trade of her tribe or band, the Indian
woman did much to familiarize the Nor'wester with Indian life
and, in teaching him the native tongue, greatly contributed to his
effectiveness as a trader. In contrast, the London Committee, the
remote ruling body of the Hudson's Bay Company, had early
forbidden any dealings between its servants and Indian women
on the grounds that the expense which would accrue from their
support plus the possible danger of affronting Indian sensibilities
outweighed any advantages to be derived. In practice, this regulation proved difficult to enforce. Although it prevented the
practice of taking Indian wives from becoming widespread

within the lower ranks of the English company, keeping an Indian woman became the prerogative of an officer in charge of a post.[1]

When forced into open competition with the Nor'Westers in the late decades of the 18th century, the Hudson's Bay Company was compelled to modify its policy towards Indian women. In attempting to recruit the highly-prized French-Canadian voyageur into its service, the Company was made aware that the right to have an Indian helpmate was not one which the Canadian would relinquish lightly,[2] and this attitude influenced its own men. In 1802, the council at York Factory appealed to the London Committee, stressing that their Indian women were in fact "your Honors Servants" and played an important economic role in the struggle against the rival concern:

> ... they clean and put into a state of preservation all Beavr. and Otter skins brought by the Indians undried and in bad Condition. They prepare Line for Snow shoes and knit them also without which your Honors servants could not give efficient opposition to the Canadian traders they make Leather shoes for the men who are obliged to travel about in search of Indians and furs and are useful in a variety of other instances...[3]

By the time of the union of the two companies in 1821, taking a native woman for a wife was a widespread social practice, known as marriage à la facon du pays. Although it might involve the payment of a bride price, a country marriage was an informal arrangement whereby a couple agreed to cohabit for an unspecified length of time. It derived from the Indian concept of marriage and was but one example of the extent to which the social mores and customs of the Indians influenced the norms of fur trade society. As the explorer Sir John Franklin remarked, the white man seemed "to find it easier to descend to the Indian customs, and modes of thinking, particularly with respect to women, than to attempt to raise the Indians to theirs."[4] The first missionaries, who arrived relatively late in Rupert's Land, were horrified by what they considered to be the Europeans' uncivilized treatment of their Indian wives.[5] Such usage, however, reflected the position of women in Indian society. Partly through economic necessity, they were subjected to an endless round of domestic drudgery, even to the extent of being reduced to beasts of burden. The excuse was advanced that if the white man displayed tender feelings towards his wife, the Indian, to whom such notions were foreign would despise him.[6] It is likely, however, that within the fur trade post, European conventions did tend to ameliorate the Indian woman's lot, particularly in the higher ranks of the service where she would have shared in her husband's privileges.

Although, there were occasions (especially during the drunken days of the trade war) when Indian women were abused by the traders, in general, an unwritten code of honour developed; marriage à la façon du pays was considered to be as binding as any church ceremony in the Indian Country. There were many examples of a lasting and honorable relationship developing between the white trader and his Indian helpmate. The domestic pleasures of family life undoubtedly did much to reconcile the European to the isolated and monotonous life of a fur trade post.[7]

The greatest social problem occurred when the trader retired from Rupert's Land. It became customary to forsake one's Indian family for it proved extremely difficult for the wife in particular to make the transition to "civilised" living whether in Great Britain or the Canadas.[8] In the early days of the fur trade, when widowed or abandoned, an Indian wife with her children had been welcomed back into her tribe. This became increasingly rare as the structure of Indian society crumbled through the effects of European contact. It was also not feasible for the half-breed woman, who knew little of life outside the fur trade post, and from whose growing ranks many wives were chosen in the early decades of the 19th century. A practice which was dubbed "turning off" arose, by which the retiring husband endeavoured to assure that his spouse was placed under the protection of or became the country wife of another fur trader. Such had been the fate of the kind-hearted washerwoman Betsey, who when Letitia Hargrave encountered her at York Factory in 1840 was not sure whether her last protector had been her fourth or fifth husband.[9] Although it was fairly common for fathers to bequeath some money for the maintenance of their country-born children, they were not legally compelled to do so. As a result, during the decades immediately preceding the union of the two companies, the number of deserted women and children being maintained at the expense of the posts, especially those of the North West Company, reached alarming proportions. In an attempt to reduce this heavy economic burden, the North West proprietors ruled as early as 1806 that in future its servants were to choose only half-breed women as wives. They also contemplated the creation of a settlement in the Rainy Lake area where their superannuated servants, particularly the French-Canadian voyageurs, could

29

retire with their Indian families.[10]

The whole question was pushed into the background by the struggle for the control of the fur trade, but when the Hudson's Bay Company absorbed its rival in 1821, the London Committee recognized that steps must be taken to solve this pressing social problem if only for reasons of economy and security:

> We understand that there are an immense number of Women and Children supported at the different Trading Posts, some belonging to men still in the Service and others who have been left by the Fathers unprotected and a burden on the Trade. It becomes . . . a serious consideration how these People are to be disposed of. . . .[11]

Philanthropic considerations also influenced Company policy at this time, mainly through the efforts of Benjamin Harrison, a prominent member of the Committee and an associate of the Clapham Sect. He played an important part in developing a plan for the settlement of these families in the fledgling colony of Red River which had been founded in the previous decade by the idealistic Lord Selkirk. A Catholic mission already existed to minister to the large French-Canadian sector and several Anglican clergymen were sent out under Company auspices who, with the help of the Church Missionary Society, were to establish a school for orphan children.[12] In a marked change of policy, the London Committee also encouraged those servants who did not wish to retire in Rupert's Land to take their families with them provided they possessed sufficient means for their support.[13]

At the same time, as part of its program of economy and consolidation, the Committee endeavoured to divest the Company of any further responsibility for the support of the families of the traders who remained at the various posts. Although they acknowledged that those few women who performed really essential services might be paid in goods or provisions, in future each man was to clothe his family on his own private account, and a proportional tax was to be imposed to cover the cost of provisions.[14] They also proposed the creation of a pro-rated benefit fund to provide for the maintenance of a wife and family in the event of the decease of the husband or his retirement from the country.[15] The men, however, objected to being forced to make an annual payment toward the present or future support of their families, the lower ranks, in particular, claiming that their salaries were not high enough to bear this additional expense. The Committee eventually acquiesced on this point, but only after it was established as a general rule:

That no Officer or Servant in the company's service be hereafter allowed to take a woman without binding himself down to such reasonable provision for the maintenance of the woman and children as on a fair and equitable principle may be considered necessary not only during their residence in the country but after their departure hence. . . .[16]

The Hudson's Bay Company gave official status to marriage *à la façon du pays* by the introduction of a marriage contract which emphasized the husband's economic responsibilities. Although there is some variation in the actual format of the certificates which survive in the Company's records, usually both parties signed or made their mark on a document which declared that the woman was recognized as one's legal wife.[17] In retrospect since the Hudson's Bay Company was vested with governmental power over Rupert's Land, these contracts can be seen as an early form of civil marriage. The prerogative of the Church in this sphere, however, was acknowledged by the proviso that the couple would undertake to be married by a clergyman at the first possible opportunity.[18]

The Company's first chaplain, the Rev. John West, considered this to be one of his most pressing duties upon his arrival in the Indian Country in the fall of 1820; "the institution of marriage", he proclaimed, along with "the security of property" were "the fundamental laws" of any civilized society.[19] When he left Rupert's Land three years later, the worthy parson had performed a total of sixty-five marriages, among them those of several prominent settlers in Red River, former Company officers who had continued to live with their Indian wives *à la façon du pays*. His success was greeted with approbation by Nicholas Garry, a visiting member of the London Committee, who considered the practices of the Indian Country most demoralizing:

. . . Mr. West has done much good in persuading these Gentlemen to marry . . . thus introducing more proper Feelings and preventing that Debasement of Mind which must, at last, have rooted out every honorable and right Feeling. Perhaps nothing shows Debasement of Mind so much as their having lived themselves in an unmarried state, giving up their Daughters to live the same Life as their Mothers, and this Feeling, or rather its Justification, had become general all over the Country. . . .[20]

Clearly the moral code of fur trade society was in a state of confusion. It was the missionaries themselves who emphasized the concept of "living in sin", for many fur traders, and certainly the Indians, considered a country marriage to be a legal and honorable union. While officially the Company was attempting to introduce accepted Christian standards into fur trade life, as can be seen in a list of regulations designed to effect "the civilization and moral improvement" of the families attached to the various posts,[21] it is difficult to estimate the actual success of these measures. Although the social and religious conventions of European society were undoubtedly taking hold in the basically agrarian settlement of Red River, the old norms of fur trade society persisted, especially in isolated areas. In 1825 George Simpson, the Governor of the Northern Department, advised that any missionary appointed to the Columbia District across the Rockies would be wise to let the custom of the country alone:

... he ought to understand in the outset that nearly all the Gentlemen & Servants have Families altho' Marriage ceremonies are unknown in the Country and that it would be all in vain to attempt breaking through this uncivilized custom.[22]

When Simpson was appointed Governor of the vast territories of the Northern Department in 1821, he had had only one year of experience in the Indian Country as a trader in opposition to the Nor'Westers on Lake Athabasca. He soon proved himself a capable administrator, and his hard-headed, often pragmatic approach to business is reflected in his official views on the position of Indian women in fur trade society.

Simpson's journal of his winter in Athabasca reveals his appreciation of the valuable economic role played by Indian women in the functioning of the fur trade. Besides performing such routine tasks as making moccasins and collecting *wattappe* for sewing the birch-bark canoes, they were essential as interpreters. In enumerating the reasons for the strong position of the Nor'Westers at Fort Chipewyan, Simpson declared:

... their Women are faithful to their cause and good Interpreters whereas we have but one in the Fort that can talk Chipewyan....[23]

This one was the crafty Madam Lamallice, the wife of the brigade guide, who was not only adept at hoarding provisions but even managed to carry on a private trade. Simpson, concerned that this couple, who possessed much influence over the Indians, might desert to the rival concern, was forced to wink at these misdemeanors and urged the disgruntled post commander to humor them with flattery and a few extra rations.[24]

In making plans to extend the Company's trade into the remote areas of New Caledonia and McKenzie's River, formerly

the preserve of the North West Company, the Governor emphasized the value of marriage alliances. Early in the spring of 1821,
he engaged the French-Canadian Pering [Perrin] to help establish a depot on Great Slave Lake primarily because his wife was
"extensively connected amongst the Yellow Knife and
Chipewyan tribes in that quarter ... and will be enabled to
remove any prejudice that our Opponents may have instilled on
their minds against us."[25] Viewing the Committee's policy of dis-
couraging liaisons with Indian women as detrimental to the
Company's expansion, he recommended that in New Caledonia
the Gentlemen should form connections with the principal families immediately upon their arrival as "the best security we can
have of the goodwill of the Natives."[26]

During his rapid tours of the posts in the early 1820s, however,
Simpson became increasingly aware of the problems caused by
the large numbers of women and children being supported in
established areas, and he favoured the Committee's proposed
economic reforms.[27] A major source of inefficiency and expense
was the practice of allowing families, particularly those of the
officers, to accompany the brigades on the long summer journey
to and from the main depot at York Factory. Simpson's low
opinion of one Chief Factor, John Clarke, was confirmed when
Clarke abandoned some of the goods destined for Athabasca en
route to make a light canoe for the better accommodation of his
half-breed wife and her servant – an extravagance which Simpson estimated had cost the Company five hundred pounds.[28]
After his visit to the Columbia in 1824-25, the Governor further
decried the extent to which family considerations hindered the
expedition of business:

> ... We must really put a stop to the practise of Gentlemen
> bringing their Women & Children from the East to the West
> side of the Mountains, it is attended with much expense and
> inconvenience on the Voyage, business itself must give way to
> domestick considerations, the Gentlemen become drones and
> are not disposable in short the evil is more serious than I am
> well able to describe.[29]

The following year, the annual session of the Council passed a
resolution stating that Gentlemen appointed to the two districts
across the Rockies were not to encumber themselves with families.

Although Indian women were relegated by custom to an inferior status, the ladies of the country appear to have exerted a
surprising influence over their fur-trader husbands. Simpson was

33

appalled by the widespread power of these "pettycoat politicians", whose interests he suspected even affected the decisions of top-ranking officers.[30] In expressing his dissatisfaction with Chief Factor James Bird's management of the Company's business at Red River, he lamented, "I find that every matter however triffling or important is discussed wh. his Copper Colld. Mate before decided on and from her it finds its way all over the Colony."[31] Likewise, he described Mrs. McDonald, the country wife of the officer in charge at Fort Qu'Appelle, as "a stout good looking Dame not master p. Force but through persuasion & cunning. . . ."[32] In the Columbia District, the Governor claimed, two out of the three Chief Traders were completely under the control of their women. They frequently neglected business in their jealous attempts to "guard against certain innocent indiscretions which these frail brown ones are so apt to indulge in."[33]

If the irregularities in the workings of the trade caused by native families disturbed Simpson, he was even more adamant that the Indian Country was no place for a white woman. In a private letter to Committee member Andrew Colvile, he expressed concern that the example of three of the Company's officers in taking wives from among the Red River settlers in the early 1820's might establish a trend which he considered most undesirable:

> . . . it not only frustrates the intentions of the Company and executors, in respect to the Colony, but is a clog on the gentlemen who take them . . . native women are a serious incumbrance but with women from the civilized world, it is quite impossible the gentlemen can do their duty.[34]

In light of his own subsequent experience, Simpson could perhaps have shown a little compassion for the marital difficulties of some of his contemporaries. His extraordinary private correspondence with his close friend Chief Factor John George McTavish reveals a Simpson curiously different from the person his official pronouncements would lead one to expect. For a novice, he adapted with ease to the social conventions of Rupert's Land, succumbing as readily as any Nor'Wester to the charms of the ladies of the country.

Sometime during his first winter, possibly at Oxford House, Simpson was attracted to a damsel called Betsey Sinclair, a daughter of the late Chief Factor William Sinclair and his native wife Nahovway.[35] Although she accompanied him to York Factory in the fall of 1821, the newly-appointed Governor soon found her presence bothersome. He left Betsey at York when he embarked on a tour of inland posts in December and shortly afterward instructed McTavish, then in charge of the Factory, to see that she was "forwarded" in the spring to the Rock Depot where her brother-in-law Thomas Bunn was stationed.[36] Simpson's rather cavalier references to this woman as "my japan helpmate" or "my article" suggest that he himself may never have thought of her as a country wife in the true sense. That many of his contemporaries considered her as such is revealed by an entry in the York Fort Journal dated 10 February 1822 which reads: "Mrs. Simpson was delivered of a Daughter."[37] Although the Governor was at York when this infant was christened Maria by the Rev. John West on August 27,[38] he was still determined to avoid the encumbrance of a family. The proposal to place Betsey under the care of Thomas Bunn had been abandoned, but Simpson departed in early September for an extensive tour of the Athabasca and Peace River districts, leaving it to McTavish to settle the matter expeditiously:

> My Family concerns I leave entirely to your kind management, if you can dispose of the Lady it will be satisfactory as she is an unnecessary and expensive appendage, I see no fun in keeping a woman without enjoying her charms which my present rambling Life does not enable me to do. . . .[39]

He needlessly expressed concern for her virtue. Not long after his departure, Betsey Sinclair became the country wife of the clerk Robert Miles, a high-minded Englishman, who had spent the winter of 1820-21 with Simpson in the Athabasca country. The match was celebrated in the customary fashion by a dance and supper where liquid cheer flowed freely, and the couple were reported to be very happy.[40]

Despite protestations that he was too busy to be bothered by domestic considerations, the Governor seems to have found time to indulge his inclination during his tours of the Company's domains. In fact, he confided to McTavish that he suspected his amours were gaining him a notorious reputation.[41] Although the identities of the recipients of his favours remain obscure, it is known that in 1823 a son named James Keith Simpson was born.[42]

Simpson, however, appears to have made a distinction between the behaviour he considered appropriate in that motley outpost of civilization, the Red River Colony, and the behaviour acceptable in the rest of the Indian Country. While wintering at Fort Garry in 1823-24, he apparently held aloof from romantic entanglements, describing himself as one of the most "exemplary

Batchelors" in the settlement.[43] Furthermore, in spite of his country romances, the intention of returning to England to marry seems to have been in the back of the Governor's mind during this period.[44] Who the object of his affection was is not known, although it is established that Simpson had another daughter in Scotland called Maria, born before he left for Rupert's Land.[45] He was cautioned by his mentor Andrew Colvile against taking any hasty action, however:

> A wife I fear would be an embarrassment to you until the business gets into more complete order & until the necessity of those distant journies is over & if it be delayed one or two years you will be able to accumulate something before the expense of a family comes upon you.

Simpson acquiesced and set off in the fall of 1824 on his tour across the Rockies to the Columbia. While at Fort George, he was at pains to prevent himself from being drawn into the system of marriage alliances which had helped to secure the loyalty of the powerful Chinook nation, especially the great Chief Concomely. It was considered most prestigious among the "aristocracy" of this highly-complex tribe to claim a fur trader for a son-in-law. A most assiduous social-climber was an influencial personage known as "Lady Calpo", who on more than one occasion had warned the fort of impending treachery. She proved a valuable source of information for Simpson, but he found himself in a delicate situation when this old dame, in order to reaffirm her rank, endeavoured to secure him as a husband for her carefully-raised daughter:

> I have therefore a difficult card to play being equally desirous to keep clear of the Daughter and continue on good terms with the Mother and by management I hope to succeed in both altho' her ladyship is most pressing & persevering. . . .[46]

Simpson seems to have succumbed somewhat, however, for if the Chinooks expressed sorrow at his departure in the spring, "the fair princess 'Chowie' ", he suspected, was not the least grieved.[47]

When Simpson returned to Red River to wind up business prior to sailing for England, he found a situation which likely made him reconsider the feasibility of bringing a European wife to Rupert's Land. The new governor of the settlement, Capt. R. P. Pelly, now felt compelled to return to England owing to the ill health of his wife, who only two short years before had accompanied her husband out to Red River. This was a great disappointment to Simpson as he had hoped Pelly would be able to effect some order and stability in the chaotic affairs of the colony. While every effort had been made to ensure the material comfort of the family, Simpson himself had noted that "Mrs. Pelly appears to be a delicate woman and does not yet seem quite at home among us."[48] When he sailed from York Factory in September 1825, the Governor was accompanied by Capt. Pelly and his ailing wife. While it is unknown how he settled any romantic attachments he may have had in Great Britain, Pelly's unhappy example undoubtedly contributed to the fact that Simpson returned to Rupert's Land still a bachelor, apparently prepared to resume former arrangements *à la façon du pays*.

Contrary to the assertions of several authors, it is only now that Margaret Taylor, the half-breed daughter of George Taylor, a former sloop master at York, appears in the Governor's life. She was definitely not the mother of either Maria or James Keith Simpson. When Simpson first became attached to her is uncertain, but she was probably introduced to him by her brother Thomas Taylor, the Governor's personal servant during these years. As was his practice when embarking on an extensive tour, Simpson left this woman at York in the fall of 1826 under the surveillance of his friend McTavish, to whom he wrote in a jocular, if rather crude fashion:

> Pray keep an Eye on the commodity and if she bring forth anything in the proper time & of the right color let them be taken care of but if any thing be amiss let the whole be bundled about their business. . . . [49]

The lady does not seem to have warranted his suspicion, and in the spring of 1827, a son was born, named George after his father.[50] Simpson honoured his responsibility for the support of his family at York, allowing Margaret the enjoyment of special rations such as tea and sugar and even providing financial assistance for her widowed mother.[51]

In his brief biography of Simpson, A. S. Morton stated that domestic concerns played no part in the Governor's life at this time, but such is not the case.[52] Although she is never mentioned in the official journals, Simpson's private correspondence reveals that Margaret Taylor accompanied him when he left York in July 1828 on another cross-country voyage, this time to New Caledonia. At first she was so unwell that he was afraid he might have to leave her in Athabasca, but she recovered and proved herself a valued companion for Simpson rapidly found his two associates Dr. Hamlyn and Chief Trader "Archy" McDonald rather tiresome. "The commodity," he confided to McTavish, "has been a great consolation to me."[53] By this time, Simpson himself seems to have regarded Margaret Taylor as his wife according to the custom of the country. While returning in the spring, he speaks of her affectionately as "my fair one" and although disgruntled at the conduct of her brother Thomas, acknowledges him as a brother-in-law.[54] Simpson, however, was now preparing for another trip to England via the Canadas. On his way east, he left Margaret, now far advanced in her second pregnancy, at Bas de la Rivière under the care of the Chief Factor John Stuart, whose country wife was her sister Mary Taylor. There, at the end of August 1829, Margaret gave birth to another boy, later christened John McKenzie Simpson. [55]

John Stuart's letters to the Governor during his absence provide a touching picture of Simpson's country wife and her little ones. Young Geordy and his baby brother were thriving; "I never saw finer or for their age more promising Children," claimed Stuart. His praise of their quiet and good-natured mother was also unstinted: ". . . in her comportment she is both decent and modest far beyond anything I could expect – or ever witnessed in any of her countrywomen."[56] Old Widow Taylor was living with the family at Bas de la Rivière, and Stuart credited her with instilling such commendable habits of cleanliness and industry in her daughters. He emphasized that Margaret was counting the days until Simpson's return:

> A little ago when at supper I was telling Geordy that in two months and ten days he would see his father. [His mother] smiled and remarked to her sister that seventy days was a long time and [she] wished it was over.[57]

It must have been a grievous shock, therefore, when the Governor did return to Rupert's Land in May 1830 – a lovely young English bride at his side! There can be little doubt that John Stuart had not the slightest intimation that Simpson intended taking a wife in England. His obsequious attempts to curry favour are much in evidence,[58] and he unquestionably described Simpson's country family in such glowing terms because he thought that was what the Governor wanted to hear.

It is extremely difficult to pinpoint the time or cause of Simpson's change of heart. In a letter dated March 1828, his cousin AEmileus Simpson advised the Governor, then contemplating retirement in Rupert's Land, that this was not likely to be a happy course of action:

> . . . rather look for some amiable companion in the civilized

world with which to conclude your days in the true comforts of a domestic life.[59]

Whatever his private feelings for Margaret Taylor, Simpson may have decided that her background and lack of education made her unsuitable for the role of "first lady" of Rupert's Land. Furthermore, his reasoning appears to have been influenced by the experience and council of his close friend John George McTavish, who in the winter of 1829-30 was also on furlough in Great Britain searching for a wife.[60]

Before becoming a Chief Factor in the Hudson's Bay Company in 1821, J. G. McTavish, the son of a Scottish chieftain, had had a long and distinguished career as a Nor'Wester. During his early days at Moose Factory, though in opposition, he formed a union with one of the daughters of Thomas Thomas, the governor of the English company's establishment. It appears to have been a particularly unhappy relationship: the woman was driven to infanticide and McTavish subsequently renounced his connection with her.[61] It should be noted that infanticide was not unknown in Indian society in times of famine or great hardship. In the case of the women of the fur traders it was perhaps symptomatic of their fear of being abandoned for it usually occurred when the husband was on furlough.

Around 1813 sometime after this unfortunate episode, McTavish took another country wife, young Nancy McKenzie, otherwise known as Matooskie, the daughter of a prominent Nor'Wester Roderic McKenzie and an Indian woman. She was to live with him for seventeen years and bear him a lively family of at least six daughters of whom McTavish seems to have been very fond. In the late 1820's, however, there are signs of a growing estrangement between himself and their mother; McTavish confided to Simpson that he contemplated packing Nancy off to Red River where her uncle, Donald McKenzie, was now governor.[62] Although his wife may have feared the outcome of such a long separation, the fact that McTavish took their young daughter Anne with him when he sailed for England in September 1829 must have been reassuring.[63]

The glimpses of the two friends' quest for a "tender exotic" in Britain reveal that the rough and ready society of the fur trade left its gentlemen ill at ease in the intricacies of genteel courtship. Simpson wrote encouragingly to McTavish who was in Scotland:

> I see you are something like myself shy with the fair, we should not be so much so with the Browns . . . muster courage "a faint heart never won a fair Lady."

Simpson was, in fact, very ill during his sojourn in England, the years of strenuous travelling having caught up with him, but he queried jauntily, "Let me know if you have any fair cousin or acquaintance likely to suit an invalid like me ..."[64] McTavish had little time to offer assistance. A few weeks later Simpson wrote ecstatically, "Would you believe it? I am in Love."[65] The middle-aged, hard-hearted Governor had fallen completely under the spell of his eighteen-year-old cousin Frances Simpson, who had been but a child when he had first started his career as a clerk in her father's firm. At first it was decided that the wedding should await Simpson's return from America in the fall of 1830, but the prospect of such a separation prompted him to persuade her parents to give their immediate consent.[66] The couple were united on February 24 and embarked on a short honeymoon to Tunbridge Wells.

McTavish, in the meantime, had not met with such immediate success. An attempt to secure the affection of a "Miss B." failed, but by February, the old Nor'Wester was able to report, much to Simpson's delight, that he too was to be wed – to a Miss Catherine Turner, daughter of the late Keith Turner of Turnerhall, Aberdeenshire.[67] They were married on February 22 in Edinburgh, their honeymoon being no more than a hasty journey to London to join the Simpsons prior to sailing for North America. Simpson, who appreciated how much the ladies would value each others' company, took pains to ensure their comfort on the voyage, reserving the sole use of the Ladies' Cabin for their party.

Although Frances Simpson was undoubtedly a very pretty and cultivated young lady, her sheltered upbringing and delicate constitution made her an unlikely candidate for the role of Governor's lady in the inhospitable wilds of Rupert's Land. Her diary of the voyage to the Indian Country reveals that parting from the close family circle of Grove House was almost more than she could bear:

> I can scarcely trust myself to think of the pang which shot thro' my heart, on taking the last "Farewell" of my beloved Father, who was equally overcome at the first parting from any of his children – suffice it to say, that this was to me a moment of bitter sorrow. . . .[68]

Shortly after the ship sailed from Liverpool on March 10, the young woman succumbed to a violent attack of sea-sickness; she was so ill that Simpson was prepared to bribe the Captain to put her ashore in Ireland, but stormy weather foiled the attempted landing. Fortunately, over the course of the voyage her health improved. The party spent several pleasant days in New York and then proceeded overland to Montreal, where the ladies divided their time between sight-seeing and being entertained by fashionable society.

Before embarking at Lachine for the canoe trip to the interior, however, an incident occurred which threw the contrasting mores of fur trade society and middle-class gentility into sharp focus. McTavish's open affection and continuing responsibility for his eldest daughters made it inevitable that his new wife would learn of their existence. In fact, his thirteen-year-old daughter Mary was at school near Montreal. One evening after dinner, the Governor's servant threw open the door and announced "Miss Mactavish" to the assembled company:

> [McTavish] rose & took her up to his wife, who got stupid, but shook hands with the Miss who was very pretty & mighty impudent . . . [Mrs. McTavish] got white & red & at last rose & left the room, all the party looking very uncomfortable except [her husband] & the girl. [Mrs. Simpson] followed & found her in a violent fit of crying, she said she knew the child was to have been home that night, but thought she would have been spared such a public introduction.[69]

Simpson seems to have endeavoured to spare his wife similar indignities. Letitia Hargrave, in recounting this episode in 1840, commented wryly that "Mrs. Simpson evidently has no idea that she has more encumbrances than Mrs. Mactavish, altho' she did say that she was always terrified to look about her in case of seeing something disagreeable."[70] (This may help to explain Simpson's relative neglect of his mixed-blood children in later years. There is no evidence that they, unlike many of the children of Company officers, were ever sent overseas or to Canada to be educated, and all were excluded from Simpson's final will of 1860.)[71]

On the long voyage into the Indian Country, the first ever for British ladies, every precaution was taken to minimize the hazards and inconveniences of canoe travel. Although Frances owned that it was not a trip "altogether pleasing or congenial to the taste of a Stranger", her diary displays much youthful enthusiasm and good humour. She was awed by the magnificence of the scenery, professed admiration for the strength and skill of their picked crew of voyageurs, two of whom were entrusted to carry the ladies over the portages, and shook hands with several of the leading Indians, to whom she was an object of great curiosity.[72] At Fort William, however, she was grieved at losing the companionship of the amiable Mrs. McTavish, who was here branching off to her new home at Moose Factory, the headquarters of the Southern Department.

The news that the Governor had returned to Rupert's Land with a genteel English wife made a great stir, especially in the upper echelons of fur trade society. As the party progressed from post to post, the Company's officers were assiduous in their attempts to appear hospitable and refined. At Lac La Pluie (which some weeks later was named Fort Frances in honour of Mrs. Simpson) Chief Trader Thomas McMurray undertook to play the gallant, and escorted the Governor's wife on a tour of fort and garden:

> ... old & weatherbeaten as he was, he surpassed all the Gentlemen I had met with in these Wilds, as a Lady's Man; but altho' our walk did not occupy an hour, it quite exhausted all his fine speeches, and the poor man seemed as much relieved when we returned to the house ... as if he had just been freed from an attack of the Night-Mare.[73]

Few were more concerned to create a favourable impression than the obsequious John Stuart who welcomed Simpson's bride to Bas de la Rivière in early June with "no ordinary degree of kindness". His efforts to appear the well-read gentlemen are conspicuous in the rapturous way he described the Governor's lady to a prominent member of the London Committee:

> The very first sight of her on landing at Bas de la Rivière strongly reminded me of the Picture Milton has drawn of our first Mother = Grace was in all her steps = heaven in her Eye = In all her gestures Dignity and love, while everything I have seen of her since – seems to denote her such as first Lord Lyttleton represented his first Lady to have been = Polite as all her life in courts had been – Yet good as she the world had never seen. [74]

Governor Simpson, he declared, had performed an immeasurable service in bringing this charming creature to the Indian Country because her coming heralded an improved standard of morality and gentility.

The extent to which Stuart enthused over the virtues of Simpson's new wife is extremely suspect when one considers that this old Nor'Wester had often taken it upon himself to champion the honour of the ladies of the country,[75] and that his own country wife was the sister of the deposed Margaret Taylor. A truer gauge of his feelings is revealed in his hostile reaction to the news that his long-time associate J. G. McTavish had also not considered his country union binding and had returned to Rupert's Land with a Scottish wife.[76]

Indeed, the news of McTavish's marriage was greeted with astonishment throughout the Indian Country. Whatever their opinion of the Governor's action, several influential fur traders were loud in denouncing McTavish's shabby treatment of Nancy McKenzie, none more so than her uncle Donald, the Governor of Red River, though he himself had quietly "turned off" his own country wife shortly before marrying a Swiss settler's daughter. Even the young clerk, James Hargrave, who disapproved of country marriages, felt great sympathy for Matooskie when she was quietly told that McTavish was not returning to York:

> The first blow was dreadful to witness ... but the poor girl here bears up wonderfully & is fast acquiring resignation. [77]

McTavish's action added to his unpopularity at York; his opponents circulated rumours, which may have originated with the grief-stricken Matooskie herself, charging him with gross cruelty and drunkeness.[78] Simpson, however, would brook no attack on his friend's character when he arrived at York in the summer of 1830. He packed Nancy McKenzie off to Bas de la Rivière where she spent the winter under the same roof as his "old concern" Margaret Taylor. Both women, who each had two children with them, were given an allowance of thirty pounds.[79]

Thus John Stuart had become the temporary guardian of both cast-off wives. Much to Simpson's annoyance, the old man now deemed it a question of honour to defend the rights of the pitiable Matooskie. He bitterly attacked McTavish for having so unfeelingly violated the custom of the country:

> ... what could be your aim in discarding her whom you ... had for 17 Years with you. She was the Wife of your choice and has born you seven Children, now Stigmatized with ignominy ... if with a view to domestick happiness you have thus acted, I fear the Aim has been Missed and that remorse will be your portion for life. ... I will never become your enemy, but ... I think it is as well ... our correspondence may cease.[80]

McTavish, now safely isolated at Moose Factory, had delegated Simpson to settle his affairs, and the Governor found himself at "hot war" with McKenzie and Stuart who demanded that

Matooskie should at least receive a large financial settlement to compensate for the years she had devoted to McTavish. Although Simpson acknowledged the necessity of some provision for both women, he considered it both economic and honorable to solve the problem by finding them new husbands. Thus while McKenzie and Stuart raged, Simpson was busy negotiating. Early in January, he silenced his opponents by securing a written promise of marriage for Matooskie: one Pierre Leblanc, a respectable French-Canadian in the Company's service at Red River had finally succumbed to the offered dowry of two hundred pounds sterling.[81] Leblanc was given a week off to go courting at Bas de la Rivière, and Matooskie, although she had declared she would never take another husband, had little alternative but to accept his offer. The couple were formally married by a priest, after Matooskie's baptism, at the Catholic Church of St. Boniface early in the morning on 7 February 1831, an event which was duly celebrated by their friends at Red River. Although McTavish's country wife was now safely disposed of, he still continued to provide some financial aid for his youngest daughters who were left under her care.[82]

The details of Simpson's own negotiations are unfortunately lacking. It is recorded, however, that on 24 March 1831 "Margarette" Taylor was married to French-Canadian Amable Hogue by the Rev. David Jones at the Red River Church.[83] The opinion was popularly expressed that these arrangements represented quite a come-down for both ladies, particularly the latter.[84] John Stuart, on the other hand, attempting to reinstate himself with the Governor, declared his relief at being rid of his charges: "I am very glad that the recent marriages are over – every one of the two Couples appear perfectly happy."[85] Simpson, however, was not about to forgive either McKenzie or Stuart for their vexatious meddling. He now considered McKenzie, whom he had come to detest, as a most unsuitable governor for Red River.[86] Old John Stuart, for all his pains, found himself banished to the wilds of the McKenzie River district in the fall of 1832.[87] The whole affair, which illustrates the influence of private matters in the closeknit society of the fur trade, did little to help the Governor and his new wife settle comfortably into life at Red River.

In the colony, Simpson endeavoured to adopt a life-style which he considered appropriate to his position as the Overseas Governor of the Hudson's Bay Company. Such refinements as a pianoforte and a shiny, new carriole appeared, and construction was begun on an impressive stone house which was to be the official residence.[88] The Governor's lady was extolled as "the brightest star" in Red River society, but her very presence tended to reinforce class distinctions in the settlement. As one mixed-blood officer in the Company observed, " . . . things are not on the same footing as formerly."[89]

By the spring of 1831, however, Simpson had become thoroughly disgusted with the "high society" of the colony, largely as a result of the gossip and intrigue occasioned by the McTavish affair. He felt there were few women even among the European ladies in Red River with whom his wife Frances could form an intimate acquaintance. The Governor lamented to McTavish:

> I am most heartily tired of Red River . . . and should be delighted to join you at Moose next Fall, indeed my better half is constantly entreating me to take her there so that she may enjoy the society of her Friend . . . Here she has formed no intimacies, [Governor] McKenzie's Wife is a silly ignorant thing, whose common place wise saws with which we are constantly persecuted are worse than a blister; Mrs. Jones [the Chaplain's wife] is a good unmeaning Woman whom we merely see for half an hour occasionally & Mrs. Cockrane [the assistant-chaplain's wife] whose assumed puritanism but ill conceals the vixen, shines only when talking of elbow Grease & the scouring of pots & pans.[90]

But if the European women left much to be desired, the ladies of the country were now definitely *personae non gratae*. This self-enforced exclusiveness of the Governor had unfortunate repercussions. Those Company officers who had mixed-blood wives were much insulted when Simpson indicated that their society was no longer acceptable. No one felt this slight more acutely than Chief Factor Colin Robertson, a proud Scotsman who had had a long if somewhat erratic career in the service of both companies. Robertson had earned Simpson's dislike partly because his genuine concern for the betterment of his half-breed wife Theresa Chalifoux and their family had often resulted in extravagance and a neglect of business. The old Chief Factor intended to take his country family with him when he retired from Rupert's Land, but his attempt to introduce his wife to the society of Mrs. Simpson when passing through Red River met with a scathing rebuff from the Governor:

> . . . Robertson brought his bit of Brown wt. him to the Settlement this Spring in hopes that She would pick up a few English manners before visiting the civilized World. . . . I told him distinctly that the thing was impossible which mortified him exceedingly.[91]

At Moose Factory, McTavish had similarly ruffled feelings by refusing to countenance certain of the officers' wives. Even Simpson expressed concern lest McTavish go too far in alienating Chief Factor Joseph Beioley whose capacities he rated highly, although the Governor fully sympathized with his friend that it was the height of impertinence for Beioley to expect that "his bit of circulating copper" should have the society of Mrs. McTavish.[92] The mixed-blood, though Anglicized families of former company officers, such as that of George Gladman at Moose, were highly incensed at such treatment as they considered themselves among the upper crust of fur trade society. Simpson, however, encouraged McTavish to keep these people in their place:

> I ... understand that the other Ladies at Moose are violent and indignant at being kept at such a distance, likewise their husbands, the Young Gladmans particularly. . . . The greater distance at which they are kept the better.[93]

Only two half-breed women had been allowed to come within a dozen yards of Mrs. Simpson, he informed McTavish, and these in a purely menial capacity.[94] The extent to which the Governor found himself avoided caused him to muse: "They do not even venture within gun Shot of me now – I have seen the time when they were not so shy."[95]

By this time, the responsibilities of married life weighed heavily on the Governor for Frances Simpson, like Mrs. Pelly before her, proved unequal to the rigours of frontier life. Despite constant medical care, her health deteriorated rapidly as her first pregnancy advanced. Simpson, who now appears the most attentive of husbands, was distraught at the necessity of leaving her during the summer of 1831 to attend the annual council at York Factory.[96] His speedy dispatch of company business was not this time motivated simply by a desire for efficiency, and he hurried back to Red River in time for the birth of a son, which his wife barely survived. During the winter, Simpson was much heartened by the steady, if slow progress of both mother and child. The christening of George Geddes Simpson in January 1832 was a considerable social event in the colony. But this happiness was short-lived; the sudden death of the little boy a few months later plunged his parents into the depths of despair.[97]

Domestic tribulations had, in fact, brought the Governor to the low point of his career: his own health was breaking down, he confessed himself little interested in business, detested most of his associates, and was only prevented from retiring from the fur

trade by the loss of a large sum of money.[98] His vision of a comfortable family life in Red River now shattered, Simpson had to
accept that his wife, who was desperately in need of skilled medical attention, could no longer remain in Rupert's Land:

> She has no Society, no Friend, no Relative here but myself,
> she cannot move wt. me on my different Journeys and I cannot
> leave her in the hands of Strangers . . . some of them very
> unfeeling. . . .[99]

He, therefore, took Frances home via Canada in the summer of
1833, and she never returned to the Indian Country. Simpson's
subsequent efforts to divide his time between his family in England and the superintendence of the fur trade in Western Canada
tended to hamper his effectiveness as Governor.[100]

Perhaps it was Catherine McTavish's Scottish constitution
which enabled her to withstand the harsh climate of Hudson Bay
because she appears to have adapted with less difficulty to life at
Moose Factory. A kind, sensible woman, "tho' not hand-
some",[101] she reconciled herself to McTavish's former arrangements. She presented the old fur trader with two more little girls
and for a time had the care of four of her stepdaughters.[102]
McTavish himself was suffering badly from gout, and Simpson,
ever solicitous of his friend's welfare, sought a more amenable
situation for the family. Thus in 1835, McTavish moved to the
Lake of Two Mountains, a post about one hundred miles from
the Chats on the Ottawa River where he had invested in a farm.
The Governor declared it the ideal solution:

> Here your Family could be reared and Educated cheaply
> while Mrs. McTavish & yourself could enjoy the comforts of
> civilized society in a moderate degree as the country is becom-
> ing closely settled all about you, a Steam Vessel plies regularly
> to your Door & there is a Church within 3 or 4 Miles of it.[103]

Although neither Mrs. Simpson nor Mrs. McTavish remained
for long in the Indian Country, their coming contributed to the
decline in the position of native women in fur trade society. The
implication was apparent that in more established areas, particularly at Red River, a country wife was no longer acceptable. In
considering possible successors to McKenzie for the
governorship of the colony, Simpson initially discounted the
highly-competent Alexander Christie because he had an Indian
family *à la façon du pays*.[104]

It now became fashionable for a Company officer to have a
European wife. As Hargrave unfeelingly observed, "this influx of

white faces has cast a still deeper shade over the faces of our Brunettes in the eyes of many."[105] When Chief Factor James McMillan brought his Scottish wife out to Red River in the fall of 1831, one old fur trader, commenting on this "novelty of getting H Bay stocked with European Ladys", conjectured that several others would avail themselves of their furlough "with no other view than that of getting Spliced to some fair Belinda & return with her" to the Indian Country.[106] Even some of those who had strongly professed a sense of duty to their country wives succumbed. Simpson commented wryly on Chief Factor William Connolly's marriage to his wealthy cousin in Montreal in 1832:

> You would have heard of Connolly's Marriage – he was one of those who considered it a most unnatural proceeding "to desert the Mother of his children" and marry another; this is all very fine, very sentimental and very kindhearted 3000 Miles from the Civilized World but is lost sight of even by Friend Connolly where a proper opportunity offers.[107]

The coming of white women to the Indian Country brought into disrepute the indigenous social customs of the fur trade. Marriage *à la façon du pays* was now no longer acceptable, especially with the presence of missionaries intolerant of any deviation. The presence of white women underlined the perceived cultural shortcomings of mixed-blood wives, particularly in more settled areas where their native skills were no longer required. European ladies themselves, by zealously guarding what they considered to be their intrinsically superior status, actively fostered an increasing stratification of fur trade society. The arrival of the white woman can be seen as symbolic of a new era: the old fur trade order was gradually giving way to agrarian settlement which was unquestioningly equated with civilization.

Chapter 3

The Feminization of Teaching

Alison Prentice

I

According to Solomon Denton, the local school inspector for the county of York in New Brunswick, many districts in his area were having trouble keeping schools open in 1856. There were many reasons, but a striking and not uncommon one mentioned by Denton was the failure in certain places to agree "as to what Teacher to employ." The problem, the inspector said, was that "one party wishes for a female, while the other insists upon a male Teacher; the end is, that they engage neither."[1]

While most such disputes probably ended less drastically, it is nevertheless clear that the same debate was taking place in many parts of British North America in the middle years of the nineteenth century. Yet, by the end of the century, the question of whether to employ a male or a female teacher had become academic, for in most places in Canada, almost the only elementary school teachers available for hire were women. What had happened between 1856 and 1900 to bring about this significant change?

The answer, as in most historical questions, is a complex one, which goes beyond either the history of women or the history of education alone, to a consideration of a series of interrelated developments in the roles played by schools, teachers and women, and in the ideology concerning them during this period. Perhaps the first point that has to be made by way of introduction is the negative one that the "feminization of teaching" does not refer to the entry of women into a role that they had never occupied before. Women did teach school before the middle of the nineteenth century in British North America; what they did not do, in most regions, is teach publicly to any great extent, that is, in large schools outside the home. The first thing to consider, then, is the making of elementary school teaching into an occupation that was conducted chiefly in non-domestic surroundings.

49

While this may seem an obvious point, it requires some discussion, largely because the movement of elementary instruction out of the home and into the larger environment of the school has been misunderstood by historians in the past. Students of educational history are now becoming increasingly aware, however, of both how momentous the movement was in the totality of western social history,[2] and how rapidly the alteration sometimes occurred in particular places during times of intense economic and social change.[3] Equally important too is the growing recognition that the movement of formal elementary instruction into institutions known in Canada as public schools, its extension to greater numbers of children, and, to more years of their lives, does not mean that, prior to this movement, most children went totally uninstructed. Many, on the contrary, we believe, were exposed to considerable "schooling" in the earlier decades of the century, and many of their teachers, furthermore, were women. How many, in both cases, it is probably impossible to know, for useful statistics did not begin to be gathered before the creation of centralized educational administrations, which, in central and eastern British North America, took place at mid-century. But we do know that before the 1840s there were, in the populated regions, a great many small "private" schools, schools located in the households of both men and women, and sometimes of married couples.[4] Male teachers were no doubt in the majority in most provinces before the 1840s, and they probably also conducted most "public" schools of that era, the schools that were too large to accommodate in households. The feminization of teaching which took place in the second half of the nineteenth century was thus, in the first place, a movement of women into *public* school teaching, at a time when elementary education itself was gradually moving out of the household and into the ever growing public institutions that would eventually almost monopolize the name of "schools."[5]

The second and better known aspect of the feminization of teaching is the fact that in the third quarter of the century in most of British North America and Canada, women became a majority among common or elementary school teachers. Less well known is that fact that this change was closely related to two contemporary educational movements: the first, a campaign to promote the grading of school children, and, as a result, to promote the consolidation of small schools into larger schools and school systems, especially in urban areas; and the second, a passionate campaign to raise the status of teaching as a profession.

The first of these movements, the physical separation of children into classes or grades within each school or school system, was undertaken largely in the name of efficiency. The chief goal was an efficient division of labour, with the more experienced teachers taking the advanced grades and the less well trained, engaged at lower rates of pay, taking the younger children or beginners. The end result of organizing schools in this way, it was claimed, was that larger numbers of pupils could thus be more cheaply and effectively taught.[6] At the same time, however, higher salaries were energetically pursued by schoolmen of the same era, as an essential part of their campaign to make the teaching profession respectable and to induce well qualified people to remain in it as a lifetime career.[7] Clearly the two goals were to some extent incompatible, as cheapness was promoted on the one hand and higher salaries and respectable careers were touted on the other. The gradual introduction of more and more female teachers at least partially solved the problem, for the employment of growing numbers of women in the lower ranks of expanded teaching staffs made it possible for school administrators to pursue both goals at once. Relatively higher salaries could be made available for male superintendents, inspectors, principal teachers and headmasters, yet money could be saved at the same time by engaging women at low salaries to teach the lower grades.[8]

As the dilemma reported by school inspector Denton illustrates, all of this could not have taken place without considerable discussion of the pros and cons of admitting women to public school teaching in the first place. Was it respectable for women to teach outside the home? More pertinent to school authorities was the question of female ability. Were women capable of governing large numbers of pupils in the not always comfortable environment of the public school? These questions were raised again and again among educators and laymen. The idea of a predominantly female elementary teaching force was one which only gradually gained acceptance in British North America.

The feminization of teaching was made possible by three conditions. One was the eventual acceptance and promotion of the idea by leading educational administrators and propagandists of the day. Another and probably more basic condition was the growing tendency on the part of money-conscious school trustees to see women as having a vital economic role to play in their rapidly expanding schools and school systems.[9] Between 1845 and 1875, more and more women were hired, and by the latter date they had become the majority among common or elementary school teachers in most provinces. Equally basic to all of this was, of course, the interest in and acceptance of their changing role by the women themselves, and by the society that financed and used the schools.

II

What was the reaction of educational administrators – a new and increasingly powerful breed during this period – to the proliferation of women teachers in the common schools? The most pressing issue as far as most of them were concerned was the question of discipline. The relative "mental ability" of females was a consideration with some concerned educators, but most nineteenth century critics of "female teaching" were far more worried about how school children could be governed by women.[10] Supporters of women in the schools also felt that the question was a crucial one. Edmund Hillyer Duval, who was principal of the Provincial Training School for teachers in St. John, New Brunswick, put forward what was to become a leading argument for feminization, when he claimed in 1855 that women might actually be better than men at schoolroom discipline. The supposition that females were "not so capable of maintaining government in Schools," he said, was a sentiment with which he could not concur, since he believed that they usually maintained "as efficient order" as did their male colleagues, and "often by gentler means." Duval pointed out that this opinion was supported by evidence not only from the province of New Brunswick, but also from England and from the New England states.[11]

But if the question of school "government" or discipline was the chief debating point, the question of cost was the more telling factor. For Duval, and for many other school authorities, the main reason for engaging female teachers was less their real or imagined qualifications, than the fact that they could be obtained relatively cheaply.[12] That this was the essential motive emerges from the literary as well as the statistical records of Upper and Lower Canada, New Brunswick and Nova Scotia. Over and over again local as well as provincial officials explained that female teachers were not only as good as male teachers, but could be had "at a saving of 50 per cent."[13] J. B. Meilleur, who was the first Chief Superintendent of Schools for Lower Canada, reported as early as 1850 that the number of schools taught by females already slightly exceeded, in that province, "the half of the whole number of Schools." The reason, he explained, was simply that the service of female teachers could be obtained more cheaply than those of males.[14]

At first this fact was received by educators with mixed feelings, and criticism of the iniquitously low salaries paid by many school trustees was the stock in trade of educational officials in every province. According to one critic, a school inspector for the New Brunswick counties of Sunbury, York, Carleton and Victoria, writing in 1867, the result of women accepting low salaries was that many of the best qualified men left the teaching profession.[15] In Nova Scotia, ambivalence regarding female teachers came out in expressions of official concern about seasonal alterations of school personnel. Two provincial superintendents of schools, J. William Dawson in 1851 and Alexander Forrester in 1859, deplored the constant changing, "from males to females, and from females to males, every half year – the males teaching in winter and the females in summer." The practice, which was widespread in other provinces (and was related to the fact that girls and younger children tended to be the majority of pupils during the summer term), was considered "in every way injurious to the cause of education". In 1851, the argument went that a good teacher, of whatever sex, should be retained. But in 1859, by referring to the ideal teacher in the masculine gender throughout his report, Alexander Forrester left no doubt about which sex he wished to see more permanently established in the schools.[16]

Forrester's views may have softened somewhat by the late 1860s, but by 1871 Nova Scotia's new Superintendent of Schools, J. B. Calkin, expressed grave misgivings once again about what he called the increasing "disproportion in numbers" between male and female teachers. Convinced that the cause was "the unreasonable desire of many sections to have cheap Schools," Calkin believed that the inevitable result of the trend would be a deterioration in education, as few women either reached the higher ranks of the profession, or were capable of taking charge of the more advanced pupils.[17]

In Upper Canada the Chief Superintendency was retained for more than a quarter of a century by one man, the dynamic Methodist propagandist, Egerton Ryerson. Political to the core, Ryerson's approach to the question of female teaching was circumspect. He stated as early as 1848 that women teachers should be "encouraged" and even went so far as to say that it might well be an "advantage" to employ females to instruct younger pupils,[18] but not until 1865 did he go into the matter fully and even then his statement was less than a complete commitment. In the annual superintendent's report for that year, official support was given to the view that female were as good as male teachers in some areas. Ryerson said he agreed with American educationists that females were "best adapted to teach small children, having, as a general rule, most heart, most tender feelings, most assiduity, and, in the order of Providence, the qualities best suited for the care, instruction and government of infancy and childhood." At the same time, however, he insisted that as many male teachers were "as painstaking to instruct, encourage, govern, and secure the attention of little children" as females. Clearly in 1865, Ryerson was still reluctant to commit himself to the view that women were in some areas superior to men. But by the following year the Chief Superintendent had capitulated. Women, the 1866 report announced, *were* best suited to teach the young; therefore the fact that more and more women teachers, proportionally, were to be found in the common schools of Upper Canada, was to be considered progress in the right direction.[19]

Ryerson's new opinion was cited in at least two provinces shortly after this as important evidence that the trend to feminization was a desirable one. In New Brunswick, where the reception of female teachers was still far from enthusiastic, it was nevertheless pointed out in the School Superintendent's Report for 1867 that many sister provinces did not share New Brunswick's aversion to female teachers, and that in Upper Canada, moreover, official opinion regarded "the increase of these Teachers as a circumstance favourable to the diffusion of good elementary instruction."[20] In British Columbia, the change was received with enthusiasm. Quoting *verbatim* much of what Ryerson had said on female teaching, British Columbia's Superintendent of Education claimed in 1872 that it was "generally conceded" that most women teachers possessed "greater aptitude for communicating knowledge," and were "usually better disciplinarians, especially among younger children, than males." Woman's mission, he went on to say, was "predominantly that of an educator."[21]

Thus in the three decades between 1845 and 1875, chief superintendents in at least three provinces had joined J. B. Meilleur of Quebec in accepting female teachers in public schools. Their acceptance, however, was clearly qualified by the tendency, in at least two cases, to stress woman's special suitability to instruct the very young. And in Nova Scotia, J. B. Calkin still refused to adopt the new stance.

Whatever their private or public opinions on the subject, however, educational administrators were, by the late 1860s, having to face the truth that the feminization of the teaching force was fast becoming a reality. In the case of Upper Canada, Ryerson's statement in 1866 anticipated by only a few years the point at which women teachers in fact became the majority in the province. A look at comparative data for the provinces of Lower Canada, Nova Scotia and New Brunswick in Table 1 reveals slightly different patterns of feminization in each, but that only Lower Canada departed radically from the experience of her sister provinces. Her departure was in having a majority of female teachers two decades earlier, reaching this state as early as 1850, and in the rapid movement of women to a position of numerical dominance. No province could match Lower Canada in this respect, but slowly in the other three provinces feminization was clearly taking place. Most similar to each other were the provinces of Upper Canada and Nova Scotia, which despite the far greater number of teachers employed in the former, exhibited almost identically changing sex ratios over the two decades. In New Brunswick, the transition appears to have been less dramatic, but there too, the balance was gradually shifting.

Table 1

Sex Ratios among Common or Public School Teachers in Lower and Upper Canada, Nova Scotia and New Brunswick, 1851 - 1871

		Lower Canada		Upper Canada		Nova Scotia		New Brunswick	
		No.	%	No.	%	No.	%	No.	%
1851	males	Females already a majority according to the Annual Report for 1850		2,251	77.8	662	80.2		
	females			726	22.2	163	19.8		
1856	males	892	32.2	2,622	71.1			485	56.0
	females	1,877	67.8	1,067	28.9			381	44.0
1861	males	1,270	29.9	3,031	69.9	649	69.6		
	females	2,980	70.1	1,305	30.1	283	30.4		
1866	males			2,925	61.1	603	62.6	422	52.5
	females			1,864	38.9	361	37.4	382	47.5
1871	males	1,115	21.8	2,641	49.8	806	52.6	402	44.2
	females	4,005	78.2	2,665	50.2	726	47.4	507	55.8

From the *Annual Reports* of the Superintendents of Public or Common Schools for the various provinces, and the *Nova Scotia Journal of Education*, No. 19 (July 1868)

If the provincial superintendents were accepting a trend, there were also a number of ways in which they were promoting it. The first and most obvious encouragement given to female teachers was the opening of normal schools to women. In Upper Canada, male students were in the majority when women were first admitted to the provincial Normal School soon after it opened in the 1840s, and remained in this position throughout the 1850s, but by the end of the 60s female students became numerically dominant, reflecting their position in the profession as a whole.[22] In Quebec too, sex ratios among normal school students seemed to reflect the provincial situation, with women in the majority at McGill Normal School when it opened in 1857, and becoming the majority provincially as soon as Laval opened its new normal school to women in the session of 1857/58.[23] In some cases, prospective women teachers received special consideration. In Upper Canada, for example, they continued to be admitted to the normal school at the age of sixteen when the minimum age for men was raised to eighteen. According to the instructions of the Chief Superintendent of Schools in that province, also, restrictions on the employment of aliens in the 1840s were not, after 1847, to be applied to women teachers. Finally, regulations of the Upper Canadian Council of Public Instruction for 1850 exempted women who were applying for first and second class teaching certificates from examination in a small number of specified areas.[24] In Lower Canada, in 1852, female teachers were to be examined by School Inspectors, but were excused from the usual examinations before Boards of Examiners.[25]

The insidious feature of such concessions of course was that they helped to ensure both the lower pay and status of many female teachers. Yet it is also true, as has been suggested, that low pay and status were probably a condition of female employment in the first place. In New Brunswick, the Chief Superintendent associated the introduction of increasing numbers of women teachers into the schools, in 1865, with two factors: the low wages offered by rural trustees on the one hand, and the classifying and grading of schools in villages and towns on the other. In the latter case, he judged, "nearly three-fourths of all the teaching could be most economically and satisfactorily performed by females."[26]

The association between feminization and the expansion of graded schools in the urban centres can be seen when the sex ratios among the teachers of Toronto and Halifax are compared with the provincial ratios of Upper Canada and Nova Scotia, respectively. (See Table 2.) While feminization took place more slowly and a little later in Halifax than in Toronto, by 1861 in Toronto and 1871 in Halifax, women outnumbered their male colleagues in the neighbourhood of two to one. In Ontario and Nova Scotia, however, the proportion of women teachers remained far lower, with only a slight majority in Ontario by 1871 and remaining still a minority in Nova Scotia in that year. Thus in both provinces, the chief urban centres were very much in advance in the process of feminization. A comparison of the city of St. John and the province of New Brunswick in 1871 gives similar results, with 52 females to 19 male teachers reported for the city, or a ratio of 73.2% to 26.8%, and a total of 507 female to 402 male teachers in the province as a whole, creating a much closer ratio of 55.8% to 44.2%.[27]

Table 2

Sex Ratios of Common or Public School Teachers in
Urban and Provincial Settings

		1851		1861		1871	
		No.	%	No.	%	No.	%
Toronto	male	12	75.0	20	33.0		
	female	4	25.0	41	67.0		
Upper Canada	male	2,551	77.8	3,031	69.9		
	female	726	22.2	1,305	30.1		
Halifax	male	9	64.3	12	48.0	27	34.6
	female	5	35.7	13	52.0	51	65.4
Nova Scotia	male	662	80.2	649	.69.6	806	52.6
	female	163	19.8	283	30.4	726	47.4

From the *Annual Reports* of the Superintendents of Common or Public Schools, Upper Canada and Nova Scotia, 1851-1871, and the *Reports of the Board of School Commissioners for the City of Halifax.*

That the more rapid feminization of urban centres reflected the development of graded school systems and professional hierarchies within the school emerges clearly from a look at the salary scales in Toronto and Halifax. In the former, a hierarchical pattern was in evidence as early as 1858 in the non-Catholic schools of the city. Headed by a superintendent whose annual salary was $1,200.00 and six headmasters who were paid $700.00

each, the city's teachers were ranked according to function, training and sex, and were paid accordingly, with two male assistants at $520.00, four headmistresses at $400.00, seven variously titled female teachers at $320.00, six female assistants at $280.00, seven other female assistants (usually titled junior) at $240.00 and three female monitor teachers at $170.00 each.[28]

The city schools of Halifax were organized in a similar way (as shown in Tables 3 and 4.) Seven male principals earned an annual salary of between $600.00 and $800.00 each, while the two female principals were paid between $400.00 and $500.00; although the thirteen first class male teachers made between $400.00 and $600.00 a year, the annual salaries of the forty-three first class female teachers ranged from $250.00 to $400.00 – and so on down the line. In one school which employed only first class teachers, all but one of the men earned $600.00 a year and the principal $800.00, while none of the women were paid more than an annual salary of $360.00.

In 1850 a trustee from Hamilton, Upper Canada, listed the benefits of centralized graded school systems as follows: (1) the

Table 3

Teachers Employed in the Public Schools of Halifax, 1870

		Number with this Status	Salary Range
Principals	male	7	$600.00 – $800.00
	female	2	400.00 – 500.00
First Class Teachers	male	13	400.00 – 600.00
	female	43	250.00 – 400.00
Second Class Teachers	male	4	360.00 – 400.00
	female	2	160.00 – 300.00
Third Class Teachers	male	2	160.00 – 320.00
	female	2	160.00 – 240.00
Not classified	male	2	300.00 – 700.00
	female	0	

"List of Teachers Employed in the Public Schools," *Report of the Board of School Commissioners for the City of Halifax for Year 1870,* pp. 33-36.

Table 4

Teachers of the Albro Street School, Halifax, 1870

Principal	Mr. McLoughlan	1st class	$800.00 *per annum*
Teachers	Mr. Sterns	1st class	600.00 *per annum*
	Mr. Daker	1st class	600.00 *per annum*
	Mr. Smith	1st class	600.00 *per annum*
	Mr. McLean	1st class	600.00 *per annum*
	Mr. Artz	1st class	440.00 *per annum*
	Miss Graham	1st class	360.00 *per annum*
	Miss McCloskey	1st class	330.00 *per annum*
	Miss M.L. Johns	1st class	330.00 *per annum*
	Mrs. Payne	1st class	330.00 *per annum*
	Miss Caldwell	1st class	250.00 *per annum*

"List of Teachers Employed in the Public Schools," *Report of the Board of School Commissioners for the City of Halifax for the Year 1870,* p.34.

attraction of more children into the school system because higher classes could be provided; (2) an improvement in the status of teachers; and (3) provision for the instruction of larger numbers of children at less cost.[29] The trustee did not elaborate further, but as has already been suggested in a general way, the second and third goals could only be achieved at the same time through the creation of hierarchies based on sex, with male teachers receiving higher salaries as principals and teachers of the upper grades, while females taught the lower grades at lower rates of pay.

In Toronto between 1851 and 1861, the relative salaries of female teachers, compared to those of their male colleagues, declined and the decline was dramatic, from 69.9% to 41.4%. In the province of Upper Canada as a whole, where hierarchical patterns had not yet made as great an impact, relative female salaries also dropped, but only from 60.3% to 50.1%. (Table 5) It is interesting to observe that during this decade the relative salaries of female teachers who boarded with their employers, or "boarded around" as the expression went, actually went up from 67% to 71.4% of the salaries of male teachers who boarded around. Only salaries "without board" worsened in comparison with men's salaries, suggesting that in Upper Canada traditional rural communities where the teacher was an itinerant who boarded with the local inhabitants, treated male and female teachers more equally than the urban centres that were coming into being.[30]

Table 5

Comparison of Male and Female Salaries in Toronto and the Province, 1851-1861

	1851		1861	
Average Male Salary, Toronto	£105.0.0		$640.00	
Average Female Salary, Toronto	£ 73.2.0	69.6% of male salary	$265.00	41.4% of male salary
Average Male Salary, Province	£ 55.2.0		$429.00	
Average Female Salary, Province	£ 33.10.0	60.3% of male salary	$215.00	50.1% of male salary

From the Statistical Tables of the *Annual Reports of the Chief Superintendent of Schools for 1851 and 1861*. Separate Schools are included. All salaries are without board.

Certainly there is no doubt that in the city of Halifax, hierarchical patterns not only were emerging, but were deliberately based on sex. A directive attached to the Halifax salary list, published in 1870, noted that from that date salaries in the city were to be rationalized so that eventually teachers in all schools would be paid on the same scale, at first appointment. The scale provided that first and second class male teachers would start at $400.00 and $350.00 respectively, while first and second class females would begin at $250.00 and $200.00.[31]

In the light of these differences, why were women willing to take on the job of teaching in city schools? Part of the answer to this question is of course the shortage of employment available to women other than domestic work. But one must add to this, first of all, the very desire to work outside the home, as the household became less and less the centre of industry and as the domestic employment which had for so long claimed large numbers of women clearly began to lose whatever attraction it may have had. Evidence from Upper Canada in the 1840s suggests, indeed, that to some observers there was little to choose between domestic service and teaching in the early years, from the point of view of either status or wages. The two occupations were frequently compared, and in tones of considerable disparagement, with some holding that female teachers were on the same (low) social and educational level as "spinsters and household servants," while others noted that teachers in general were no better than the "lowest menials."[32] It was not surprising, such critics felt, that the wages of the two occupations were similar.

If domestic work and teaching commanded similar wages in the 1840s, any improvement, however little, in the salaries or status of the latter would be bound to make teaching seem an attractive possibility. The salaries of female teachers in Halifax and Toronto, furthermore, were so much higher than the provincial averages for teachers in Nova Scotia and Upper Canada, that they must have held a special allure for women coming from outside these cities, in spite of the fact that they compared so poorly with the salaries of urban male teachers. For many women, then, even the lowest ranks of city school hierarchies may have provided opportunities for respectable employment, and, as time went on, both a higher status and higher wages than had been available to them in the past.

Whether it amounted to the rationalization of what had already happened, or a prediction of things to come, the portrayal of women as ideally suited to the instruction and government of the very young must also have had an impact on prospective teachers. In the inspirational text for teachers published by Alexander Forrester in 1867 when he was Chief Superintendent of Schools in Nova Scotia, the author noted that while formerly, "female teaching" had been "confined to private families, or private schools, or matrons' village schools," it had now become prevalent in public schools in both the old world and the new. The superintendent was not anxious to discuss the prejudices that existed against women teachers, but to make a point regarding their "qualifications and position." It was sufficient, he claimed, to note that "both by the law of nature and revelation," there was "a position of subordination and of dependence" assigned to women, and that thus there ought to be "situations in educational establishments better adapted to the one sex than the other." Accordingly, it was generally admitted that the infant and primary departments were "best fitted for the female," while "the head masterships, and the more advanced sections" ought to be reserved for the male teachers in schools. [33]

If elementary school teaching, even at comparatively low rates of pay, nevertheless opened up opportunities to work outside the home for women who, before, had largely devoted their lives to the domestic sphere, and if the propaganda and discussion of the period also helped to steer women into subordinate positions in urban school systems, a third force helped to ensure that they would remain in the lower ranks. This was the reputation, deserved or otherwise, that women had for retiring from the profession after a few years, just as experience was "beginning to make them really efficient" as the Superintendent of Schools for New Brunswick put it. The problem, in this administrator's view, was that their places were then filled by "younger and less experienced recruits from the Training School," the ultimate effect of which was to lower the reputation of all female teachers, whether they were experienced or not.[34] Men too, however, were accused of treating the profession as temporary employment, undertaken only for quick money during bad times, and there seems, at this stage of the research, no way of knowing whether or not the tendency was really more pronounced among women. It remains sufficient, perhaps, to know that at least one influential superintendent thought this to be the case, for, once again, the spread of such opinions was bound to suggest to women as well as to their male colleagues that the lower salaries for female teachers were justified.

So far this essay has cited the views of men on the subject of women teachers. What were the opinions of the women themselves? As might be expected, statements by women teachers are hard to come by, but the few that are to be found suggest that, if the majority accepted their low status and low pay, some women at least were far from satisfied with their position.

Elizabeth Ann Inglis, a teacher who wrote complaining of her lot to the Chief Superintendent of Schools for Upper Canada in 1849, blamed her male colleagues and their poor opinion of women for the low status of female teachers. Although, according to Inglis, some of her school trustee employers had candidly admitted that her work was superior to that of most men, her salary, in the course of a ten year career, had never reflected this fact.[35]

A "female teacher" writing anonymously for the *Journal of Education for the Province of Nova Scotia* several decades later, also felt that instruction by women was "undervalued." Basing her opinion on what she believed to be woman's dominant role as educator within the home, this teacher claimed for women superiority not just as instructors of the very young, but of all ages of children, typing them "natural educators." Female teachers were, in far larger proportion than men, "suited to the work, and from a consciousness of their adapation to it" continued "to teach and love the profession, while by far the greater number of males, conscious of their want of adaptation to the work they have assumed" left the profession "for something more congenial." The fact that women received less pay for the same labour was, in the view of this writer, "a sad commentary" on the chivalry and gallantry of male Nova Scotians. Although women's claim to equal pay for equal work was the chief message that the *Journal's* anonymous correspondent wished to convey, she also wanted to see women promoted to positions of leadership in the schools. In her view, it could only be to the benefit of schools in Nova Scotia if, in some cases, "active, energetic female teachers were placed over them."[36]

It could be said that the leap to leadership had already been made, for there were of course female principals in public schools where the school population was divided according to sex. Thus two of the public schools in the city of Halifax boasted women teachers at the top by 1870.[37] But mixed schools rarely if ever had female principals in the 1870's. Furthermore, it was not really until the end of the century that Canadian women teachers felt secure enough in the profession to speak out strongly on the subject of their inequality.

A paper called "The Financial Outlook of the Women Teachers of Montreal," which was published in 1893 by Miss E. Binmore in *The Education Record of the Province of Quebec,* is in sharp contrast with the muted and anonymous statement of "a Female Teacher" and outlines provocative views on the gradually evolving position of women in the teaching profession. At first, according to Binmore, women had worked, as in any new field, virtually "on suffrance," for trustees who could not afford to pay the usual salaries, because opportunities for female employment were only gradually thrown open, and because there were always more women seeking work than there were positions. In the long run, however, "efficiency and success" would always be recognized and women paid accordingly. In the light of this scenario, the author felt that it was especially regrettable that the city of Montreal had failed either to promote women to principalships or to remunerate them adequately, and that in this respect the city lagged far behind other cities on the continent. Citing a recent petition of Montreal women teachers on the subject of their exploitation, Binmore noted that salaries for women were so low and board and room so high in certain localities of the city, that some of the teachers concerned were unable to pay for basic necessities like clothing or medical care; nor could they afford books, church contributions or further education.[38]

While the author of this 1893 discussion felt it necessary to dis-associate herself from some of the more radical opinions on women current in her period, her analysis of the role of women in teaching nevertheless went far beyond the defensive positions taken by either Elizabeth Ann Inglis in 1849 or the anonymous "Female Teacher" in 1871. The abilities of women teachers are not even discussed; Binmore obviously took them for granted. Equal rights for these teachers were demanded openly and a paper printed, in the author's own name, in a widely circulated educational journal. Another small point that should be noted is that the expressions "female teacher," furthermore, was deliber-ately chosen instead of "lady teacher," for, as the author explained, not only had the word "lady" lost much of its original meaning, it also, insofar as it retained that meaning, implied membership in a leisured class. Binmore did not believe that teaching in Montreal in the 1890s amounted to leisure; it was for equal work that she was demanding equal pay for women.

The position of women teachers in the decades between 1845 and 1875 would not have permitted such a strong expression of women's rights or needs. Only just emerging from the world of domestic and private instruction into the world of the public school, women faced much prejudice. Prejudice was caused by fear of female competition generally, or by the belief that women teachers, by accepting low salaries, degraded the profession and drove out competent men. It was caused by the genuine belief that women were constitutionally ill-adapted to the public class-room, either because of inferior mental aptitude or training, or, more often, because the disciplinary and organizational demands of the public school were too great. Prejudice also arose from the belief that many women did not intend to make a life-time career of teaching.

Such prejudice was overcome by admitting women to teaching as assistants, as instructors of the younger children and lower grades, and portraying them as dependent on the guidance of male principals and head teachers. Both women and men were encouraged in this by the perpetration of the myths that the spe-cial mission of women was the instruction of the very young, and that nature dictated their dependent status. Prejudice was also overcome by the fundamental fact that women teachers cost less. Expanding school systems could often hire two female teachers for the price of one male; male teachers at the same time could claim as a result of the employment of women, the salaries and status that so many school promoters felt was their due and an essential aspect of educational reform.

The entry of large numbers of women into public school teaching was thus accepted because their position in the schools was generally a subordinate one. Their move into public teaching facilitated – and was facilitated by – the emergence of the public school systems, in which hierarchical professional patterns were feasible. To the extent that school children absorbed messages from the organization of the institutions in which they were educated, Canadian children were exposed to a powerful image of woman's inferior position in society. One must not discount, moreover, the impact on the women themselves. The experience of public school teaching, the experience of its discipline and of its hierarchical organization, became the experience of large numbers of Canadian women by the end of the nineteenth century.

Chapter 4

The Neglected Majority:
The Changing Role of Women in
19th Century Montreal*

D. Suzanne Cross

I

The nineteenth century was generally speaking a period of rapid urban growth characterized by large scale migrations of men and women into the towns from the surrounding countryside. Immigration from the British Isles also contributed to the increasing population of cities, although the evidence suggests that it was of much less importance in Montreal than in some North American towns. Periodically, as in the early twenties, the thirties, the late forties and again in the early eighties, the stream of immigrants to Montreal turned to a flood, yet comparatively few remained to make the city their home, and the majority passed on to Canada West or the United States.

The first part of this paper examines the growth of the female population in Montreal and the distribution of women by age and location in the different parts of the city and its suburbs. As the countryside probably offered even less opportunity for young girls than for young men, women participated in the movement from over-populated rural areas to the towns of Quebec and New England, thereby greatly increasing the female proportion of the urban population. This trend was not peculiar to Quebec.

The predominance of women in many American towns in the second half of the century has been noted elsewhere.[1] There was a great demand for servants in Brookline, Pasadena and Newton, all towns with a high *per capita* income, and the textiles towns of Lowell, New Bedford and Fall River offered employment in the mills.

Women moved to the towns and cities in order to earn their living, and the second part of this paper discusses the opportuni-

*The helpful comments of Professors J. T. Copp and Micheline Dumont Johnson in the preparation of this paper are gratefully acknowledged.

ties for employment which Montreal afforded. The establishment of manufacturing on a relatively large scale created employment, and women became the mainstay of the labour force in at least one industry and formed an important sector in several others. Women, many of them married, worked out of necessity in order that they and their dependents might survive. The seriousness of the plight of many working class families was recognized by the religious orders who established a number of day care centres thus enabling many women with children to supplement the family income by working outside the home. It will be shown that Protestant and Catholic women did not share the same experiences, as several of the roads open to the former were closed to the latter. Occasional reference is made to the women's religious orders and the charitable organizations run by women, but only within the context of their effect on the employment scene.

II

Sex ratios indicating the number of females per hundred males have been computed for Montreal, Quebec City and the Province of Quebec, and are given in Graph 1. In a population with an equal number of males and females the ratio is 100 when females predominate the figure is above 100; where males are in the majority the ratio drops below 100. Throughout the period

Table 1

Sex Ratios (Number of Females per 100 Males) by Age Group for
Montreal, 1844-1901

	Under 15	15-19	20-29	Over 30
1844	98.5	128.2	106.6	95.7
1851	101.3	126.4	134.0	95.5
1861	97.5	114.6	126.5	101.9
1871	100.6	138.8	132.8	111.8
1881	100.0	127.6	136.2	115.2
1891	102.9	119.6	122.4	112.2
1901	102.3	116.8	120.2	112.6
x^2	.24	46.39*	51.99*	7.20

Source: *Census of Lower Canada,* 1844; *Census of Canadas* 1851, vol. I, table 3; 1861, vol. I table 5; *Census of Canada,* 1871, vol II, table 7; 1881, vol II, table 8; 1891, vol II, table 1; 1901, vol. I, table 7.
*Significant at or beyond the .05 level of confidence.

women outnumbered men in Montreal and Quebec, and the overall proportion of women increased steadily from 1851 to 1881. In 1891 and 1901 the proportion of women continued to increase in Quebec, whereas there was a slight decrease in Montreal. The ratios for the cities contrasted with those for the Province as a whole: at mid-century there were fewer women than men in the Province, but from 1871 to the end of the century, the ratios remained stable.

The sex ratios for the different age groups in Montreal are shown in Table 1. The ratios were calculated for four groups: children under the age of 15; girls between 15 and 19; young women from 20 to 29 and mature women over 30. The most striking feature was the high proportion of girls and young women. The ratios in the children's group were all very close to 100, whereas the ratios for the girls and young women's groups were well above 100. In these two age groups women outnumbered men for every year studied. The high ratios among the girls could not be attributed to a carry-over effect from the children's group in the previous decade, as there were almost equal numbers of males and females in the children's group. The arrival of large numbers of young girls in Montreal was the cause of the high ratios in that group. The ratios for the young and mature women's groups were, at least in part, due to the carry-over effects from the girl's group for the previous decade. The ratios for the mature women's groups were noticeably higher from 1871 onwards, but did not equal those of the girls and young women, and it seems likely that they were due to the carry-over effects already mentioned rather than to large scale migrations of older women. As early as 1844 there were already a large number of young girls in the city, and it seems safe to assume that the majority of women who continued to come to Montreal throughout the century were, upon arrival, in their mid and late teens or early twenties.

The male and female population were distributed unevenly throughout the city, as can be seen by the sex ratios for the wards shown in Table 2. Women greatly outnumbered men in St. Antoine, St. Lawrence, St. Louis and St. James throughout the second half of the century. St. Antoine was essentially a middle- and upper-class residential area, although labourers and artisans resided in the lower part of the ward. Industrial establishments were restricted to the extreme south east corner. Large numbers of domestic servants were employed in the wealthy Protestant homes along St. Antoine Street. In 1871, 66 per cent of the total number of servants for the whole city were employed in Mont-

Table 2

Sex Ratios (Number of Females per 100 Males) for the Wards of
Montreal, 1861-1901

	1861	1871	1881	1891	1901
East	82.5	105.5	107.0	105.7	61.0
Centre	98.0	141.8	100.7	128.8	186.3
West	100.0	149.0	98.1	95.5	95.1
St. Anne	98.7	101.5	103.1	98.5	97.9
St. Antoine	113.2	114.3	124.3	118.6	120.5
St. Lawrence	110.4	118.0	120.7	115.5	111.7
St. Louis	110.7	120.5	117.0	118.6	113.1
St. James	102.1	118.6	118.8	115.7	114.1
St. Marys	103.1	108.6	108.9	104.9	108.2

Source: *Census of Canadas* 1861, vol. I, table 5; *Census of Canada,*
1871, vol. I, table 1; 1881, vol. I, table 4; 1891, vol. I, table 1; 1901, vol.
I, table 7.

real West.[2] A cursory examination of the census returns for 1861
and 1871 revealed that most of these servants were young Irish
Catholic girls. The location of a number of factories employing
women which were within walking distance of the central area
largely explained the high proportion of women in St. Lawrence,
St. Louis and even St. James. It was important for women to live
close to their jobs, because .05¢ car fares were a major item for
the worker who earned only .50¢ to .75¢ a day. Tickets were available at six for .25¢ and twenty-five for $1.00, but these sums rep-
resented a large outlay for the poor. Special workingmen's tickets
for use in the early morning and evening were not introduced
until 1892. Even the new rate of eight tickets for .25¢ was beyond
the means of most working women.

The proportion of women in St. Anne's and St. Mary's wards
was lower than in the wards already mentioned. St. Mary's in the
east end was an area of rapid population growth and appeared to
share the characteristics of the new suburbs which are discussed
below. The situation of St. Anne, a well-established and predominantly Irish Catholic ward, was different. The ward was close to
the Lachine canal, the harbour and the Grand Trunk Railway
yards, all of which attracted male labour. There were some local
factories employing women, but many daughters from homes in
St. Anne's went into domestic service in neighbouring St.
Antoine.

The population of West and Centre wards, which, together

69

with East ward, formed the core of old Montreal, declined steadily in the second half of the century. These wards constituted the
commercial and retail centre of the city, but there was also a concentration of garment and shoe factories in West and Centre. In
the 1850's merchants and their male clerks lived over the
business premises, but when the Montreal City Passenger Railway began operations in 1860, many left the area to reside away
from the centre of the city. It is difficult to account for the fluctuations in the ratios in these wards, but it should be pointed out
that the differences were not very important because the
populations were small. A majority of only a few hundred of
either sex in a small population can produce extreme ratios, but
would be of little significance in a larger population. The small
proportion of women in East ward in 1861 was due to the presence of the garrison at the Quebec Gate Barracks, but satisfactory explanations for the other fluctuations have not been found.

During the last thirty years of the century, population growth
was more rapid in the suburban villages of Hochelaga, Côte St.
Louis, St. Louis de Mile End, St. Jean Baptiste, Ste. Cunégonde,
St. Henri and St. Gabriel than in Montreal itself. With the
exception of Hochelaga, the sex ratios were similar to those in St.
Mary's ward falling between 102 and 108, although in a few
instances there were as low as 98. The ratio for Hochelaga village
was 103.2 in 1871 and 115.7 a decade later. The Hudson Cotton
Company and the W. C. MacDonald Tobacco Company were
both located in Hochelaga, and many women were employed in
their factories. During the 1880's, however, the Canadian Pacific
Railway attracted over a thousand men to work in its shops and
yards which were constructed in the east end. Part of the area
was annexed to Montreal in 1883 and the ratio for Hochelaga
ward was 105.7 in 1891 and 103.9 in 1901. There were few
employment opportunities for women in St. Louis de Mile End,
Côte St. Louis, St. Jean Baptiste and St. Gabriel. The stone quar-
ries in Côte St. Louis attracted men to those suburbs and industry on the Lachine Canal and the nearby Grand Trunk shops
provided plenty of employent for men in St. Gabriel. Ste.
Cunégonde and St. Henri were industrial suburbs: the Belding
Paul silk mill, the Merchants Cotton Company, the Montreal
Woollen Mill and several establishments manufacturing food
employed considerable numbers of females, but many were married women which tended to maintain an even sex ratio. These
opportunities for women were also counter-balanced by the
numerous industries along the Lachine Canal which created
work for men. Although a few wealthy citizens employed ser-

vants in their suburban homes, the demand for domestics was small in the lower middle- and working-class districts.

III

Information on the employment of women in the 19th century is fragmentary, and for the early years almost non-existent. Prior to the establishment of factories, working class women had to rely on domestic service, cleaning, washing, sewing and caring for children. According to the 1861 Census, two per cent of women were engaged in sewing as seamstresses of dressmakers. Domestic service was a major source of employment as indicated by Table 3. No explanation has been found for the great drop in the number of servants between 1844 and 1851, and bearing in mind the arrival of thousands of Irish immigrants in the late 1840's, an increase rather than a decrease in the number of servants would have been expected. Some women were already moving into factory work, but it is doubtful if this adequately explains the decline in the number of servants between 1844 and 1851. It is unwise to place too much confidence in the early census, and it is possible that the number of servants given for 1844 is too high or that for 1851 is too low. The number of servants had increased by 1871 but so had the population, and contemporaries commented on the shortage of servants.[3] Throughout the 1870's the "servant problem" agitated the ladies of Montreal, and there was probably truth in the complaint that girls preferred working in the factories.[4] Hours of work were extremely long and conditions bad in the factories, but at the end of the day a girl was her own mistress which was far from the case with the servant who was subject to the rules of the household at all times.

Table 3

The Number and Percentage of Female Servants in Montreal

	No. of servants	% of female population
1844	3,013	9.2
1851	915	3.1
1861	2,770	6.0
1871	3,657	6.4
1881	5,898	7.9

Source: *Census of Lower Canada,* 1844; *Census of Canadas,* 1851, vol. I, table 4; 1861, vol. I, table 7; *Census of Canada,* 1871, vol. II, table 8; 1881, vol. II, table 14.

At least one editor thought that the ladies were to blame for the reluctance of young girls to enter domestic service. Servants, he said, were badly paid, over-worked, given little or no time off, inadequately housed and fed and subjected at all hours to the capricious demands of the mistress.[5] From the point of view of the employers, matters had improved slightly by 1881, and there was one servant per 4.8 families as compared with one per 5.8 families in 1861.[6]

Domestic service created employment for some women and at the same time released others from devoting all their time to the cares of the household. Increasing numbers of middle- and upper-class women had leisure to devote to social and recreational activities and also to charitable organizations and higher education as witnessed by the foundation of the Montreal Ladies Educational Association in 1871. The shortage of servants was a matter of real concern to the ladies of the upper classes. Various attempts were made to alleviate the problem, but even so supply could not keep up with the demand. The Misses Rye and McPherson, who ran one of several servant registry offices, periodically arranged for young girls to come from England to take up domestic work in Montreal. In 1871, J. E. Pell of the St. George Society suggested that he be given financial assistance in order to tour the villages of England and persuade girls to come to Montreal.[7] Several charitable organizations concerned themselves with finding employment, particularly in domestic service, for women. The Protestant House of Industry and Refuge established a servants' register in 1867[8] and the Y.W.C.A., which began its work in Montreal in 1874, immediately set up a committee for domestic servants.[9] The Women's Protective Immigration Society also tried to channel immigrants in this direction and occasionally advanced passage money to suitable girls.[10] The Montreal Day Nursery functioned as an informal employment office by the end of the century. Anyone wanting charwomen on a daily basis informed the Nursery, and when mothers brought their children in, they were directed to the available work.

The shortage of servants was only one aspect of the problem. Most girls entering service lacked any experience, and few employers wanted to invest the time and effort in training them. Attempts to provide some preliminary training were made periodically, but it is doubtful that these efforts were very satisfactory. In 1860 the Home and School of Industry made the training of young girls for domestic service one of their principal objectives.[11] Later they instituted a special class for girls of eight years and up in order to train them in housework.[12] Kitchen Garden classes were organized for little girls below the age of seven, and the class at the Day Nursery was reported to be one of several operating in the city. Kitchen Gardens originated in the United States and the idea was introduced to Montreal by a Miss Huntingdon of New York.[13]

IV

A separate listing for men and women in industrial occupations was first introduced in the Census of 1871. Although the number of servants in Montreal declined between 1844 and 1861 and did not reach the 1844 level until 1871, the female population rose from just under 33,000 to over 57,000. It can be seen from Graph 2 that by 1871 women played an important role in a number of industries, and we can infer that they had been doing so for some time. Many of the industrial establishments employing women were founded in the 1850's and 1860's, and some even earlier. J. & T. Bell began manufacturing boots and shoes in 1819, and the business was still flourishing in 1894.[14] Brown and Childs employed some 800 hands in the boot trade by 1856.[15] During the 1850's, at least six more sizeable factories were established, and another four in the 1860's.[16] The location of these and most of the factories mentioned below can be seen on the map.

Several garment factories, some of which were very large, were in operation in the mid-century. Messrs. Moss and Brothers dated from 1836, the shirt manufacturer John Aitken and Co. from 1851 and the clothing firm of Messrs. McMillan and Carson from 1854.[17] H. Shorey and Co., which later became one of Montreal's largest clothing factories was established in 1865.[18] Two textile mills, one for woolen and the other for cotton cloth, began manufacturing in 1852 and 1853 respectively in the vicinity of St. Gabriel's Locks.[19] The tobacco factory of the W. C. MacDonald Co.,[20] the "Stonewall Jackson" Cigar factory[21] and S. Davis and Sons[22] were all in operation before 1860. It is reasonable to suppose that increasing numbers of women were employed in these factories from the 1850's or possibly earlier. Manufacturers knew that women and children could do this work just as well as men and would accept less pay.

Most industrial work was located in factories, but this was not the case in the garment trade where diverse conditions existed. There were many small dressmakers', milliners' and tailors' shops, and seamstresses and dressmakers worked in private homes on a daily basis. In the manufacture of men's clothing, although some work was done in the factory, more was farmed out to women working in their own homes on machines that were either rented or supplied by the manufacturer.[23] In 1892 the J. W. Mackedie Company had 900 hands on their outside payroll, and the H. Shorey Company 1,400 in addition to 130 employed in the factory.[24]

Graph 2 indicates those industries in Montreal which relied extensively on female labour. Several occupations, which are listed separately in the industrial schedules of the census, have been combined to form the garment trade.[25] The number of women declined in this trade between 1881 and 1891: most of the sub-groups remained unchanged, but tailoresses gave place to tailors. There was also a reduction in the number of men and women in the boot and shoes factories. This industry was experiencing difficulties in the late eighties, and by 1891 the value of products was down by close to $2 million and salaries by a quater of a million. There were 129 establishments compared with 171 in 1881. Many factories were established in response to the "National Policy," but limited Canadian markets restricted growth, and it is clear from accounts of the individual factories that few were able to produce at their full capacity.[26] In the tobacco, cotton, silk and rubber industries there was a steady increase in the number of females employed, but the garment trade remained the major source of work.

Only industries which employed more than 100 women were included in Graph 2, but smaller numbers worked in other industries. In 1871, just under 23,000 men, women and children were classified as industrial workers in Montreal and Hochelaga. Of this number over 7,000 or approximately 33 per cent of the work force were women and girls. There were over 42,000 employed in industry in 1891 of whom approximately 12,000 were women and girls. The number of men in industry had doubled, whereas there were only 4,500 more women working in 1891 than in 1871, and they comprised 28 per cent of the work force as compared with 33 per cent in 1871.[27] During these years new jobs for women were opening up more slowly than for men. The above figures indicate the number of women working on census day, and probably under-represent the number who worked during part of the year. There is no way of estimating the number who worked temporarily when the main bread winner was unemployed or ill. The wage books for the Molson Brewery showed a rapid turnover among the girls in the bottling factory.[28]

V

There is strong evidence that as early as the 1850's, it was increasingly common for French Canadian married women to go out to work. As an illustration, in 1855 the Sisters of Providence began caring for young children who had been refused admission to schools in the Quebec suburbs, and they established a separate *salle d'asile* in connection with the Hospice St. Joseph in 1860.[29] Children between the ages of two and seven were left by their parents early in the morning and picked up in the late afternoon. In 1858 the Grey Nuns opened the first of five similar centres – the *salle d'asile* St. Joseph. The response on the part of parents was immediate, and *l'asile* Nazareth followed in 1861, *l'asile* Bethléem in 1868, *l'asile* St. Henri in 1885 and finally *l'asile* Ste. Cunégonde in 1889. As might be expected, *l'asile* St. Vincent de Paul, *l'asile* St. Joseph and *l'asile* Ste. Cunégonde were located in working-class districts. In contrast *l'asile* Nazareth and *l'asile* Bethléem were on St. Catherine Street and Richmond Square, both of which were prestigious addresses. St. Catherine Street was moderately convenient for women in the lower ports of St. Lawrence and St. Louis and also for those who walked in from the village of St. Jean Baptiste to the north. The Richmond Square site was made available by the Hon. C. S. Rodier, and was no great distance from St. Joseph and St. Bonaventure streets. The decline in the number of children at *l'asile* Bethléem after 1887 suggests that a number came from the parishes of Ste. Cunégonde and St. Henri and later attended the local *salles d'asile*.

The number of children who were registered at the *salles d'asile* run by the Grey Nuns can be seen in Table 4 and Table 5 gives the totals who attended during five-year periods. A glance shows that considerable numbers of young children frequented *salles d'asile*. It must, however, be asked whether these were children of widowed mothers or of parents who were both living. The registers for *l'asile* St. Joseph for 1858 to 1869 and for *l'asile* Ste. Cunégonde for 1889 to 1891 have been preserved.[30] The name and age of each child was inscribed together with the address and occupation of the parent. Very few widows registered their children. It appears certain that many families in which both parents were employed sent their children to the *salles d'asile*. In 1878 the Grey Nuns stated that *"Le but principal de cette oeuvre [les salles d'asile] est de donner aux parents de la classe peu aisée, la libre disposition de leurs journées afin qu'ils puissent se livrer à un travail fructueux pour la famille...."*[31] At the opening of *l'asile* St. Henri, the curé Mr. Remi-Clotaire Decary remarked that *"Les parents pauvres qui travaillent en dehors de leur maison ont le privilège d'aller placer leurs enfants sous la protection bienveillante des Soeurs de l'asile Saint Henri."*[32]

Table 4

Number of Children Attending the "Salles d'Asile" Run by the
Grey Nuns

	L'asile St. Joseph	L'asile Nazareth	L'asile Bethléem	L'asile St. Henri	L'asile Ste. Cunégonde
1863	408	334			
1868	604	795	33		
1872	512	500	100		
1877	484	220	360		
1882	348	400	280		
1887	429	187	324	450	
1892	110	387	312	542	352
1897	130	314	256	604	550
1902	*	298	246	404	380

Source: "Les Rapports des Chapitres Généraux," vol. II, Archives des
Soeurs Grises.
*Figures missing.

Table 5

Total Number of Children Attending the "Salles d'Asile" During
5-Year Periods.

1858-63	1,704
1864-68	3,408
1869-72*	2,848**
1873-77	2,959**
1878-82	6,401
1883-87	5,387
1888-92	7,907
1893-97	9,608
1898-1902	10,126

Source: "Les Rapports des Chapitres Généraux, vol. II
*4-year period.
**Figures missing for *L'asile Bethléem.*

The registers of St. Joseph and Ste. Cunégonde show that almost without exception the children were French Canadian: the Irish and English did not send their children to these particular institutions. The Grey Nuns did not make a regular charge for the care of children, but some parents were able to contribute. For revenue the Sisters depended on donations, bazaars and a small subsidy which amounted to approximately 25 cents per child per year from the Provincial Legislature.[33]

The role of the *salles d'asile* in enabling married women with children to go to work needs further consideration. Children below the age of two were not admitted, and the registers show that most of those attending were over the age of three. Although the evidence is not conclusive, it does not appear that the presence of an infant in the family prevented the mother from working. According to contemporary accounts, French Canadian mothers frequently resorted to artificial feeding instead of breast feeding which made possible an early return to work after childbirth provided that some care could be provided.[34] It is suggested that children between the ages of 10 and 13 were used to look after the children who were too young to attend the *salles d'asile.* The registers of the parish school of St. Joseph which was run by the Sisters of the Congregation of Notre Dame show that the majority of children left after the third grade, but at this age, probably 10 or 11, very few went out to work.[35] There were certainly considerable numbers of children available who could function as baby sitters in their own families or possibly for neighbours, thus releasing the mother for work outside the home.

There were few day care centres for pre-school children in the English-speaking community, lending substance to the claim that only French Canadian mothers went out to work. In 1886 a group of ladies approached the Y.W.C.A. and asked for their support in setting up a day nursery. A building was rented on Fortification Lane, and two years later the Day Nursery moved to larger premises on Mountain Street. A comparatively small number of children frequented the nursery: in 1899 attendance averaged twenty-five daily,[36] although earlier in the decade it had been as high as forty.[37] The charge of ten cents a day per child and fifty cents a week may have kept mothers away. From the annual reports, it appears that the nursery was used by women who were the sole bread winners of the family. [38] It is possible that some of the other Protestant charitable organizations took in a few children while their mothers worked, but the facilities did not compare in size or number with those of the Grey Nuns.

VI

Other avenues of employent were open to women who had come capital or had the benefit of a sound basic education. The Montreal Street Directories show many women running boarding houses, grocery stores and other small businesses. Other women worked as clerks in retail stores or offices. The typewriter and the telephone were coming into use in the 1880's and 1890's, but were still by no means common. It does not seem likely that many women depended on the typewriter and telephone before 1900.

The care of people, particularly the sick, the destitute and the orphaned, has traditionally been the work of women. The Grey Nuns and the Hospital Sisters of St. Joseph had long undertaken this work in Montreal, and the Congregation of Notre Dame had been involved in education from the earliest days. These orders expanded their work in an attempt to keep up with the rapidly growing city, but the need for additional services became apparent. The 1840's and the 1850's saw many new communities emerge under the direction of Bishop Bourget, and the Catholic charitable organizations became institutionalized by the Church. It is not within the scope of this paper to examine the role of the religious orders, but it should be pointed out that during the 1830's Catholic lay women as well as Protestants were involved in charitable work. The Catholic Orphanage, which was established by the Sulpicians in 1832, was confided to the care of the *Société des Dames de Charité.*[39] During the lifetime of the foundresses, the lay administration was vigorous in meeting the needs of the orphanage, but their successors were confronted with serious financial problems in the 1880's and considered disbanding. Assistance from the Sulpicians enabled them to carry on, but in 1889 Mlle Morin, who had run the orphanage for many years, retired, and the Grey Nuns were invited to assume charge of the children.[40] In 1847 the Sulpicians founded a second institution known in its first days as "The House", which was the forerunner of the St. Parick's Orphan Asylum.[41] The Irish Ladies of Charity were interested in this work from its inception, and during the first years lay women cared for the orphans. The Grey Nuns took over at an early date, but the Irish Ladies of Charity maintained their patronage for many years. *Le Refuge de la Passion,* also established by the Sulpicians in 1861, was directed by the Misses Pratt and Cassant until 1866. It was then taken over by les *Petites Servantes des Pauvres,* and after serveral changes in management it came under the care of the Grey Nuns who renamed it *Le Patronage d'Youville* in 1895.[42]

In the 1820's and 1830's Catholic lay women were obviously willing to respond to the needs of society. Bishop Bourget, however, intended all social institutions in the Catholic Community to be controlled by the Church, and *"l'élan de piété imprimé à tous les fidèles de son diocèse par l'Evêque de Montréal a fait surgir des nouvelles communautés."*[43] A group of ladies led by Mme Gamelin had been caring for sick and destitute women since 1828. The Bishop invited les Soeurs de la Charité de la Providence to send members of their order from France to undertake this work. When the order was unable to accede to his request, he established a local order, and six ladies already involved in the work place themselves under the direction of Mme Gamelin.[44] In 1844 *l'Institut des Soeurs de Charité de la Providence* was established canonically in Montreal. The lay apostolate of Mme Marie Rosalie Cadron and her companions was of shorter duration. In 1845 she left her family, and set up *le refuge Ste. Pélagie* for unmarried mothers. She and Sophie Desmarêts took in eleven girls the first year, but the work grew rapidly and nearly four hundred infants were born at the refuge during the first six years. The Bishop instituted a rule for the ladies in 1846, and the novitiate of *les Soeurs de la Miséricorde* accepted six of those who were already engaged in the work.[45] One can but speculate on what might have happened had the Bishop been a man of less drive and determination. It is possible that much of the charitable work would have continued in the hands of Catholic lay women working alongside the existing religious orders. As it turned out, the religious communities took over the care of the orphans, the old and destitute, the mentally and physically sick, the blind, deaf and mute, the unmarried mothers and the female prisoners, and Catholic lay women were gradually excluded, from all but a supporting role.

In the Protestant community, women were involved in numerous charitable institutions.[46] The role of women in these societies varied considerably. In the larger organizations such as the House of Industry and Refuge, there was a board of directors usually composed of prominent businessmen who looked after the financial and legal matters. Various women's committees set the policy and generally directed different aspects of the work. These ladies were usually from the upper classes and gave of their services freely. Finally a respectable older woman was employed as matron to take charge of the daily running of the institution, possible with the assistance of two or three general servants. Smaller societies like the Y.W.C.A., the Women's Protective Immigration Society and the Women's Christian Temperance Union were run exclusively by women.

VII

The greatest progress made by Protestant women in Montreal was in the field of education and nursing. *Ecole Jacques Cartier,* the Catholic normal school in Montreal, did not admit female students until a women's annex was added in 1899.[47] In 1869 Mme Médéric Marchand opened a private school which later received a subsidy from the Catholic School Commission. This school made an attempt to prepare girls for careers in teaching and office work. Between 1881 and 1901 nearly a thousand girls gained their *brevet d'enseignement* for elementary, model or academic teaching.[48] It is not known how many of these girls taught, but it does not seem likely that they had much impact on the teaching profession, as lay teachers were in the minority. In 1893 there were 142 teaching sisters and 43 women teachers in the schools controlled by the Commission, and another 400 sisters were engaged in independent schools.[49] The McGill Normal School opened its doors to student teachers of both sexes in 1857. Women always greatly outnumbered men, although this had not originally been anticipated. The low salaries paid to teachers failed to attract men. The school had some unusual features: tuition was free and financial assistance in the form of small bursaries was given for living expenses. Students whose homes were more than ninety miles from Montreal also received a travel allowance. Male students who had a good academic standing in the school were admitted to McGill College but this privilege did not extend to women. The aim of the school was first and foremost to produce teachers: students had to sign a pledge that committed them to teaching for three years after graduation.[50] The original prospectus was not clear on this point: students were required to promise to comply with Regulation 23, but the meaning of the regulation was not explained. At least one student in the first class did not understand this obligation, and Principal William Dawson received a request from a parent that his daughter should be released from teaching for three years.[51] Dawson's reply has not been found, but an application form used at a later date made the rules of the school more explicit. The applicant promised to pay £10 to the Principal of the Normal School if he or she failed to comply with the regulations which were spelled out and included the three-year pledge to teach.[52]

The financial assistance to normal school students varied from year to year. In 1857 the sum of £8 or £9 was offered.[53] The prospectus for 1867 refers to a sum of $36 for students in the elementary and model course and $80 to those in the academy class.[54]

The following year nineteen female students received $24 each.[55]

During the nineteenth century 1,664 women obtained the elementary diploma, 978 the model and 160 the academic diploma from the McGill Normal School.[56] The classes steadily increased in size from an initial group of eleven girls, six of whom came from Montreal, to one of 149 in the 1898-99 session.[57] Free tuition and the modest bursaries opened a career to many girls who otherwise could not have afforded a college education. Although the pay for teachers was extremely poor, teaching was considered a socially acceptable occupation for respectable girls. It remains a mystery how they managed to maintain their social position on salaries of less than $100 a year. Teaching was the only career open to women that led to a pension. The average salary for women with diplomas was $99 in 1899,[58] but as some teachers at the Montreal High School for Girls received salaries ranging from $350 to $600 a year,[59] many salaries must have been well below the average. Pensions were even more modest than salaries. In 1900 there were twenty-three women in Montreal receiving pensions which averaged $67.34 for an average of twenty-three years' service. The lowest pension was $21.87 a year after twenty years of teaching and the highest $218.77 also after the same length of service.[60]

Before 1871, the McGill Normal School was the only institution concerned with the higher education of women, but in 1884 McGill College opened its doors to women on a regular basis. This enabled graduates of the Normal School, the Montreal High School for Girls and also ladies who attended courses organized by the Montreal Ladies Educational Association to continue their education. A degree from McGill did not, however, immediately open the doors of opportunity to women. As one editor pointed out in 1875, there was no demand for highly educated women outside the teaching profession.[61] The admission of women to McGill had important consequences for the twentieth rather than the nineteenth century.[62] Only a very small number of women attended McGill College particularly in comparison with the Normal School. The faculties of medicine and law refused to accept women and those who wished to study medicine went to the medical school of Bishop's College which was located in Montreal. This institution accepted women after 1890 and ten completed their training before the school merged with the McGill medical school in 1905.[63]

The Montreal School of Nursing had greater impact in creating opportunities for women in the medical field. By mid-century Florence Nightingale had largely succeeded in establishing nursing as a career for respectable women, although the term nurse was still used synonymously with that of servant in Montreal. As the advantages of trained nurses became increasingly apparent, the medical staff and management committee of the Montreal General Hospital began to examine ways of training nurses and in 1874 the committee corresponded with Miss Maria Machin one of the Nightingale nurses at St. Thomas' Hospital, London. The following year Miss Machin arrived in Montreal for the purpose of establishing a school at the General. She was later joined by several trained nurses.[64] Financial difficulties prevented the foundation of a school at that time, and several of the trained nurses left. The Y.M.C.A. proposed a course for nurses in 1877, but the hospital was unable to co-operate, and the project was abandoned.[65] Miss Anna Caroline Maxwell, a graduate of the Boston City Hospital, was engaged in 1879. A circular was prepared announcing that a school offering a two-year course would open in 1880, but it also failed to materialize.[66] Miss Rimmer, who was in charge of the hospital during the 1880's, had no formal training in nursing, but was a lady of good sense and organizing ability and she improved conditions and attracted a better class of women to hospital work.[67].

In 1889 the hospital management committee again resolved on the necessity of a training school, and advertisements were placed in the local papers and in American medical journals. Miss Gertrude Elizabeth Livingstone, who had graduated from the New York Hospital's Training School for Nurses, was appointed, together with two trained assistants. In April 1890 the school opened. Nursing as a career immediately attracted women in Montreal: in the first year, one hundred and sixty applications were received. Eighty candidates were admitted on probation and forty-two were finally accepted.[68] The two-year programme place emphasis on practical experience, and the curriculum contained only twenty-two hours of lectures. Students were rotated through the different wards and departments, spending a few months in each.[69] In spite of the large enrolment only six nurses graduated from the first class.

VIII

By 1900 Montreal was the home of thousands of women whose place of birth was in rural Quebec or the British Isles. The demand for female labour had drawn them to the city, and they had made the transition to a totally new environment. Girls who grew up on the farm surrounded by the warmth and affection of a large family had adapted to working in a factory and living in a cramped room or a shack euphemistically called a rear dwelling. Young Irish girls, some newly arrived from Ireland and others the daughters of Irish settlers in the counties north and south of Montreal, had learned to conform to the demands of wealthy Protestant families. These women left no testimony of their loneliness, discouragement and homesickness, but there is no reason to believe they escaped such feelings.

One of the most striking features of the period was the emergence of the French Canadian working mother. We do not know what effect this had on the relationship within the family, but it was probably considerable. The influence of the religious orders in the moral and religious development of French Canadian children was more important than has previously been recognized, as it is now clear that large numbers of very young children passed their formative years in the care of the sisters whose first concern was to instil a set of standards rooted in the catholicism of nineteenth century Quebec. Prayers and catechism were part of the daily fare of the *salles d'asile,* and the importance of this in the formation of religious, moral and social attitudes should not be underestimated.

In a sense this paper raises more questions than it attempts to answer. One of the most interesting relates to the reasons why French Canadian mothers worked, when apparently those of English, Scottish and Irish origin did not. Was poverty generally more prevalent among French Canadians or did the large family make it necessary to have a second wage corner? Alternatively, was a second wage needed because some French Canadian artisans were buying homes in the suburbs as suggested by the rhetoric in the newspapers? The picture tends to confirm the writer's earlier contention that the Irish made a satisfactory adjustment in Montreal, and were no longer at the bottom of the economic ladder in the post-Confederation years.[70]

As the religious orders proliferated, Catholic lay women were increasingly excluded from a variety of occupations. Within the religious community, however, it was possible for women to rise to positions of great authority and responsibility that had no counterpart in the Protestant community. A high degree of administrative ability and business acumen was required to meet the temporal as well as the spiritual needs of a community. The necessity of accommodating the wishes of the bishop, the chaplain and the sisters while conforming to the civil code, called for diplomacy of a high order on the part of the superior.

Industrial expansion created jobs for women and lessened their dependence on domestic service. At the same time, the existence of a pool of cheap female labour encouraged the growth of the garment, boot and shoe, textile and tobacco trades. The number of women employed in industry reached a peak in 1881, when nearly 16 per cent of the female population were employed in manufacturing as compared with 8 per cent in domestic service. It would be interesting to know why the proportion of women employed in industry had dropped to 11 per cent in 1891.[71] One wonders, also, if these figures do not underestimate the total number of women employed in manufacturing over a given period. To what extent did the responsibilities of marriage and raising a family contribute to creating a highly mobile female work force in which women moved frequently between the factory and the home?

In conclusion it can be said that during the nineteenth century the role of women in Montreal underwent considerable change. At the end of the period they constituted an important but docile element in the labour force. In the unlikely event of a general strike of women, one suspects that the extent of disruption would have astonished Montrealers. As it was women raised no voice against the undoubted hardships of their existence, and few spoke on their behalf.

Graph 1

Sex Ratios for Montreal, Quebec City and the Province of Quebec, 1844-1901

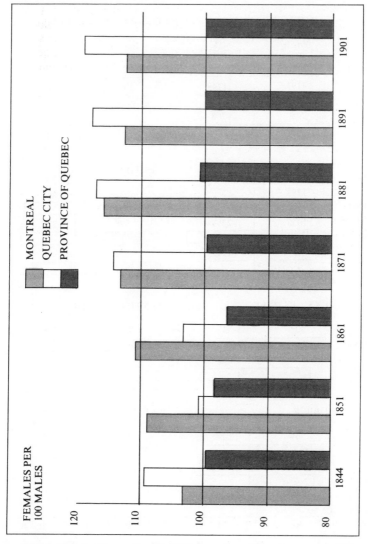

Source: *Census of Lower Canada 1844*, Jour. Leg. Ass., vol. v, app. 1, 1846; *Census of Canada 1851*, vol. I, table 3; 1861, vol I, table 5; *Census of Canada 1871*, vol I, table 1; 1881, vol I, table 1; vol. I, table 3; 1901, vol. I, table 7.

Graph 2
Proportion of Women Industrial Occupations

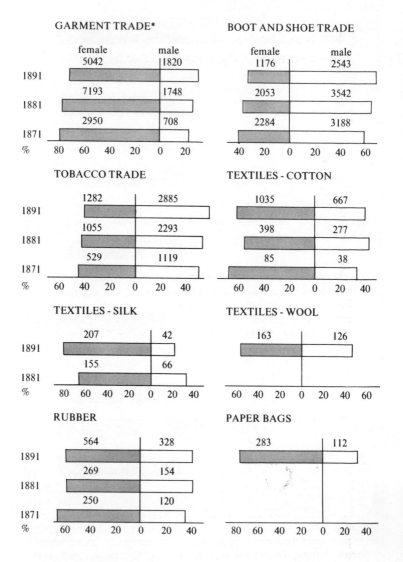

GARMENT TRADE*

	female	male
1891	5042	1820
1881	7193	1748
1871	2950	708

% 80 60 40 20 0 20

BOOT AND SHOE TRADE

	female	male
1891	1176	2543
1881	2053	3542
1871	2284	3188

40 20 0 20 40 60

TOBACCO TRADE

1891	1282	2885
1881	1055	2293
1871	529	1119

% 60 40 20 0 20 40

TEXTILES - COTTON

1891	1035	667
1881	398	277
1871	85	38

60 40 20 0 20 40

TEXTILES - SILK

1891	207	42
1881	155	66

% 80 60 40 20 0 20 40

TEXTILES - WOOL

1891	163	126

60 40 20 0 20 40 60

RUBBER

1891	564	328
1881	269	154
1871	250	120

% 60 40 20 0 20 40

PAPER BAGS

1891	283	112

80 60 40 20 0 20 40

Source: Industrial schedules. *Census of Canada,* 1871, 1881 and 1891.
*Composite figure for related occupations.

86

Chapter 5

'Setting the Stage':
National Organization and the Women's
Movement in the Late 19th Century

Veronica Strong-Boag

Canadian life in the late nineteenth century was marked by an important change in scale. Voluntary organizations once largely restricted to the local community or, in rare instances, the province, now achieved national stature,[1] as fears of immigration, industrialization and urbanization aroused increasing numbers of Canadians to band together for reassurance and remedy. Businessmen sought relief in nation-wide combines and associations.[2] Working men established provincial and national unions.[3] Protestant churchmen also set their hopes on wider alliances.[4] Great partnerships like the Canadian Manufacturers' Association, the Canadian Labour Union and the Methodist Church of Canada represented attempts to find collective solutions to the similar problems of the Dominion's 'island communities'.[5] At the same time, these new structures gave an aspiring national elite its chance for recognition. Common problems, whether commercial, industrial or religious, justified common leadership. Business, labour or religious alliances reflected and encouraged growth in national feeling. Not only the churches but all these associations can be "closely related to the development of a united, autonomous nation."[6] Their efforts helped to give Canadians a heightened sense of group identity just as the twentieth century – Canada's century – dawned.

Women – particularly those from the middle class – were not unmoved by the forces which propelled their male relatives into joint activity. They too were shocked by urban poverty, industrial unrest and social disease; they too responded to the call of religion, to the warning of British and American reformers and to the pleas of Canadian nationalists. New access to universities and professions gave them still more reasons for cooperation.[7] As a result, Canada's female citizens shared in the organizational expansion of the late nineteenth century. By the mid-1890s club women were right in the midst of a Dominion-wide campaign for national unity and moral uplift.[8] "Superior" women had their own blueprint for Canada's future.[9]

Women banded together early in the Dominion's history but the major feminine partnerships date from the 1870s.[10] In this decade women began, cautiously at first, to test the value of more than purely local assemblies. Religious faith usually sustained these pioneers in their unfamiliar task and missionary societies were the most important of the first great female alliances. Church women had formed small groups some years previously but they founded provincial and national associations in the 1870s. Determined to give concrete expression to their religious faith and to evangelize the non-Christian world, female church-goers enlarged the scope of their organizational efforts and strengthened the financial bases of their churches. The Woman's Missionary Societies of the Methodist Episcopal Church and of the Methodist Church appeared in 1876 and 1880 respectively. Following the Methodist union of 1884, these two united as the Methodist Woman's Missionary Society. Female Presbyterians, invigorated by the fusion of their churches in 1875, established the Woman's Foreign Missionary Society in 1876. The Baptists set up the Women's Baptist Home Missionary Union of the Maritime Provinces in 1884. Three years later the Women's Baptist Home and Foreign Mission Society was formed from groups in Manitoba and the Northwest Territories. The Congregational Churches created a Woman's Board of Missions in 1886. Anglicans were somewhat different. Since 1883 every baptised person, male and female, belonged to the Domestic and Foreign Missionary Society. Unlike other Protestants who established independent female associations, the more conservative Anglicans formed a Woman's Auxiliary to the Missionary Society in 1886.[11]

Methodism also offered women roles as Sunday School teachers and deaconesses. This latter group appeared in both Canada and the United States in 1887. Intended originally for evangelical work these Methodist women soon responded to the urgent need for urban charity, quickly taking on the role of social workers.[12] The Church of England added religious orders to its shorter list of similar activities.[13] An extensive network of women's religious orders and lay confraternities existed for Roman Catholics. The Nuns of the Good Shepherd, the Sisters of Providence and a host of other sisterhoods were the major dispensers of charity among the Catholic poor.[14]

Although interdenominational operations were beginning in

city missions, most women worked along side their co-religion-
ists. The lack of interdenominational experience was particularly
true of Catholics as one club woman explained: "the R.C. ladies
... say quite frankly that they have not been accustomed to work
with others and do not know their methods of procedure ..."[15]
Indeed, the strength of religious affiliations reflected the
restricted nature of most women's lives. The church, the strongest institution in young communities, offered middle-class
women in particular one of their few opportunities to escape the
household's confines. There, sustained by spiritual authority,
they could regularly socialize in the performance of unimpeach-
able tasks. Since church membership was an essential factor in
determining an individual's place in nineteenth century society,
women did not easily trespass beyond its borders. Only some
overriding sentiment, like nationalism, could counteract the
weight of religious differences.

While missionary societies were the most powerful instances of
women's ordering impulse in the 1870s and 1880s, Canadians
were also graduating to more secular, if still conscientiously sectarian, organizations. The Woman's Christian Temperance
Union, the Young Women's Christian Association, the Girls'
Friendly Society and the Dominion Order of King's Daughters
were all products of these two decades, testaments to women's
growing awareness of social, and particularly urban, problems.
They were the tools with which middle-class women intended to
rehabilitate the poor and the degenerate. In this great task they
epitomized the widespread faith in female moral superiority.

For many years the Women's Christian Temperance Union
(WCTU) attracted the most publicity, the most criticism and the
most support. Inspired by the woman's temperance movement in
the United States and the men's crusade in Canada, the first
union, then known as the Prohibition Woman's League, was
founded in Owen Sound in May of 1874. The League immediately demonstrated the energy for which the WCTU would be
famous. Pickets, placards and petitions crowded city streets and
municipal offices to demand a reduction in the number of liquor
licences, the closing of billiard saloons where there was gambling, and temperance education for children.[16] While Owen
Sound's women were thus busily occupied, the influential American women were launching the WCTU of the United States. A
Canadian representative at the founding meeting of that body
returned home to establish the Dominion's first official Union, in
Picton, Ontario in December of 1874. This intrepid lady, Mrs.
Letitia Youmans, became the single most important figure in the

WCTU's early history. First president of the Ontario WCTU in 1877 and of the Dominion body in 1883, she engineered mammoth organizing drives until her death in 1896. A strong, energetic and perhaps authoritarian executive knit together widely separated women who were often unfamiliar with club procedure. As was the case with many voluntary undertakings, local bodies were frequently intermittent and uncertain in their efforts.[17] Nevertheless, guided by deeply dedicated leaders, the WCTU grew steadily. In 1891 the Ontario body counted 175 unions with 4,318 members.[18]

In addition to the major goal – prohibition – WCTU'ers crusaded for Protestant missions, domestic science instruction for the poor, anti-tobacco legislation, stronger drug laws, social purity, school temperance textbooks and woman suffrage. Nor were they without encouragement. In 1886, under pressure from the WCTU, Ontario introduced the first temperance manual into schools. Seven years later the provincial Minister of Education authorized a textbook on temperance physiology. For the most part, however, official reception was disappointing. Each rebuff served only to drum up support for a suffrage platform. In 1890 a motion asking for its adoption was sent before the Ontario Resolutions Committee which passed it on to the Provincial Convention. Wary of the repercussions of such a radical policy, this body in turn forwarded the resolution to the Dominion command where it was finally adopted. The WCTU's Franchise Department became the major focus for women's first efforts to gain the vote.[19] The first superintendent of the Ontario Department justified her work in a manner most of the Dominion's suffragists, then and later, would have understood:

> It is not the clamor of ambition, ignorance, or frivolity trying to gain position. It is the prayer of earnest, thoughtful Christian women on behalf of their children and their children's children. It is in the interest of our homes, our divinely appointed place, to protect the home against the licensed evil which is the enemy of the home, and also to aid in our efforts to advance God's Kingdom beyond the bounds of our homes.
>
> It is only by legislation that the roots of great evils can be touched, and for want of the ballot we stand powerless in face of our most terrible foe, the legalized liquor traffic. The liquor sellers are not afraid of our conventions, but they are afraid of our ballots.[20]

Although not all women were prepared to campaign for prohibition or the franchise, the 'WCTU'er' struck a popular note in her defense of the home. Concern for the domestic institution was a bond which united the great majority of organized women.

Yet, while many women were politicized by the Union, many others were offended by its harsh condemnation of opposition and its refusal to condone even moderate drinking. Catholics were only the largest of many groups to reject the WCTU's pretensions. By the 1890s the WCTU was clearly not going to recruit or unite all the nation's women. For all its limitations, however, the WCTU had identified many of the problems which would obsess feminine activists for many years to come. Its "attack on the male as the leader of the family and the bulwark of middle-class respectability."[21] also introduced a theme of considerable significance. Championship of an activist maternalism was only the positive side of the same coin.[22]

Unlike the WCTU, the Young Women's Christian Association (YWCA) was modelled on a British experiment. Originating as a prayer union in the 1850s, the British organization had, over time, assumed responsibilities for the housing, domestic training and religious instruction of poor urban girls. The first Canadian branch was established in St. John in 1870. Three years later Toronto became the second 'Y' city followed by Montreal in 1874. Quebec formed its Association in 1875. Membership grew steadily throughout the 1870s and 1880s feeding on the spreading urban poverty. In December of 1893, under the stimulus of women's meetings held at the Chicago World's Fair, a national body was organized to coordinate efforts in various cities.

The constitution of the St. John 'Y' set the tone for subsequent groups:

> The objects of this Association shall be, the mutual spiritual improvement of its members, the systematic circulation of suitable Religious Literature, the regular visitation of the poor and suffering and the promotion, whenever and wherever possible, of the knowledge and love of Christ Jesus our Lord.[23]

As this pledge suggests, the YWCA recruited heavily from the same Protestant evangelical churches which were so well represented in the WCTU. By the 1890s the 'Y' had become a major instrument of Protestant benevolence. Although much good was done, paternalism is the key word in describing its attitude to young members. One symptom of this was the training of girls for domestic service, sometimes in the homes of their benefactors. Home-oriented work was prized for its morals rather than its wages. It also constituted the cheapest of occupational training that the 'Y', and other budget-conscious agencies dealing with women (the penal institutions included) could provide. The YWCA also served as a labour bureau for the new urban settler. By using its services girls could quickly contact employers and thereby protect themselves from the moral dangers of city life. Like other women's organizations, the 'Y' emphasized the importance of family life for the Dominion. The girl had to be protected because she represented a future mother, the guardian of a household. Summer and holiday camps, recreation and study programmes and urban housing for working women were all intended to guide girls into a disciplined and moral woman-hood. By 1893 the YWCA was the single most important agency dealing with the urban working girl. This prominence, like that of the WCTU, helped engender a self-confident isolationism which discouraged support for some broader alliance of the nation's women. The 'Y''s strongly espoused sectarianism had the same effect. Despite this independence the YWCA established an influ-ential tradition of 'maternalistic' intervention, a tradition few Canadian feminists would entirely escape.[24]

Unlike the broadly Protestant WCTU and YWCA, the Girls' Friendly Society (GFS) was an Anglican organization formed in 1882 as a national branch of the British parent society.[25] Its ranks included the middle-class 'associate' and the unmarried working girl 'member'. The ideal bond between the two was that of a mother and daughter – this inegalitarian association symbolizing the preferable relationship between the upper and lower classes. The GFS in both Britain and Canada also maintained a socially conservative attitude to the poorer family: "It aimed to prop up the family where it was still performing its function, and to pro-vide a substitute family [with mother and sisters, but not father or brothers] for girls who were orphaned or some reason separ-ated from their relatives."[26] A wide variety of programmes set out to stabilize and control working-class life-styles. As its first duty the GFS took on the reception and shelter of immigrant girls. Such assistance was supplemented by labour bureaus, adult edu-cation classes, lunch rooms, recreation centres, vacation homes and sick funds. In addition, members were urged to support domestic and overseas missions. All GFS activities stressed moral purity; loss of a member's character brought immediate expul-sion. Exercising their *noblesse oblige* sentiments on a carefully chosen group, these Anglicans did not view themselves as "refor-matory ... we seek rather by love and friendship to protect young, innocent lives, and to guard them and train them for Christ."[27]Although the Society's British traditions made it attrac-tive and familiar to some Canadians, it was never as powerful as the Anglican Woman's Auxiliary. In time, this relatively weak position made it receptive to plans for greater cooperation among Canadian women.[28]

The Dominion Order of King's Daughters (DOKD) sprang from an American parent established in New York City in 1886. By the close of the same year 'circles' had been established in Canada. Like the GFS it was particularly strong in Ontario but, unlike the Anglican body, it was broadly Protestant in membership. Founded expressly to develop spiritual life, it soon responded to the same urban problems which concerned the YWCA and the GFS. Comparable services included educational classes, lunch rooms, mothers' meetings, fresh air camps, summer creches, girls' clubs and convalescent homes. Such assistance was "not of a reformative, but of a formative character."[29] The debauched and the degenerate were not in its keeping. Although the DOKD's ranks embraced both rich and poor, there was not so formalized a relationship as that which distinguished the Friendly Society. There was still, however, more than a touch of patronage involved in the efforts of these middle-class women to remake the lives of the poorer urban inhabitant. Unlike the WCTU and, in time, the YWCA, neither the GFS nor the DOKD, appeared to view themselves as major proponents of legislative reform, instead they worked most comfortably in the older, more *ad hoc,* charitable tradition. It was a mode of operation which very few feminine charities would entirely reject.[30] In the 1890s the Dominion Order was probably the smallest of the broadly Protestant national societies. Like the GFS, it would welcome opportunities for some wider association of women.

Spiritual and welfare interests were not the only matters to engage Canadian women. Cultural societies supplied another prominent element in the club movement. Although many town musical, artistic and literary groups sprang up in the 1870s and 1880s none grew to national proportions. The first years of the 1890s were more fertile, producing both the Aberdeen Association and the Women's Art Association of Canada. Like many other societies founded in this decade each deliberately rejected sectarianism and espoused patriotism, perhaps in its stead. In the case of these Associations, nationalistic sentiment took the form of a crusade to improve the cultural level of the Dominion.

The Aberdeen Association (AA), familiarly known as the "mission of the old magazine", laboured to overcome the effects of geographic isolation. While on a western holiday in 1890, Lady Ishbel Aberdeen, wife of a future Governor-General, encouraged Winnipeg women to distribute literature to the widely-separated households of the Northwest. Her enthusiasm, later so influential for other, more ambitious, feminist projects in Canada, was contagious. Volunteers across the Dominion soon busily supported this informal Canadianization campaign. The AA's mailing list eventually grew to include readers in mines, lumber camps, sealing vessels and lighthouses. The Association helped compensate for the cultural and material proverty of a young land. Its messengers reminded recipients of national and religious loyalties. Where communication was poor and distances great, the AA affirmed a common identity. Its workers were of necessity particularly conscious of the need to strengthen ties between the different regions; they would be easy converts to plans for a national confederation of women.[31]

The Women's Art Association of Canada (WAAC) did not originate for philanthropic purposes like the majority of its contemporaries. Growing out of the Women's Art Club of Toronto established in 1890, it planned both to promote a more general interest in art and to offer mutual help and encouragement to female artists and art-lovers. Its aims suggest an important distinction between 'professional' and 'honorary' membership. The former was made up of serious artists; the latter's interest in art was largely a leisure time activity. The division between the two groups was reflected in the operations of the Association, which, on the one hand, offered *ateliers* and live models and, on the other, held exhibitions and lectures on the Canadian and foreign art worlds. Both aspects of its labours appear to have been generally successful. The WAAC provided female artists with a sympathetic milieu, including a potential market for their work[32] and sponsored shows which brought international exhibits to culturally isolated towns. By 1893 the Club had already asserted its national ambitions by changing its name to the Women's Art Association of Canada but, like other Toronto-based bodies, it could use assistance in substantiating this claim. As a representative of the non-sectarian minority in a club world deeply divided by religion the Association also had every reason to welcome a more interdenominational spirit among Canadian women.[33]

Although never as widespread as local cultural societies, woman's rights' associations also appeared as early as the 1870s.[34] Suffragists made up the least publicly acceptable elements of the club movement in the early years. Hampered by persistent opprobium, they endeavoured to create forums for women's discussion of political issues. So long as female citizens were denied the vote, suffragists conducted their campaigns on a largely non-partisan level. Appealing to all parties, they emphasized that enfranchisement would protect women and not desex them as some feared. Their oft-repeated promise that feminine votes would improve the entire community was part and parcel of the widespread belief in masculine immorality and feminine purity.[35] The Dominion Women's Enfranchisement Association (DWEA) was the most ambitious suffrage society operating in the 1890s. Relying heavily on its Toronto base, it had little real claim to national stature but its two powerful spokesmen, Dr. Emily Howard Stowe and her daughter, Dr. Augusta Stowe Gullen, gave the DWEA a powerful advantage. Very conscious of their weakness in a conservative community, such women were increasingly receptive to new ways of broadening their appeal and educating Canadian womanhood.[36]

By 1893 a number of Canada's female associations had achieved national dimensions. The strongest of these were the missionary societies but more secular groups like the WCTU, the YWCA, the GFS and the DOKD were also attracting supporters. Cultural and political interests were enshrined within separate organizations. Canadians were often intensely conscious of these new female initiatives. The Victoria *Times* gave an extravagant but not untypical appraisal of developments:

> Ten years ago people were much more content to lead a vegetable life, troubling heads but little over what are now considered to be the burning questions of the day. There was a stifling air of "laissez-faire" in those times, and a strong tendency towards the suppression and ridiculing of all women's higher aims and ambitions; but in this fin-de-siecle much of that is changed, and the ability of the gentler sex to cope with and successfully master many of the deeper problems of life is becoming an established and recognized fact.[37]

Women in substantial numbers had rejected purely individual solutions to the problems of their time. As patriots they recognized the value of Dominion-wide alliances. By the early 1890s many club women were prepared to advance beyond their first relatively restricted national partnerships to some wider association.

By their failings and by their virtues the early feminine associations had laid the essential groundwork for the creation of the National Council of Women of Canada (NCWC) in 1893. Citizens were becoming accustomed to a maternalistic activism. Issues like working girls, urban housing, public creches, children's recreation, cultural improvement and social purity had been identified as belonging, although not exclusively, to female reformers.

The work of the NCWC's precursors had highlighted the role of women in society and in the family. It was up to new organizations, including the National Council, to expand upon these efforts. Women had also received an important lesson in organizational procedures. The pioneers had taught

> ... women to take part in business, to be methodical and orderly, and to subordinate individual opinions to those of the majority. But, on the other hand, [they] ... also erected new barriers between us and new rivalries, and it is often inexpressibly sad to find members of one charitable or philanthropic institution carrying on in a spirit of jealousy and enmity towards some other kindred organization with similar objects, but different methods, and both overlapping one another's work, and hindering instead of helping the common good.[38]

Although numerous women, particularly those in the labour force, were unheard from, the Club movement did show considerable diversity and duplication by the last decade of the nineteenth century. The need for some kind of clearing house for the Dominion's feminine activities was becoming apparent. Patriotism could be best served by furthering the co-operation of the nation's women.

Sentiments in favour of a coordinating mechanism were fostered by events in the United States and elsewhere. Sharing beliefs in the efficacy of maternal influence, the distinctiveness of the female character and the injustice of much in society, women began to form international partnerships by the last quarter of the nineteenth century. The pioneer American feminists, Elizabeth Cady Stanton and Susan B. Anthony, crossed to England in 1882-3 to lay the first ambitious plans for an international meeting of suffragists. Tactical considerations soon caused the National Woman Suffrage Association planners in the United States to broaden the scope of the proposed meetings to include "all associations of women in the trades, professions and reforms as well as those advocating political rights."[39] This change insured the future cooperation of Canadian women who, for the most part, could not have supported an outright suffrage platform.

Stanton's and Anthony's first proposals were premature. The founding meeting of the International Council of Women (ICW) did not take place until 1888 in Washington, D.C. It was just as well. Several promising developments had occurred since 1883. Unions of Women Workers in Great Britain now provided the nucleus around which the National Council of that country could be formed.[40] In North America, temperance, philanthropic and suffrage forces were reaching national dimensions. Delegates from England, France, Denmark, Norway, Finland, India, the United States and Canada were present at the 1888 assembly.

Canadian representatives in Washington included Bessie Starr Keefer of the WCTU, Dr. Emily Howard Stowe of the Dominion Women's Enfranchisement Association and Emily Willoughby Cummings of the Anglican Woman's Auxiliary. The latter was chosen by the ICW to form a branch in the Dominion. This, however, was not an auspicious moment to begin Canadian involvement in the wider movement and no more was heard, for the time being, from Mrs. Cummings.[41] The National Council of Women of the United States (NCWUS), formed in 1888, was itself a rather overly ambitious undertaking. [42] Its weakness permitted the General Federation of Women's Clubs (GFWC), founded in 1890, to assume the most prestigious national position in the Republic and, in time, to charter its own affiliates in such places as India, the Philippines and Korea.[43] The NCWUS was never to have the authority of its younger Canadian counterpart.

The ICW symbolized feminism's first 'era of sisterhood' but it was another word, motherhood, which most often rallied women of every nation.[44] In many ways the ICW was a gigantic maternal union. According to many female activists within its ranks women's distinctive biology equipped them for a wide range of activities outside the home. The International's preoccupation with this aspect of femininity reinforced the similar beliefs of Canadian women.

The ICW meeting convened at the Columbian Exposition in Chicago in 1893 supplied the immediate impulse behind the formation of the Canadian Council. The wife of the Dominion's Governor-General, Lady Ishbel Aberdeen, unexpectedly became international president at this congress.[45] Canadian women including Emily Willoughby Cummings again attended the ICW's gatherings. One Toronto participant afterwards recalled the superior attitude of some Americans:

> . . . a female shook her umbrella at me and bawled, (although I was very near her), "You Canadians are indifferent. You must be aroused. You must vote![46]

Such attacks were irritating but fairness had earlier forced the same writer to admit that "The American woman's mind is made up on lots of questions which we are just beginning to tackle . . ."[47] The Canadian spectators in Chicago could hardly avoid some awareness of their own relative immaturity in feminist matters. They could, however, console themselves with the election of a Canadian resident, Lady Ishbel Aberdeen, to the presidency.

Returning to Toronto the Canadian representatives asked the Governor-General's wife to undertake the leadership of a national Council. Already a well-known personality because of her earlier travels in the Dominion and her much-publicized reform efforts in Great Britain,[48] Lady Aberdeen could lend the fledgling organization the prestige it would need to overcome the rivalries and divisions of the Canadian club movement, not to mention the hostility of anti-feminists. The problems of national unity in a country wracked by the Jesuit Estates' Bill and the 'Manitoba Schools' Question' made the Chicago visitors all the more eager to acquire a

> president who would be outside all party politics and creed rivalries, and who would yet be sympathetic with all the different sections of thought and work with which women of various races and creeds were connected, throughout the Dominion. [49]

Aberdeen's religious tolerance had been demonstrated while her husband was Lord High Commissioner to the General Assembly of the Church of Scotland. The breadth of her sympathies had been proven by her work for Sunday Schools, the Society for the Prevention of Cruelty to Children, working girls' homes, and Canning Town Women's Settlement, Omnibus Suppers, the Home Reading Union, the Mission to the Costermongers, the Associated Workers' League, George Holland's Mission to Whitechapel, the Strand Rescue Mission, and the Society for the Improvement of Dress for Women Workers.[50] It was harder to believe that a woman who decorated every room with a picture of Gladstone was politically impartial. No one else, however, had the social rank or the organizing abilities to give the NCWC a sound start. As it was, "... the identification of Lady Aberdeen with the local councils ... made cohesive organization so much easier than in the United States."[51]

Having secured Aberdeen as their chief officer, interested women held a few small preliminary meetings in Toronto. Finally, in October of 1893, a mass assembly of the Queen City's women met in the Horticultural Pavilion to inaugurate the National Council of Women of Canada. Here Aberdeen was welcomed as the first president, Mary Macdonell of Toronto as vice-president for Ontario, Mary English of London as recording secretary, Adelaide Hoodless of Hamilton as treasurer and Emily Willoughby Cummings of Toronto as corresponding secretary.

Lady Thompson, wife of the Prime Minister, joined Madame Laurier, wife of the Leader of the Opposition, as a vice-president-at-large, an honorary position. The wives of the lieutenant-governors were to become honorary vice-presidents for their provinces. The same October meeting approved the constitutions for the National and Local Councils.

The enthusiasm generated at the NCWC's founding encouraged the converted to organize Local Councils. Early in November of 1893, two hundred representative women from forty-nine individual societies met to organize the Toronto Local Council of Women.[52] Montreal's Victoria Armories was packed to the doors for a similar gathering on the night of November 30th, 1893.[53] Less than three months later over one thousand people clamoured fruitlessly at the entrance of the Grand Opera House in London, Ontario, and envied the "fully thirty-five hundred" who presided over the formation of a new Council.[54] That same February of 1894, Lady Ishbel Aberdeen, the key speaker in Toronto, Montreal and London, returned to Ontario's capital to address yet another public meeting, this time of nearly 3000 women.[55] Throughout the winter of 1893 and into 1894 large groups met for similar purposes in Hamilton, Ottawa, Quebec City, Winnipeg and Kingston. The skeleton of the NCWC was taking shape just as feminine nationalists had wished.

These Local Councils took in representatives from branches of nationally organized societies like the WCTU, the YWCA and the DOKD and from groups restricted to a single town like literary societies, teachers' associations, and governing boards of orphans' homes. During its first year of existence, 1893-94, the Council was also able to lure a number, although not the most powerful, of Dominion-wide societies in at the national level – the Aberdeen Association, the Women's Art Association, the Girls' Friendly Society, the Dominion Order of King's Daughters and the Dominion Women's Enfranchisement Association. These first affiliates, Local Councils and nationally organized societies were those who appreciated "with a sense 'of much comfort' that we are not alone, that in 'union is strength', and that our endeavours for the good of our beloved country cover the land like a network."[56]

In 1893 the National Council of Women of Canada endeavoured to rally a club movement whose basic divisions were religious in nature. To do this it had to declare itself non-sectarian. This cautious stance did not go uncriticized. The London Local Council under the influence of the WCTU spoke for those who wished membership limited to "Certain Associations of Women who believe in God and in His Son our Saviour, the Lord Jesus Christ".[57] Failing this, hardliners desired to further the cause of righteousness by introducing meetings with an audible rendition of the Lord's Prayer. One spokesman for this point of view pleaded: "Surely not with London only lies the duty of combatting and giving open denial to the idea alas, so generally and rapidly gaining ground that National Council is an irreligious body . . ."[58] The 'non-denominationalists' captained by Lady Aberdeen advocated meetings opened only with silent worship. The Governor-General's wife eventually carried the day since audible repetition of the Lord's name antagonized potential members among the Catholic and Jewish ladies. The London Local Council, however, was nearly destroyed by the bitter controversy. In Toronto, the Council repeated the Prayer aloud for many years despite continued objections. Finally, by about 1900, all the Councils appear to have adopted a form of silent prayer.[59] This decision was a major factor in the WCTU's and YWCA's refusal to affiliate.[60]

The Constitution also included a non-partisan pledge. The NCWC was "organized in the interest of no one propaganda".[61] Politics and religion were too closely interwoven in Canada to be safely separated. In an era marked by exaggerated party spirit the NCWC faced a special difficulty. Its membership quickly came to rely on an urban elite whose masculine counterparts – husbands, fathers, brothers – were often deeply involved in the Conservative and Liberal hierarchies. The appointment of both Mesdames Thompson and Laurier to the executive was intended to disarm those who feared political attachments. The first president, Aberdeen, was determined to secure at least an initial political balance within the NCWC. Her own Liberal sympathies made her very much suspect in Conservative circles and she wished to save the Council similar difficulties.[62] Her efforts were largely successful. Not until World War One was there a real problem of maintaining political neutrality although the strength of Aberdeen's personal sympathies for Gladstonian liberalism must have raised some eyebrows among Conservatives.

The NCWC's carefully emphasized federal structure constituted a third guarantee to members. Article II of the Constitution soothed the worst fears of those who jealously guarded their autonomous peculiarities. It made reassuring reading:

This Council . . . has no power over the organizations which constitute it beyond that of suggestion and sympathy; therefore, no Society voting to enter this Council shall render itself liable to be interfered with in respect to its complete organic unity, independence, or methods of work, or be committed to any principle or method of any other Society, or to any act or utterance of the Council itself, beyond compliance with the terms of this Constitution.[63]

Ill-equipped for combat the NCWC had to rely on conciliation. Only diplomacy could preserve a national union of women.

Although the requirements of survival caused the Council to acknowledge modern secular trends, in other ways it took a more traditional stand. The NCWC pledged itself to the preservation of two of the three major institutions in society: the family and the state. The Preamble to the Constitution set forth this allegiance in no uncertain terms:

> We, Women of Canada, sincerely believing that the best good of our homes and nation will be advanced by our own greater unity of thought, sympathy, and purpose, and that an organized movement of women will best conserve the greatest good of the Family and the State, do hereby band ourselves together to further the application of the Golden Rule to society, custom and law.[64]

This association of "homes and Nation" and "the Family and the State" was to become the leitmotif of Council policy. Since these institutions could not be separated without endangering each, the survival and betterment of one insured, at least according to most NCWC'ers, the improvement of the other. This credo formed the popular cornerstone of NCWC programmes.

The Council's founders believed that the state, under the impact of industrialization and urbanization, was being weakened at its most crucial point – the family. Modern civilization took the father out of the home into the corrupting world of business; it removed traditional feminine tasks from the same home. The woman was left isolated and unable to determine either the food her family consumed or the clothes it wore. Under the impact of an increasingly materialistic male management, the outside world was contaminating family life itself. Aberdeen and her Canadian co-workers saw women in this critical situation as the divinely appointed guardians of an institution which in its inculcation of the virtues of kindness, love, duty, respect and honour was essential to the best kind of human development. "Working in harmony with God's laws of the family", women were "the centre through which all healthy influence should spread."[65]

The role of women outside the family network sprang from their role within that primary group. Feminine influence was to improve man, to draw him back to family-rooted virtues. Too much involved with business, men had often failed to acknowledge human needs.[66] Women had to realize that no walls could keep out worldly corruption. To protect themselves and guarantee a better future for their offspring women had "to be in touch with every side of our manifold life."[67] There was general agreement that "the solidarity of the home interests finds its only salvation in woman's comprehension of civil and religious affairs as they reflect in her home."[68]

In 1893 the NCWC staked out a strong position within the Canadian club movement. Unlike the missionary societies, the WCTU, the YWCA, the GFS and the DOKD it planted a non-sectarian standard. Criticism was still further defused, except from the most hard-line elements, by political non-partisanship. At the same time, the Council's altruistic patriotism with its commitment to family and state was attractive to female activists both within and without the existing societies. The appeal of the NCWC was both simple and, to an important degree, familiar. Adherence to the Golden Rule united women of diverse backgrounds and beliefs providing a "platform, large, strong and broad enough to furnish standing room for all."[69] It also avoided potentially divisive ideological questions and united the largest possible number of women. It would be some time before the Canadian woman's movement outgrew this platform.

But the formation of the NCWC in 1893 also reflected the growing national self-confidence of the last decade of the nineteenth century. During its first meetings, the Council announced its responsibility for the promotion of national enthusiasm and affection.[70] Women in every province felt, like the Halifax president, that

> We are too provincial in this province, and we forget the duty we owe to the rest of Canada; perhaps because we are too well satisfied with ourselves. We do not seem to have felt the great heart-beat of the Dominion as we should. This Council is going to bring us into touch with other parts of the Dominion, and we shall be the "Foremothers" of a great nation.[71]

The NCWC would return to this theme often in the next thirty and more years.

Buoyed up by such patriotic aspirations, many women had high hopes for coordinating feminine policies at the national level. The NCWC would broaden the perspective of workers too preoccupied with purely local issues. At the same time, by informing groups of one another's activities, it could end the needless duplication which beset women's work. And there were still more important tasks confronting the federation. One prominent leader spoke of this much later: ". . . the changing and moulding of public opinion is . . . the greatest thing the Council has done. It is before all else a federation of ideas or ideals, and an educative force." It existed "to suggest and initiate rather than to carry out."[72] The founders of the NCWC intended to extend feminine influence over all the operations of Canadian society. Previously employed in a multitude of smaller associations this power would now be exercised on the largest possible scale. This enlargement was essential because the community had outgrown all less comprehensive solutions to its problems.

In the last half of the nineteenth century Canadian women joined wholeheartedly in the organizational boom which swept the Dominion. Like businessmen, working men and church men, they increasingly relied on Dominion-wide partnerships to express social concern and unite the country. The strongest of the early alliances were fervently sectarian. Secularly-minded groups were a small minority. Leading club women, however, were not long satisfied with their much divided realm. The benefits of greater cooperation were clear. So long as feminine patriots were distracted by religious rivalries so long would patriotic womanhood be weak. The NCWC – a giant confederation – admitted nationalists of every religious or political stripe. Under its aegis the Dominion's women would be strengthened in their struggle for Canada's improvement. At the same time, the Council would raise up a new crop of feminist leaders to succeed those who were rooted in sectarianism and provincialism. After 1894 the National Council would be a major instrument of feminine nationalism, reform and ambition. The stage for this work had been well prepared. The birth of the Council represented the culmination of a trend toward national unity in the Canadian woman's movement. This unity, imperfect as it was in some ways, contributed to the growing sense of group identity with which Canadians of both sexes entered the new century.

Chapter 6

Henri Bourassa and
"the Woman Question"

Susan Mann Trofimenkoff

In the 1960s English Canadians rediscovered Henri Bourassa and made of him a man ahead of his time, a prophet of bilingualism and biculturalism, a salve for the Canadian conscience, pestered as it was by ever-increasing signs of unhappiness from Quebec. Earlier generations of English Canadians had known him too, particularly those living in the 1900s and 1910s. They made of Bourassa a traitor to the Canadian cause; they feared, distrusted, even hated him. In both instances, Bourassa's penchant for going against the majority made of him a 'force to be reckoned with,' and a radical one at that, to English and French Canadians alike. Whether provided by our grandparents or our teachers, the popular image of Henri Bourassa has thus always been a *rouge* image.

But Laurier, who knew him well, had called Bourassa a *castor rouge*. The *castor* in Bourassa has largely been taken for granted by historians, with a nod to his ultramontanism and a quick passing on to more exciting things. It is perhaps time to have a closer look at the *castor* side of Bourassa, and where better to find it than in his attitudes to women?

On three separate occasions, in 1913, 1918, and 1925, Bourassa filled his pen with vitriol and denounced what modern society seemed to be doing to women. Indeed, according to Bourassa's logic, each occasion led inexorably to the next; he could well have written everything he had to say on "the woman question" in 1913. Instead he awaited circumstances, rushed into print, probably muttering to himself "I told you so" and then after 1925 never said another word on the subject. The three issues which prompted his ire were feminism in 1913, woman suffrage in 1918 and divorce in 1925. In each case the circumstances, Bourassa's ideas and the echoes those ideas created reveal a particular view of women, a particular view of men and a particular, albeit partial, view of the *castor* Bourassa.

Of the three aspects of the "woman question" with which Bourassa dealt, feminism had the largest geographical setting. Feminism was "in the air" internationally and any Québécois newspaper reader would have been aware of it. Of course, militant feminism received the most publicity for this was the heyday of British suffragettes' use of 'violence' and subjection to it, and Québécois press readers were not spared any of the grisly details.[1] Indeed some of the leading British suffragettes had visited Montreal,[2] making speeches and urging on the more hesitant colonials. "Don't be submissive. Don't be docile. Don't be ladylike. Don't dread being conspicuous . . ." shouted Mrs. Barbara Wylie[3] to the consternation of Canadian *castors* like Henri Bourassa.

This "plague of women" as the *Gazette* called it[4] appeared to be descending even closer to home. In February 1913 the Local Council of Women in Montreal organized a two-week Montreal Suffrage Exhibition, in March a Canadian contingent joined a mass march in Washington in favour of woman suffrage,[5] in April the Montreal Suffrage Association was formed,[6] in May the National Council of Women held week-long meetings in Montreal and among the main topics of discussion were the suffrage and the legal status of women in Quebec.[7] And in November the Montreal *Herald* had the audacity to publish a special woman's edition and to have women hawking it on the streets!

In the midst of all this feminist activity, Bourassa took to his editorial desk, penning a series of articles partially in response to provocation on the part of a Montreal suffragette and partly to state his case in opposition to feminism and to the suffrage.[8]

For Bourassa feminism constituted another foreign import, spelling danger and disorder for French Canada. For all his respect for British political and constitutional principles, he had no use whatsoever for this latest Anglo-Saxon export. He therefore traced feminism to its Protestant roots, lumped it with socialism, and condemned it roundly as a danger to the French-Canadian family and thus to French-Canadian civilization. Just look at those countries where feminism is rampant; there, Bourassa contended, you will find female drunks, unmarried mothers, divorcées, and "angel makers."[9] Of course no such vile creatures existed in Quebec! What did exist in Quebec and what would be most threatened by feminism was the vast ideological construct which had been building since at least the 1840s. This "official ideology" had made of Quebec a cultural haven in a materialist sea, an exemplar of superior virtues, religious, moral, educational, familial. And the guardian of it all was woman. If she should change, and feminism would surely change her, then the whole construct would tumble. What then?

So very important was the maintenance of this construct and of the woman's place in it, that Bourassa hauled out every conceivable argument to stamp out feminism. From religion to ridicule, from principles to propriety, from pseudo-scientific laws to a personal distaste for political practices, Bourassa touched on them all hoping that their combination would make his case irrefutable. Certainly they made it comprehensive: there was Eve at the origin of all the evil that had befallen the human race because she desired to be the equal of God; there was the skirt revolting against the pants; there was the unchanging principle of order and unity and hence of woman's everlasting and unchanging role within it; there was Bourassa's personal sense of decorum outraged by women taking an active part in public life; [10] there were the pseudo-scientific notions of the day that people develop in accordance with their inner, natural laws and hence the view that the inner space (and therefore law) of women was the womb; and finally there was Bourassa's own disdain for the corruption, intimidation, blackmail and general scurrilousness of political activity. Once you gave women the vote you would expose them to all that!

Bourassa's arguments harbour a few peculiarities. For one thing he possessed a highly developed sense of history but he tended to use it only when it suited his purposes. He was, for example, more than willing to argue that Christianity had rescued women from their state of slavery to men in pagan days but he would not carry his historical sense any further to wonder whether the subsequent position of women – on a pedestal of purity, virginity and spirituality – might not require some revision twenty centuries later. Then again, Bourassa obviously knew very few feminists and understood them even less. For most feminists of his day whether in Great Britain, the United States, Canada or Quebec would all have accepted the notion of *given* differences between men and women, of female superiority in the realms of caring, loving and nurturing. All they wanted to do was extend these very attributes into the public realm for the betterment of all mankind.

Since Bourassa in fact shared some of the same tenets with the women he decried, it is not surprising to find echoes of the same kinds of ideas throughout the press and the pulpit of the time. The women's pages in newspapers all propagated the image of the homey, introspective, emotional, light hearted (and light headed), devoted mother and wife.[11] Fadette in *Le Devoir* warned women against the feminist dream of being the rival of men;[12] Colette in *La Presse* sanctioned a division of womankind into *femmes* (the real women, devoted to their maternal mission, the ornament of their families), *suffragettes* (the moderate ones, mistaken but permitted to express their views) and *furies* (the violent suffragettes who had simply ceased being women).[13] Even letters to the editor expressed the view that the political emancipation of women would bring about a total disruption of society.[14] Perhaps even more pleasing to Bourassa was the appearance within a few years of a series of articles on feminism by the renowned theologian Mgr. L. A. Paquet. Paquet drew not only upon every theological source he could muster but also quoted Henri Bourassa to denounce the freedom young girls had, their audacity in questioning the authority of their parents, their exposure to doctrines and activities at variance with family traditions, their very dress which defied all sense of decency.[15] Farther afield, in English Canada, if Bourassa had cared to look, he would have discovered the women editors of a new publication the *Canadian Woman's Annual* repeating the same notion of women as "the conservers of life, the natural guardians of the young, the creators of the home. . . "[16]

With so many people echoing the same ideas, why did Bourassa feel the necessity to be so vehement? Probably because he saw feminism as the thin edge of the wedge; the worst was yet to come: first there would be the suffrage and then there would be divorce.

Five years later, in 1918, the Canadian Parliament was in fact in the midst of a debate over a government-sponsored bill to extend the suffrage in federal elections to women. Unlike the earlier occasion when feminism had had an international setting, the suffrage question was much more a domestic one. The international scene was overshadowed by the war and although the Canadian government was aware of other countries' interest in the issue, it took its cue from some of the Canadian provinces and from its own Wartime Elections Act of 1917.[17] The suffrage bill was introduced quietly, debated decorously and passed promptly.

The press too, inundated with war copy, gave scarcely a mention to this latest aspect of the "woman question." It recognized, along with Borden, that women had engaged publicly and visibly in war work; whether, as Borden argued, this warranted their receiving the vote as recompense was another question. Indeed one journalist expressed his uneasiness about a delegation of women descending upon Ottawa for the Women's War Conference in February 1918: they may have been charming but they caused more apprehension than any delegation of western farmers or trade unionists![18] The *Gazette* was much less alarmed and when the suffrage bill was introduced, remarked calmly that "this epochal legislation" seemed to be receiving general acceptance.[19]

Perhaps that was what stirred Bourassa to action. Without even waiting for the major debate on the question (indeed perhaps hoping to influence it), Bourassa jumped into the fray with a series of articles denouncing woman suffrage.[20] Extremely revealing of the importance Bourassa accorded the question of social order now being undermined for a second time, was the fact that his articles were written at the very time of the conscription riots in Quebec city. Bourassa said not a word about them, leaving the commentary on that ugly situation to his second-in-command, Omer Héroux.

Like its forbear feminism, the suffrage was another foreign import. It was the logical result of the Reformation and the Anglo-Saxon break with tradition, with true Christianity, with the family and with society. From then on, rampant individualism held sway; once one had accepted the notion of "every man for himself," there was no reason for objecting to "every woman for herself." Moreover, Anglo-Saxon women had long since lost their feminine charm and natural means of influence; it was to be expected that they would therefore seek political means to affect society. But of course none of this applied to French-Canadian women who had maintained the true traditions, the true faith, the true sense of the family (thanks to their "glorious fecundity") and hence their proper sphere of influence.

Bourassa then proceeded to draw a distinction between the vote as a privilege and the vote as a function. He categorically denied any element of privilege in the suffrage; rather it was a function, a function of those whose duty it was to protect society. Needless to say that particular duty belonged to men. Women's duty lay elsewhere, in motherhood and therefore in private. Indeed, maternity was such a high calling that women, like judges, were granted the right not to vote. For all his intellectual posturing, Bourassa was in fact voicing the commonplace notion that sexual differences not only entail but determine social differences.

Just in case his readers could not follow his historical and philosophical reasoning, Bourassa took to name calling. He granted that women might have a sense of morality superior to that of men, but only in private and only when sustained by motherhood; in public their intuition, emotionalism and passion would only lead them into trouble. They could exercise their moral influence quite effectively without voting; indeed it was only by not becoming "public women" that they could exercise any influence at all. And those women who did not conform to Bourassa's rule for them (essential motherhood no matter what their civil state) were *monstres*.

Presumably the federal suffrage bill would create all these "public women," all these "*monstres*." Once women had the vote they would become party hacks, MPs, senators, lawyers, in short "women-men," a hybrid which would destroy the woman-mother, the "woman-woman." At that point women would cease marrying, cease having children, cease caring for and educating the young. Having tossed away all such privileges, women would return to the state of slavery they endured twenty centuries ago. Something then that the suffragists saw as a mark of freedom – the vote – Bourassa saw as a sure step to slavery.

The best place to find echoes of such ideas is in the House of Commons during committee stage discussion of the Woman Suffrage Bill. This occurred after the publication of Bourassa's series of articles, and although only a few speakers echoed Bourassa verbatim, all of the opponents of the bill, and they were mostly French Canadian, would have acceded heartily to his views. The opponents dreaded the prospect of women being dragged away from their homes.[21] They saw only evil resulting: men and women would become alike; conflict between them would ensue with the eventual disruption of homes; the birthrate would decline; family ties would be broken; parental authority would be destroyed and respect for women would vanish.[22] Moreover, as was well known, woman's constitution could not stand up to the excitement of political life; they would succumb to the "foul vapours of politics."[23] One MP who managed to demolish his case no sooner than he had stated it was nonetheless able to put into one sentence what all the other opponents, Bourassa included, took pages to articulate:

I say that Holy Scriptures, theology, ancient philosophy, Christian philosophy, history, anatomy, physiology, political economy, and feminine psychology, all seem to indicate that the place of women in this world is not amid the strife of the political arena, but in her home.[24]

What more could anyone say? The opponents tried valiantly but the debate was over within a few hours and the bill passed easily. The senators subsequently made a few brave attempts to amend the bill but to no avail. Canadian women were to have the vote in spite of, or perhaps because of, what the *Gazette* called the "mouldy ideas" which were used to oppose it.[25]

Québécois, however, went on espousing these "mouldy ideas" by refusing the provincial suffrage to women until 1940. And again, just as in 1913, Bourassa could be gratified to find his province maintaining the true path, as outlined and expressed by journalists, politicians and theologians.[26]

Behind the "mouldy ideas" was something which no one recognized at the time[27]: the opponents of woman suffrage were not talking about women at all, but about an image of women. All those angels and queens and ornaments and objects of respect were not real women at all but rather ideas that these men entertained about women. What the suffrage bill implied was that there was something wrong with the image; votes for women would in fact tarnish the image men had of women. Indeed, one could stretch the point even further: the debate over the Woman Suffrage Bill may well have been a debate over the manliness of the MPs. Their whole notion of themselves as heads, protectors, leaders, chivalrous and gallant descendents of God's initial creation was under attack and, I think, subconsciously they knew it. Votes for women was destroying not only man's image of woman but his own self-image. Hence, the verbal violence of both Bourassa and the politicians who opposed woman suffrage.

As Bourassa had predicted in 1913 and as the opponents of the suffrage bill foresaw in 1918, the next stage in this dangerous "woman question" would be the break up of families – divorce. In fact, by 1925 the Canadian House of Commons was openly debating the question. Of the three occasions when Bourassa wrote on "the woman question," this one was the least discussed publicly. Perhaps the subject was still taboo, as the divorce statistics in Canada climbed slowly but surely every year through the 1920s. Certainly it was constitutionally complicated in that the Federal Government had final control but some provinces had divorce courts, others (Ontario and Quebec) did not and had to take cases to the Federal Parliament, and others still (in the west) were in the process of establishing them. The question was also legally complicated with different criteria for obtaining a divorce in different parts of the country. And finally, the question was socially complicated, with varying religious and social sanctions surrounding marriage. No wonder few public speakers wished to broach such a topic! Then too, for those who were looking for such things, there were some ominous signs surrounding the debate in the House of Commons: the bill was introduced on Friday the 13th; and a few days after it passed, an earthquake shook the eastern part of North America. Three women in Quebec actually died of fright![28] When only a few years earlier, serious people could be found to suggest that the First World War had been inflicted upon mankind as punishment for his sins, who would be surprised if someone should think that the very earth itself was objecting to this latest impertinent challenge to the social order?

The challenge this time came from western Canada. Joseph Shaw, a Progressive MP from Calgary, finally was allowed to present a bill which he had been urging for some years: a bill to equalize the criteria for obtaining a divorce in the four western provinces. Prior to 1925, men in the west could obtain a divorce on the grounds of a wife's adultery, but women had to prove not only adultery on their husband's part, but also desertion in order to obtain a divorce in the west.[29] Poor Shaw merely wanted to remove a small anomaly in the law and although he had the backing of most of the MPs and some major associations[30] and even the precedent of a recent British Law,[31] he may well have been unaware of the veritable Pandora's box of vile humours his bill would open, particularly among the French Canadians.

Of course those same French Canadians had been sensitized to the issue by two *causes célèbres* in the marital field. Both the Despatie-Tremblay case, which had dragged through the courts from 1909 until 1921 and which journalists like Bourassa recalled on every possible occasion, and the Plante-Zannis case between 1918 and 1925 emphasized the growing secularization of marriage, the ever-increasing civil control and hence the diminishing ecclesiastical sanction of marriage.[32] A sure way to damnation[33] – and now the Parliament of Canada was further emphasizing the purely civil, legalistic, secular nature of one of man's God-given institutions.

On this occasion Bourassa waited to express his views until after the major debate in the House of Commons, to add his voice to the substantial minority that had opposed the second reading of the bill and to urge Senate rejection of it.[34]

Just like feminism and woman suffrage, divorce was also another foreign import, this time from the United States and France. And if Canada accepted such an import, the country would follow the same path toward national degradation and suicide, the latter caused by the current euphemism for birth control: "voluntary sterility." Divorce would undermine the very foundation of the family and as the family goes so goes the nation.

Like most of the parliamentary opponents of the Shaw bill, Bourassa tended to skirt the particular import of the bill – a simple equalization of the sexes in a given state of affairs – in order to denounce the very principle of divorce. He did this deliberately in order to show by example what he felt Catholic and Quebec spokesmen had been neglecting to do ever since Confederation. Bourassa was appalled at the total lack of concern expressed by Quebec's Confederation makers about the distribution of powers regarding marriage and divorce between the federal and provincial governments. Quebec had been left with the "frills," the mere celebration of marriage, whereas the federal government could make any laws it pleased regarding marriage and divorce. The Confederation agreement of 1867 had thus sanctioned the legal validity of divorce for the whole of Canada and Québécois of the time had quietly acquiesced. No wonder, claimed Bourassa, we have had difficulty having our Catholic social views accepted in the rest of Canada. And he proceeded to trace all the blows French Canadians outside Quebec had experienced to the spinelessness of French-Canadian leaders in the 1860s on the divorce issue! The only remedy lay in French Canadians loudly proclaiming the Catholic social truths by which they were supposed to be living and by putting some order into Quebec's own marriage laws where civil marriage was gradually replacing religious marriage. Civil marriage would lead directly to divorce.

Of course Bourassa could not avoid the question of equality between men and women that was at the heart of the Shaw bill. Nor would he want to, since the question permitted him to refurbish all his old arguments on the "anatomy is destiny" theme which he had used in combatting feminism in 1913 and woman suffrage in 1918. If we really want equality between men and women on this divorce issue, he stated bluntly, we should abolish divorce completely.[35] But since that was probably impracticable in 1925 Bourassa justified the legal inequality between men and women in the matter of divorce. Adultery was in fact different for men and women; the social consequences were different (Bourassa did not dare utter his precise meaning: men could get away with it whereas women would become pregnant). And since undefiled maternity (again the unspecified meaning: nobody else in there) was woman's greatest honour, an honour no man could achieve, then her fall from such a height warranted a penalty heavier than that placed upon the man. The existing laws then simply sanctioned what was obviously a natural, a social truth. Add to that Christ's saying that a husband may cast off an adulterous wife and Bourassa had what he considered an airtight case for the legal inequality of men and women in the matter of divorce.

Echoes of Bourassa's views reverberated in French-Canadian circles for some time. Indeed, so much interest was expressed in his articles that *Le Devoir* put them together in a pamphlet which seems to have sold quickly and well.[36] Of course the debate in the House of Commons preceeded the publication of his articles but the opponents of the divorce bill differed little in their arguments. Indeed one MP, C. A. Fournier, went to great lyrical lengths about the results of divorce, in a manner Bourassa could never achieve:

> Legalized lechery, adultery by due process of law, concubinage upheld by the constitution, all aspects of present day divorce, being sanctioned, flourishing in rank growth and their foul affects rise, like the exhalations of a noisome slough, which scatters to the winds the propagating plague that poisons the nation.[37]

If most MPs did not go quite so far, there was a distinct feeling in the debate, even among the proponents of the bill, that the world of the 1920s was disintegrating with more crime, more women out of their homes, more divorce.[38] The Senate debate on the bill, three months after Bourassa's articles, bestirred fourteen opponents, three of whom had obviously read and digested Bourassa's arguments.[39] But they could not manage what Bourassa had hoped for, the defeat of the bill.

Other indications of a general approval of the ideas Bourassa was expressing can be found in the women's pages of the French press where the maternal and subordinate role of the woman was repeatedly stressed.[40] And "all of intellectual Montreal" poured out to hear a French priest speak on feminism later in March of 1925. Chanoine Coubé too made the case for male superiority, quite charmingly it must be admitted; the women in the audience, were they not already convinced of their own inferiority, would easily have been flattered into it.[41] Then too of course, Bourassa's views were no different from those much more dryly expressed in the Quebec civil code which allowed separation, not divorce, for the man on the grounds of his wife's adultery but not for the woman on similar grounds unless the husband happened to be keeping his concubine in the family home.[42]

Except for a lengthy series of articles on the religio-legalistic history of divorce in 1929 at the time of the establishment of divorce courts in Ontario,[43] those were the final words of

Bourassa on "the woman question." What do they reveal?

In the first place, Bourassa harboured a particular image of women. For him women were delicate creatures of intuition, nobility and dignity; they were emotional but at the same time full of good sense. They were the gentle, pure, charming, queens of the home, preservers of tradition, educators of *sons*. Their primary function was marriage and maternity. Thanks to the Church's intercession on their behalf, they were the agents of redemption of man and society. A charming image and an important role. There is, however, one peculiarity in it. Bourassa defined women solely in terms of their sexual relation to men whether it be a specific relation, that of wives and mothers of sons, a rejected relation, that of nuns, or a negative relation, that of spinsters. In other words, for Bourassa, women had no other reason for being except as sexual adjuncts of men.

Behind this particular image of women lurks a particular image of men. Men, in Bourassa's view, were beings of reason and logic; to them therefore belonged the roles of leadership in society. Yet at the same time Bourassa allowed that men were brutal, corrupt and passionate. In this case the image is a strong one, perhaps even contradictory. Needless to say the redeeming function – soothing, softening, curtailing and reconciling the sharpness and contradition in the image – is to be carried out by the woman.

Still within the realm of images, the man-woman relationship thus becomes very important although its importance is of value only to the man. Bourassa seems to imply a latent struggle between men and women which is only held in check by the very strict division, even opposition, of their natures, roles, tasks, means and methods. Indeed, for people of Bourassa's ilk, all the opposites, all the bifurcations in the world could be made into a sexual bifurcation: reason/emotion; authority/obedience; culture/nature; head/heart, outside/inside, etc., etc. Now Freud may have claimed that nothing was to be gained by this kind of sexual attribution to qualities and characteristics but it is revealing of a tenaciously held image. And it perhaps explains the intensity of Bourassa's hostility to feminism. If society is in fact maintained by that kind of tension, then any break in the tension will truly destroy society. Bourassa may jokingly have talked of women wishing to rival men, but what really bothered him was that "the woman question" implied a challenge to his image of women. If women left their ideal role then society would collapse. As long as women were the redemptors then men could engage in all manner of scurrilous activities, however ambitious, egotistical, envious or brutal; their nastiness would always be tempered by the opposite qualities in women and the much-lauded social equilibrium would result. Thus feminism had to be fought with every weapon at hand in order to sustain an image of men, which in turn upheld a social order, the defence of which, according to Bourassa, was more important than anything else.[44] What truer mark could be found of a *castor*?

But there is still more of the *castor* in Bourassa. The man that emerges here is a rather bitter, humourless, rigid, self-righteous person. He held a static world view, a world of rules and regulations, of hierarchy and order with everyone in his place, fulfilling a pre-ordained role. He confused given social situations with truths of nature for all time. Indeed, one suspects that part of the horror he expressed about the feminists stemmed from the fact that they had forced him to talk in public about matters of which he probably never would have uttered a word in private. Again, a true *castor*.

Henri Bourassa is by no means the only person then or since to have expressed such views. Many of his arguments are still common currency today, a fact which suggests something about the pace at which society changes. Historians and sociologists interested in the question of change over time have found the topic so complex that they have been forced to swallow their mutual suspicions and lean on each other. Perhaps one of the difficulties of the question lies in the fact that much of mankind's energies are summoned not to bring about change but to resist it.[45] Certainly Henri Bourassa is a case in point, with his vehement denunciation of any change in *his* image of women. The fact that many of his views sound familiar in the 1970s may suggest that we are all somewhat *castor*.

Chapter 7

The Image of Women in Mass Circulation Magazines in the 1920s

Mary Vipond

The 1920s was an ambiguous decade, a decade of change and contradiction. In many respects it was a very conservative period, when Canadians clung to traditional values and institutions for stability and security. At the same time, however, Canadians in the twenties were fully conscious that the past was irretrievable.They were aware that society was in a state of flux, and that they were living in the first years of new era. Simultaneously they looked both back and ahead.

An examination of the image of women in the mass circulation magazine press reveals the ambivalence of beliefs and assumptions in Canada in the 1920s. The argument of William Henry Chafe in his study *The American Woman,* that the image of women does not shift until the reality of their lives does, is applicable to Canada in the 1920s; both were inconsistent, both paradoxical. But World War I had not had the broad effect on the reality of women's lives for which it has sometimes been given credit. More Canadian women were being educated in the twenties than ever before, more were in the labour force, and there were more opportunities and choices open to them. But these changes had been coming for some time, and they were tempered by the fact that women continued to be concentrated in traditionally female occupations and by the reality that marriage remained the career of most women. Neither had the suffrage movement had the impact on men's or women's attitudes which some of its proponents had assumed it would. What the War *had* brought, to some at least, was disillusionment with reform and idealism. The vote had been won by the alliance of reformers with dedicated suffragists.[2] But in the 1920s, the prevailing mood was a desire to return to what the American president, Warren Harding, called "normalcy," of the good old days, and the wartime reform spirit withered away. There was much talk of flappers in the 1920s, but almost everyone still assumed that femininity, innocence and passivity were the true characteristics of women, and that sexual differences determined and defined political and economic roles.[3]

Canadian mass circulation magazines (both those of general interest and those intended primarily for women) were written by and for the middle class.[4] In them one finds no recognition of the fact that more Canadian women worked as domestic servants than at any other paid job. The only interest the magazines showed in servants was in how to get them and keep them.[5] The editors of these magazines were not only themselves middle class but middle aged and male.[6] Judging both from their editorials and from the articles and stories they chose to publish, these men retained traditional attitudes towards women, but at the same time were more bemused by than opposed to the birth of the New Woman. They were in no sense leaders of public opinion. Rather, following the tradition of the mass ciruclation press, they catered to conventional assumptions and to the prevailing opinions of the average reader. They reflected the economic and social reality of the day, and by so doing reinforced and helped justify the status quo.

In this examination of the image of women in Canadian magazines, the main focus will be on the assumptions which they made about women's work. Because the evolution of the status of women within our society has been so closely tied to changes in the nature of their work, the images presented of women as workers are particularly revealing of the manner in which old and new attitudes clashed and coalesced in the 1920s.

Women represented about 15.5% of the total labour force over the age of 10 in Canada in 1921 and 17.0% in 1931. The 36% increase in the number of employed women during the 1920s was greater than that in the decade to follow, the depressed 1930s, and it was also greater than that in the decade which included World War I. It was considerably below the rate of 47% attained during the first decade of the twentieth century.[7] The occupational categories which contained the highest proportion of women were personal service, clerical, professional and manufacturing. The vast majority – about 90% – of the women who were gainfully employed were single. Thirty-two per cent of single women over 10 were in the labour force in 1931, almost half of them being between the ages of 20 and 24.[8] By the 1920s it was generally assumed that a girl worked for a few years before she married. There were still occasional references in the magazines to middle class fathers who prohibited their daughters from working because it reflected on their ability to support the family.[9] But for the most part it was taken for granted not only that girls *could* be gainfully employed but that they *should* be. The rationale was straightforward. As one columnist wrote, "a few years of business experience . . .serve to make [a woman] a more efficient home-maker, a more companionable wife and a better balanced mother." Young women were advised that they should look for a fulfilling, satisfying career; success in a job would stand them in good stead when they became wives and mothers. They would then be better prepared as well, of course, for the exigencies of spinsterhood or early widowhood.[10]

Middle class girls were urged in the 1920s to obtain a good education. In 1919-20, 13.9% of university undergraduates in Canada were women; by 1929-30, their proportion had risen significantly, to 23.5%. Graduate enrolments showed a slight decline during the decade, but the proportion of women in graduate school remained over 25%.[11] The expenditure of $400 to $700 a year to send a girl to university was justified by the magazines in the same way as they justified her employment: a well-educated woman could secure a better job before she married, if she were widowed, or if she never married. Above all, a well-educated woman would be a more capable, a more self-confident, and therefore a *better* wife and mother. That women in the universities were still almost all in traditionally female faculties was not disturbing to the magazine writers. On the contrary, those professions which most closely approximated the woman's function as homemaker were the most highly regarded. Great pride was taken in the trebling of the number of women studying Household Science during the decade. Household Science, after all, was the perfect field for women, for it gave them a "scientific" career while at the same time preparing them to be housewives and mothers.[12]

Only about 3% of married women were in the labour force in Canada in the 1920s.[13] Social pressure combined with more formal restrictions to keep that number low. Although it was generally accepted that a middle class girl should work before marriage, it was also assumed that she resigned, not when her first child arrived, but the day she married, in order to take on her new full-time job of caring for a house and a husband. There was still a definite stigma attached to the employment of middle class wives, for a husband's status was measured in part by his ability to keep his wife "idle" at home.[14] As well, many school boards insisted that their women employees resign on marriage, and the Canadian civil service adopted a similar rule in 1921.[15]

For the working class, of course, it was different. A relatively large proportion of domestic servants, for example, were married women. Work for them was a stark necessity.

Some married middle class women did manage, despite the difficulties, to work full time. But articles in the magazine press always stressed how exceptional such "Super-Women" were. For the average woman, it was made very clear, it would be almost impossible to combine a career with housekeeping.[16] No help could be expected from one's husband, for he was already making a large enough sacrifice in giving up his full-time wife. A woman columnist in the *Canadian Home Journal* queried:

> What about the husband in all this clamour for a career? Is he a poor thing without any rights at all? ... He must feel rather desolate when he returns, tired, from a busy office, to find that his wage-earning wife is still down town, absorbed by office cares .... Surely a man's pride must suffer injury when his wife turns wage-earner, too, and his home becomes merely a lodging-house.[17]

Thus a clear-cut choice faced women of the day: either a career or marriage, but not both. The magazines left no doubt that in their view every *true* woman chose marriage if she could. Short stories told again and again of independent young flappers who happily threw up their careers in order to settle down to marital bliss with the right man.[18] Sufficient economic or social change, then, had not occurred to permit or to demand that married women become gainfully employed. Their role remained a traditional one.

During the years they were present in the labour force, women were paid less than men. Not only did predominantly female jobs have lower wage scales, but there was rarely even lip service paid to the idea of equal pay for equal work. It was routinely accepted, for example, that women teachers received 25% less than men with equal qualifications and experience.[19] Although there were occasional articles in some of the smaller Canadian magazines which argued the case for equal pay, the mass circulation press hardly ever mentioned the idea. In general, the popular magazines simply reported that the differential existed, warned women to expect it and not to be resentful, and explained why it was so. There were two principal justifications offered: men were permanent employees who took their careers seriously while women were only filling in time until they married, and secondly, men had to support wives and families while working women usually lived at home and really needed only "pin money."[20] Despite evidence that many working women were actually supporting dependents and needed their meagre incomes badly, the prevailing belief that women's primary role was maternal, with its two corollaries that women were only temporarily in the labour force and that men must earn more because they had wives and children to support, made general acceptance of the idea of equal pay impossible.

At the average age of twenty-five, Canadian women in the 1920s turned to their real careers – marriage and motherhood. One of the most difficult circumstances with which the young women of the decade had to cope was the contradiction between what was expected of them before and after marriage. They were encouraged to obtain a good education and to find a stimulating career, but then to turn their attention solely to housework, husband and children when they married. They were encouraged to be independent and self-sufficient before marriage, but warned that in order to find and keep a husband they must become docile clinging vines.[21]

It was partly in order to make the housewife's work more challenging and satisfying to ex-career women that the mass circulation magazines placed so much emphasis on the home as a business and on the homemaker as a professional.[22] The "modern" housewife, they insisted, was "scientific" and "efficient"; she was an "engineer," a "manager," a "domestic supervisor"; when she shopped she became a "purchasing agent"; her kitchen was her "plant" and her utensils were her "tools." Repeatedly it was stressed that a man and wife had a "business partnership" – he managed the office, she the home. An article in *Saturday Night* put it concisely:

> The housewife of today is to her home what her husband is to his office. She is a house manager. To be successful in that sphere she must apply the same principles of management to her work that her husband does to his.[23]

The magazines also tried to make housework more palatable by stressing how much easier it was to do than in the past. Undoubtedly it was, even given the passing of the servant, and much was legitimately made of the "electric servants" which made women's work lighter – sewing machines, irons, toasters, ranges, frying pans, coffee percolators and even dishwashers.[24] The advertisers emphasized that the "modern" woman was always seeking those household appliances and products which reduced her workload the most. The advertisers, of course, were seeking as many purchasers of as many new products as possible.

An advertisement for new, easy, healthy Fels Naphtha soap summed up the twenties' image of the housewife. It pictured a gray-haired mother advising her daughter:

> Now that you are married, dear, your job will be to run the house just as well as John hopes to run his business. At first you'll have to do most of the work yourself – even the washing and the cleaning.
> But don't let that worry you. It isn't work, my dear, that takes the bloom from pretty cheeks. It's the work women do needlessly – the down-right drudgeries.[25]

With the purchase of the latest in household equipment, the advertisers and columnists both promised their women readers, drudgery would be at an end, and housework would become a job as respectable as that of any man.

One of the important demographic trends of the 1920s was the steady decrease in family size. The crude birth rate fell gradually during the decade from 29.3/1000 in 1921 to 23.5/1000 in 1929. Some of this decline was due to such factors as a drop in the number of women of childbearing age, but a substantial portion of it was attributable to deliberate choice, as well as to socio-economic factors like urbanization and the assimilation of immigrants.[26] Women were having fewer children, but they were urged by the magazines to devote more and more attention to them. If there was pressure on women in the 1920s to be efficient and competent in their housework, there was far more on them to be perfect mothers. It was no longer assumed that natural instinct, trial and error, or practice with younger siblings taught a woman to be a mother. Now a professional approach must be taken; women must be trained for the task. "Undeveloped maternal instinct," prominent Canadian educator Aletta E. Marty declared, would no longer suffice "to teach women to bring up sons and daughters worthily in a society so complex and exacting as that of today." Motherhood must now be regarded as "a science for which some intelligent preparation is required, just as it is for any other skilled occupation."[27]

The emphasis which one finds in the mass magazines of the 1920s on efficiency, professionalism and management was not unique to that decade. The scientific management movement of Frederick Winslow Taylor had peaked in the United States before the War, and its application to housework dated from that period too.[28] By the 1920s, however, the general acceptance of the idea that housework must be performed in the "modern" manner, efficiently and without waste of resources, had led to the conclusion that a new type of housewife was needed. The "modern" homemaker, according to the popular press, required the kind of experience which could be gained only by education and by exposure to the business world, where organizational principles had been long established. While the increasing demand for workers with particular kinds of skills was probably the most important factor in bringing more and more young women into the labour force in the 1920s, a new rationalization made their employment acceptable to the middle class – the argument that pre-marital employment would make them more competent, self-confident and efficient wives and mothers.

But while the image of the homemaker became more professional in the twenties, traditional assumptions about women's nature had had no difficulty in surviving the War and the suffrage movement. Indeed the tendency of some of the most prominent Canadian suffragists to argue their case on the basis of the superiority and distinctiveness of women bolstered rather than hindered the perpetuation of these attitudes into the post-war decade and beyond. The image of women as feminine, ladylike, and maternal continued to thrive. Women were, according to the magazines, delicate creatures who were morally superior to men, purer and more noble. They were also more excitable, highly-strung, liable to hysteria and attacks of 'nerves', temperamental, irrational, conservative, more primitive and more ruled by instinct than men. They preferred to be protected and cared for by men; "primarily" they were "mothers of men."[29]

Thus two contradictory images existed simultaneously. While on the one hand the magazines lauded the "modern" housewife, on the other they expressed concern that too much education and work experience might destroy women's maternal instincts.[30] The image of efficiency was one which emphasized hard work, discipline and "masculinity" over feeling, sympathy and "femininity." It was an image appropriate to urban twentieth century life. But the middle class were afraid to face the full social implications of the technological society which they otherwise so heartily endorsed. Fearing the application of the principles of scientific management to family life, they inconsistently tried to preserve traditional sexual roles at the same time as they endorsed modernity and efficiency in other aspects of life and work.[31]

The contradictions between the two images of women became obvious in those magazine columns which attempted to advise young women on how to behave in the business world. Although claiming they believed that women should strive for success, the authors of these articles gave only the most cautious praise to such unfeminine qualities as initiative and enterprise. A young woman, they advised, should never be aggressive, but rather "consistently pleasant and obliging." She should co-operate with others, never complain, be as attractive as possible, and when she was not promoted or given a raise she should "show some of the female patience for which we are famous."[32] Time after time when a proficient businesswoman was mentioned in a magazine article, it was pointed out that despite her success she was "still at heart a woman." To cite just one of innumerable examples, the editor of the *Canadian Magazine* introduced Miss Margaret Pennell, newly-appointed woman's editor, as follows:

> Miss Pennell is one of Canada's most successful business women and yet has retained and developed in her self and in her work all the charms of viewpoint and domestic feeling that are sometimes considered old fashioned to-day.

Much emphasis was placed on the vase of flowers which a woman executive placed on her immaculate desk, and on the paintings and mirrors she hung on her office walls. Even more stress was placed on how "serene," "womanly" and innocent she was able to remain despite her career.[33]

The same contradiciton emerged in the two views of marriage which were presented by the magazines. In one, husband and wife were equal partners in a common enterprise; in the other, the unity of the family was preserved by traditional roles, with the husband as "seigneur et maître."[34] But the two pictures were not given equal emphasis. Occasional articles suggested that men preferred as wives women with spirit and independence.[35] Much more typical, however, were those which cautioned women to efface themselves for the sake of the family. A long-running series in *MacLean's* called "The Bride's Club," for example, gave advice to newly-wed women about how to cope with the various problems of married life. Without exception it recommended that the job of the wife was to cater to her husband's every whim, however unreasonable.[36] Short story after short story as well told of housewives fed up with the toil and monotony of their daily round who tried to escape either by taking a job or by running away. Inevitably, however, the heroine learned her lesson and returned in the end, happy to do her duty.[37] Attempting to combat the rising divorce rate in Canada in the 1920s, the popular magazines deliberately fostered those values which held that the welfare of the nation rested on the stability and permanence of the family, and counselled that it was a woman's duty, indeed her honour and her privilege, to submerge her own selfish desires to that end.

According to the mass circulation magazines of the 1920s, the position of women in society had undergone a revolution since the nineteenth century. Editors and writers alike were firmly convinced that "there were never so many opportunities for women as now," that the world was theirs.[38] More sensitive observers, both men and women, were aware that only a mid-point had been reached, that there was still a long way to go before Canadians – men and women – really accepted the idea of independence and equality for women. Anne Anderson Perry, a feminist and one of the few to write for the popular magazines on the subject of women in politics in the twenties, commented:

> We are, in fact, very confused in our minds between old ideals of shrinking, dependent femininity, and the more modern conception of woman as an independent entity with a destiny of her own, both political and economic.

And Canadian author Madge Macbeth wrote in the same vein:

> Woman is passing through a cultural transition. Instinctively, she is bound to the old order of things; intellectually, she clamours for the new. And vacillating, she stands between them.[39]

The changes which had occurred in the lives of women since before the War were more of degree than of kind.[40] Women did have the vote, but they had little political influence. More women did work at more kinds of jobs – but economic equality did not exist. Women's lives had not changed much, nor had prevailing assumptions about their role. The "new" image of woman as scientific home manager could coexist with the "old" image of woman as lady for the simple reason that both reflected the reality of the day – that women were still "primarily mothers of men."

Chapter 8

Women's Emancipation and the Recruitment of Women into the Labour Force in World War II

Ruth Pierson

It is often assumed that the employment of women in the labour force during World War II greatly advanced the women's struggle to achieve equal status with men in Canada.[1] Since then feminists have lamented the ease with which many of the gains were lost at the war's end. One famous account, concerned with U.S. society but considered relevant to Canadian society as well, postulated the propagation of a "feminine mystique" to account for the postwar reverses in women's struggle for equality.[2]

I should like to argue that both the assumption of great gains made by women during World War II and the bewilderment over the postwar reversals rest on an inadequate examination of the context of women's wartime employment and an inaccurate assessment of the degree to which attitudes towards women's proper role in society changed during the war. Canada's war effort, rather than any consideration of women's right to work, determined the recruitment of women into the labour force. The recruitment of women was part of a large-scale intervention by Government into the labour market to control allocation of labour for effective prosecution of war.

Firstly, National Selective Service (NSS) and the federal Department of Labour, in the wartime mobilization of the work force, regarded women as a large labour reserve, to be dipped into more and more deeply as the labour pool dried up. The recruitment would first catch young "girls" and single women and then childless married women for full-time employment, next women with home responsibilities for part-time employment, and finally women with children for full-time employment. Starting with the most mobile, NSS pulled in these groups successively as the war effort intensified. Government officials publicly expressed a reluctance to draw upon those people in the female labour reserve whose mobilization would disrupt the traditional family system.

Secondly, the government recruiting agencies viewed their task as service to Canada's war effort. Thus in recruitment campaigns they appealed to patriotic duty and the need to make sacrifices for the nation at war. Not women's right to work, but women's obligation to work in war time was the major theme.

Finally, concessions to the special needs of working women were made only within the context of the war effort. These were introduced as temporary measures, to remain in effect only so long as the nation was at war.

I

Canada was not out of the Depression when World War II began. There were about 900,000 registered unemployed in a work force of approximately 3.8 million. In the following two years these unemployed persons largely met the increased demand for workers created by military recruitment and wartime production. By 1942 the slack had been taken up. With war industry in full production and the Armed Forces drawing large numbers of males from the labour force, the labour market had changed from one of surplus and unemployment to one of shortage. "To meet the pressure of war needs, attention, therefore, became focussed on the reserve of potential women workers who had not yet been drawn into employment."[3]

By thirteen Orders in Council, the NSS programme was established in March 1942 under the jurisdiction of the Minister of Labour.[4] Prime Minister Mackenzie King, in his address to Parliament on National Selective Service, declared that "recruitment of women for employment was 'the most important single feature of the program.' "[5] He went on to outline a ten-point plan for drawing women into industry.[6] In May 1942 a division of NSS was created to deal with employment of women and related services. Mrs. Rex (Fraudena) Eaton of Vancouver was appointed Assistant (later Associate) Director of NSS in charge of the Women's Division.

One of NSS's first steps was to measure the top layer of the female labour reserve. "It was decided to conduct a compulsory registration of *younger* women in order to ascertain more definitely what resources of woman power were available."[7] Labour Minister Humphrey Mitchell ordered the registration of all females aged twenty to twenty-four, except members of religious orders, hospital patients, prison inmates, and women in insurable employment.[8] The registration was held from September 14 to September 19, 1942. Although both married and unmarried women were required to register, the main aim of this inventory of Canada's womanpower was to measure the labour reserve of young single women. The age group twenty to twenty-four had been chosen because: "Single women would compose a higher percentage of the total than would be found in older age groups."[9]

On August 20, 1942, Mrs. Eaton had met in Ottawa with executive representatives of twenty-one national women's organizations to enlist their support for NSS and the September Registration of Canadian Women. She explained that this Registration:

> will show us exactly how many single women we have available to meet the increasing shortage of workers in our war industries. Then we will have a pool of single workers from which to draw when an employer asks for additional staff, and single women can be supplied immediately.[10]

The policy was not merely to mobilize single women, but to make unnecessary the employment of family women. Mrs. Eaton stated emphatically: "We shall not urge married women with children to go into industry." Married women had been drifting into work in war industries because "no known reservoir of single workers existed." It was hoped that the Registration would enable NSS "to direct single women into essential war industries rather than to have employers building up huge staffs of married women with children."[11]

On December 15, 1942, A. Chapman of the Research and Statistics Branch of the Department of Labour submitted a report on the "Female Labour Supply Situation." From the results of the Women's Registration, interviews by local employment and Selective Service Offices, and analyses by local offices of the relation of unfilled vacancies to unplaced applicants, she concluded:

> Study of the available information regarding the supply of and demand for female labour clearly indicates the existence of a large reserve of female labour throughout the country.[12]

Beyond "the overall surplus of female labour," the figures showed "that the bulk of the readily available surplus of female labour is concentrated in those areas where war industry is least developed." Even allowing for regional variation of response to the Registration, Chapman found that the figures "do emphasize the tremendous reservoir of female labour in areas such as the Maritimes and the Prairies where development of war industry has been slight."[13] The information from the Registration and follow-up interviews led to a programme for transferring young unmarried women from areas of surplus to areas of labour scarcity.

In May 1942 a survey of the anticipated demand for female labour had shown "that at least 75,000 additional women would be required in war industries before the end of the year."[14] The Registration itself stimulated young women to apply for employment.[15] In addition, NSS began a nationwide publicity campaign to urge upon women "the need to engage in some phase of the war effort."[16] Editors agreed to give space in their publications to pictures of women working in war production and to stories of accomplishments by individual women. Papers published news releases on NSS and its aims. The CBC presented over the national network "a series of dramatic plays, written expressly for National Selective Service around the theme of women war workers."[17] The campaign paid off. By January 1943, the additional 75,000 women had been recruited. Indeed between January 1942, and June 1943, 159,000 women had joined the industrial war effort, bringing the number of women engaged in war industries to 255,000. In the same period, several thousand women had volunteered for the Women's Divisions of the Armed Forces.[18] The "readily available surplus of female labour"[19] had evaporated.

By mid-1943 there were labour shortages in service jobs long dependent on female labour. Women were leaving these for higher paying employment in war industries. Hospitals, restaurants, hotels, laundries and dry cleaners were clamouring for help,[20] but the labour pool of single women available for full-time employment was exhausted. "It became necessary to appeal to housewives and those groups who would not ordinarily appear in the labour market."[21] While the first recruitment had sought young unmarried women and then childless married women for full-time work, in mid-1943, NSS (Women's Division) decided to launch a campaign to recruit women with home responsibilities for part-time employment.

The need for part-time workers had been foreseen as early as November 1942.[22] Supervisors of the Women's Divisions of local Employment and Selective Service Offices were instructed to persuade employers to plan for employing women part-time. At first employers resisted the idea. Mary Eadie, Women's Division Supervisor, Toronto, reported that, although some had "undertaken to use it with success, ... the employer as a whole 'will not be bothered' ... with part-time help."[23] Employers cited higher administrative costs and a feared rise in absenteeism and turn-over as reasons for their opposition. But when firms producing non-essentials, such as candy, tobacco, soft drinks and luxury items, were informed that NSS would not send them "full-time workers while essential services and war industries were short of labour"[24] and when by the spring of 1943 even firms providing essential civilian services were short of labour, many employers became more willing to employ women part-time.

The first campaign for part-time women workers was mounted in Toronto from July 12 to July 26, 1943. To prepare for it, Toronto Selective Service set up several conferences with employers in hospitals, restaurants, hotels, laundries and dry cleaning establishments.[25] On May 22, 1943, Mary Eadie reported to Mrs. Eaton that "the Ontario Restaurant Associa-tion, the Laundry and Dry Cleaning Association of Toronto and the Hospital Association of Toronto will cooperate with us because they are in such dire straits for help these days."[26] The Toronto Selective Service also won for the campaign the spon-sorship of the Local Council of Women.[27]

The campaign was "particularly directed to housewives."[28] At the same time "no women with important home responsibilities were unduly urged to register." Furthermore "no appeal was made for women to work part-time in addition to a full-time job." However, "many women without children and with few home responsibilities consented, under pressure of the campaign, to accept full-time work."[29]

In her report of July 29, 1943, to the NSS Advisory Board, Mrs. Eaton applauded the results of the campaign. Nearly 2,300 women had responded, of whom 55% were referred to full-time jobs, 39% to part-time, and about 6% were yet to be placed. For Mrs. Eaton, "the success of the campaign offered some assurance that there is still a pool of women ready and willing to fill a breach when emergencies arise."[30]

The Toronto campaign served as a model for similar cam-paigns in other Canadian cities. NSS Circular No. 270-1 (August 18, 1943) outlined the campaign. It was to relieve a labour shor-tage in "essential services such as hospitals, restaurants, hotels, laundries and dry cleaning establishments", and was directed at "a new type of recruit," namely "the housewife or others *who will do a Part-time Paid Job* for six days per week, perhaps only four hours per day, or perhaps three full days each week." Not only was the campaign aimed at housewives, but the work they were being asked to do was also seen as an extension of housework outside the home. As the Circular stated: "it is possible for many women to streamline their housekeeping at home to do the housekeeping in the community for standard wages."[31]

The President of the National Council of Women, Mrs. Edgar Hardy, endorsed these campaigns. NSS Director Arthur MacNamara and Mrs. Rex Eaton sent a letter (31 August 1943) to all Local Councils of Women enlisting their support, stating: "There is no reserve of men in Canada today. In fact there is little reserve of either men or women."[32]

In co-operation with the Local Council of Women, NSS launched special recruiting campaigns for part-time women workers in the fall of 1943 in Edmonton, Saskatoon, Regina, Brandon, Ottawa, Moncton, and Halifax. The drives sought part-time workers for the essential services already mentioned, but also in some centres, such as Edmonton, for jobs in the garment industry. In some places, such as Brandon and Edmonton, the part-time campaign was combined with a campaign for full-time women workers. The aim of the Ottawa campaign was to encourage former female employees of the Civil Service, now married, to return to part-time or full-time work to overcome the shortage of workers in war departments of Government.[33]

Even before the end of the part-time campaign in Toronto on July 26, 1943, NSS faced an acute labour shortage in war industries there. About 3,500 women were needed to fill full-time high-priority jobs in war production.[34] The urgency of the need ruled out transferring women workers from other parts of Canada.[35] To help meet this need, the Toronto Selective Service proposed that management "recruit women for employment in war industries for full-time work for a period of not less than three months." Although employers thought they needed long-term full-time workers, they saw advantages to a special appeal for three-month service: it would give the media "a new publicity angle to emphasize the need of war industries for more workers" and would counteract "the fear of being frozen to the job" which deterred many women from "employment full time in essential industry." Also women once hired might stay employed.[36]

The key note of this special campaign was "three months' service".[37] The call went out to all women, but especially to housewives, with the promise of counselling service for mothers and endeavours to place women in war plants near their homes.[38] Preceded in early August by radio publicity on the need for women in war industry, the campaign ran from August 30 to September 11. During the first week a "war industrial show" was put on at the T. Eaton Company Auditorium. "Girls" from war plants demonstrated operations they performed "in their ordinary work at the plant" and "a fashion show was given in which the girls wore their plant uniforms."[39] After the campaign, Mrs. Eaton reported that 4,330 women had been referred to war industries, 168 were awaiting referral until day nursery care for their children had been arranged, and 300 who had applied for part-time work were yet to be placed.[40]

Through the autumn of 1943 NSS continued its recruitment campaigns for full-time women workers as labour demands dictated. In October and November special drives to recruit female workers for full-time jobs in textile factories and other high priority manufacturing firms were carried out in the textile centres of Peterborough, Hamilton, Welland, St. Catharines, and Dunville.[41] In Montreal, NSS officials began planning in late September a massive recruitment campaign to alleviate a recorded labour shortage of 19,000. But in November a meeting of Montreal employers with the NSS Regional Superintendent for Quebec decided to postpone the large-scale campaign. As opposition to women's employment still persisted in Quebec, it was felt that the public would sooner accept small, separate drives specifically for "hotels, laundries, hospitals, textiles, etc."[42]

In December 1943 the urgency for recruitment campaigns subsided[43] and the first months of 1944 saw "a slow but noticeable reduction in war industry."[44] The number of women in the labour force actually declined by 10-15,000 in the first three months of the year. Although the end of the war was in sight, NSS would not allow any slackening of the war effort until victory was secured. Some were worried women might leave war industry in greater numbers than the slow-down in production warranted.[45] Married women might want to return to their homes "and a less strenuous life," single women might want to secure post-war jobs. NSS countered with publicity asking "women [to] remain steadily on their jobs throughout the year"; and instructed Women's Divisions of local Employment and Selective Service Offices to persuade women requesting separation notices to stay at their posts. To the reluctant they were to suggest a brief holiday, or transfer to a more convenient shift, or "a part-time job in essential work near their homes". These efforts were successful: "there was no general exodus [of women] from war industries and essential services."[46]

Then in June 1944 came a new emergency. The invasion of France, the Department of Munitions and Supply informed NSS, required ammunition plants in Ontario and Quebec to operate at peak production. The need for an estimated 10,000 new women workers made necessary a last large-scale recruitment campaign.

It was organized by the Public Relations Office of the Department of Labour[47] and "promoted co-operatively by the plants concerned"[48] with every assistance from NSS. Local Employment and Selective Service Offices "redoubled their efforts to persuade women to accept jobs" in nearby ammunition plants; and, working with recruiting agents of the munition firms, NSS resumed the transfer of women from East and West to central Canada.[49]

Along with recruitment of women into industries and services, there was also recruitment of women into agriculture "to fill some of the gaps in farm power with female labour." In all provinces farmers' wives and daughters took over farm work in the absence of male relatives and farm workers who had left the land to join the Armed Forces or to work in industry. In two provinces, however, special programmes were organized to recruit farm labour on the basis of the Dominion-Provincial Farm Labour Agreement, entered into by Ontario in 1941 and by British Columbia in 1943. The Ontario Farm Service Force divided female farm labour volunteers into three brigades: the Farmerette Brigade for female students (over fifteen) and teachers during their summer holidays; the Women's Land Brigade for housewives and business and professional women on a day to day basis; and the Farm Girls' Brigade for farm women (under twenty-six) to lend a hand where necessary. The work was hard, nine to ten hours a day, and the wage rate low, 25 cents an hour. In 1943, "12,793 girls in addition to a considerable number of teachers" were enrolled in the Farmerette Brigade; approximately 4,200 women in the Women's Land Brigade; and about 1,000 in the Farm Girls' Brigade. After its creation, NSS helped to publicize the appeals for Farm Labour Service.[50]

II

Labour Department officials, NSS Officers, and Farm Service officials, charged with recruiting women into the labour force during World War II, viewed their task as service to the war effort. Accordingly, in their recruitment campaigns, they appealed primarily to patriotic duty and the necessity to make sacrifices for the nation in war time.

This note was struck in the NSS Report on the Employment of Women of November 1, 1943. Next to determining the size of the existing labour reserve of women, the NSS's main task was "to outline to all Canadian women the part they would be expected to play in the anticipated expansion of all war demands."[51] NSS's job was to convince women "that it was their duty to go to work" and to persuade women "that work in war industries offered the most direct contribution which could be made to the prosecution of the war, apart from enlistment in the Armed Forces."[52] The overalls and bandana of the woman war worker "became a symbol of service."[53] The vigorous publicity campaigns of the Ontario Farm Labour Service laid "considerable stress on patriotic services."[54]

"There must be no let up in the supply of vital arms and equipment – no let up in food production – no let up in essential services" stated the letter sent by the Director of NSS and Mrs. Eaton to the Local Councils of Women enlisting their help for the campaigns to recruit women workers in the autumn of 1943. The letter made two suggestions:

> Arrange for an inspirational address in which the prestige and importance of any work essential to the war or to the home front is stressed, as well as a tribute to women now so employed.

> Stress the need of women for the armed services but point out essential employment as an opportunity for women not of military age to serve with equal effect.[55]

The NSS Circular of August 18, 1943, outlining the Campaign for Part-time Women Workers, ended with this ringing declaration: "The health and well-being of the Canadian people must be maintained while they participate in the March to Victory. The civilian essential services in the community are of vital importance."[56]

"Roll up Your Sleeves for VICTORY!" was the headline of a design, prepared by the Department of Labour's Information Division in December 1943, for a full-page newspaper advertisement to recruit women for war industry. In the centre of the ad was a drawing of a woman, shoulders squared, rolling up her sleeves. Behind her, a montage of photographs of women working, one a taxi driver, another a nurse, and the rest on production lines in war industry. The caption read:

> The women of Canada are doing a magnificent job . . . in the Munitions factories, making the tools of war, in the nursing services . . . in the women's active service units, on the land, and in many other essential industries. But the tempo of war is increasing, and will continue to increase until Victory is won. We need more and more women to take full or part time war work . . . Even if you can only spare an hour or two a day, you will be making an important contribution to the war effort.[57]

In May 1944, when it was feared that women were growing weary of war work and might be leaving the labour force altogether or changing to more promising jobs, Mrs. Eaton drafted a letter to the local Employment and Selective Service Offices. It contained this directive:

> Try to change the attitude of mind represented in the words: "I want to get a post-war job" or "I am tired of making munitions." We need to remind ourselves and others that the war has yet to be won and completed. It is too early to express other ideas. Service and sacrifice are yet the key words.[58]

Finally, in the campaign of July 1944 to recruit women for labour in the Ontario ammunition plants, the slogan was: "Women! Back Them Up – To Bring Them Back." This slogan appeared on advertisements placed in the major newspapers, reprints of which were delivered to thousands of homes in the neighbourhoods of war plants, and on posters attached to street cars, displayed in store windows, outside movie theatres and in theatre lobbies. A press release prepared for Moffats Ltd., manufacturer of ammunition boxes for the 25-Pounder gun, carried this appeal:

> Only by the single and married women coming forward and offering their help will it be possible to get these ammunition boxes out in the required time and thus keep faith with the boys at the front.[59]

The call to patriotism, to sacrifice for the nation at war, to loyalty and service to the troops fighting overseas – that appeal dominated the recruitment of women workers from beginning to end.

At the same time Labour Department and NSS officials were aware that many women were in the labour force, or applying to enter it, out of economic rather than patriotic motives. Renée Morin of the Montreal NSS reported the observations of a personnel officer for the Dominion Rubber Company:

> Most of the married women with children who seek work in our factory are in need of money to help their family. Those who are working merely to buy luxuries have not the courage to stick to their work. Very few have in mind a contribution to the war effort.[60]

On March 30, 1943, the Women's Division of the Toronto Employment and Selective Service Office ran a questionnaire on married female applicants over thirty-five years of age. The fifth question asked: "What is the prime object in your securing employment?" Of the women questioned, 9% indicated patriotic motives, 59% "desire to supplement family income," and 32% "personal needs."[61] *Relations* in May 1943 disclosed the results of an investigation carried out by the Quebec *Jeunesse ouvrière catholique* into the working experience of 700 of its gainfully employed female members: 31.4% of the women had given "as their reason for working economic necessity – no other source of revenue."[62] Obviously some discrepancy existed between the official emphasis on patriotism and the real motivation of women workers.

Actually advertisements for women workers appealed to economic incentives. The caption on the "Roll Up Your Sleeves for Victory" ad ended: "By taking up some form of war work you will not only be showing your patriotism in a practical way, but you will also be adding to the family income."[63] Besides the slogan "Back Them Up – To Bring Them Back" the advertisements in July 1944 spoke of: "Opportunity for Women in Modern War Plant ... doing an important job and at the same time making that extra money which you can use to plan your future."[64] Nonetheless, patriotic service to the war effort was the main motive of campaigns to recruit women workers.

III

It was realized from the start that the needs of working women, especially those married and those with young children, would have to be accommodated. By and large, however, such accommodation was justified by the war emergency, and would not outlast it.

One accommodation, an economic incentive to married women, was the Amendment to the Income War Tax Act in July 1942. Up to July 1942, a married woman, whose husband also had an income, could earn up to $750 without her husband's losing claim to full married status exemption. The revision of the tax law granted the husband of a working wife the full married status exemption "regardless of how large his wife's earned income might be."[65] The "special concession" was a "wartime provision,"[66] designed "to keep married women from quitting employment"[67] and to "encourage the entry of married women into gainful employment."[68]

The "concession" came to an end after the war. As of January 1, 1947, once a wife's income exceeded $250, the married status exemption of her husband would be reduced by the amount of her income over $250. Many married working women figured that the tax change would seriously diminish their actual contribution to the family income. Many employers of married women feared the change would deplete their skilled female labour force. Representations poured in to the Federal Departments of Labour, Finance and National Revenue. Fruit-packing and canning firms complained that their most skilled female packers and sorters were quitting once their earnings reached $250.[69] Textile firms complained that they were losing many of their most experienced power sewing machine operators, silk cutters, winders, and carders.[70] Similarly firms reported losing stenographer-typists;[71] hospitals, married nurses;[72] school boards, married women teachers;[73] department stores, married female employees.[74] The Deputy Minister of Labour, Arthur MacNamara, denied that his Department had intended the tax change "to drive married women out of employment," and certainly not "out of nursing, teaching or any other line of employment where their services are so seriously needed."[75] But as the spokesman for the Primary Textiles Institute, Toronto, reasoned: since the 1942 revision had been designed to draw married women into industry, its cancellation would drive them out.[76] And the Federal Government admitted as much: the tax concession of 1942 had been a war measure, "justified only by the extreme state of emergency which then existed."[77]

Perhaps the major wartime accommodation to the needs of working women was the establishment by the Dominion-Provincial Wartime Day Nurseries Agreement of child care facilities in Ontario and Quebec. But this too was a bow to the war emergency and viewed as right only so long as that emergency lasted.

In 1942, when it was realized that the Canadian economy would have to draw extensively on women's labour, it was also recognized that government provision of child care facilities for working mothers might become necessary. The Prime Minister's address to Parliament on March 24, 1942, explaining NSS and outlining a programme for bringing women into industry, had called for: "The provision of nurseries and other means of caring for children."[78]

Although the Women's Division of NSS did not campaign in 1942 for the employment of mothers, women with young children had been in the labour force before the war and had continued to enter it as production quickened. As Mrs. Eaton wrote in June 1942, "without any urging on the part of Government, married women, usually on the basis of need of further income, have already gone into industry and are doing a good job."[79] The mothers among these had had to make their own arrangements for the care of their children, with the help of relatives and neigh-bours.[80] "But these unorganized arrangements do not always work out so well and break down for days and weeks at a time."[81] There were private nurseries, run by churches and chari-table organizations, but not enough of them. In 1942, in Ontario, especially in the Toronto area, public pressure for government provision of nurseries and after-school supervision of children increased. There was concern over "latch-key" children and the possible connection between working mothers and juvenile delinquency.[82] Asked by the Minister of Labour for ideas on child care for his upcoming meeting with Ontario and Quebec Ministers, Mrs. Eaton replied that:

> Consistent and well-founded reports lead one to believe that children are neglected – thus becoming unhappy, undernour-ished and delinquent. Such a situation must be accepted as a responsibility of government in these days, when it has become a burden too heavy for private agencies.[83]

In April 1942, the Director of NSS wrote to the Ontario Govern-ment concerning "the setting-up of nurseries in co-operation with the provinces as needed."[84] In May Mrs. Eaton conferred with the Welfare Ministers of Ontario and Quebec.[85] Experts in child care, such as George F. Davidson, Executive Director of the Canadian Welfare Council,[86] and Dr. W. E. Blatz, Director of the Institute of Child Study of the University of Toronto,[87] were consulted. On the basis of these talks, a draft for a Domin-ion-Provincial agreement on child care was drawn up, which the federal Minister of Labour and the Ontario and Quebec Welfare Ministers approved on June 16, 1942.[88]

Then on July 20, 1942, through Order-in-Council P.C. 6242, the Federal Minister of Labour was authorized to co-operate with any of the Provinces to establish day-care facilities for chil-dren of mothers in war industries, in accordance with the draft agreement. The two most industrialized provinces signed that summer: Ontario on July 29, 1942; Quebec on August 3.[89] The only other province to sign was Alberta, in September 1943.[90] But the Alberta Advisory Committee on Day Nurseries, set up to assess the need in that province, voted on April 26, 1944, that there was none,[91] despite pressure from groups in Edmonton and Calgary for day nurseries in those two cities.[92]

In the meantime, Ontario and Quebec, the only two provinces which would make use of the Agreement, began to act on it. The Agreement provided that Dominion and Province would share capital and operating costs equally. * The initiative for establishing particular day nurseries rested with the Provinces.[94] Ontario and Quebec each created an Advisory Committee on Day Nurseries, and local committees in cities, to determine where need existed. Provincial directors were appointed, and in Toronto, a director for the city.[95] At the federal level, Miss Margaret Grier was appointed in October 1942 Assistant Associate Director of NSS, under Mrs. Eaton, to administer the Dominion-Provincial Wartime Day Nurseries Agreement.[96] Local Employment and Selective Service Offices were to interview applicants on need for child care, determine their eligibility, make referrals to operating child care facilities, and keep records of applicants and referrals.[97]

The programme was slow in getting off the ground. In fact, the first day nursery to open, at 95 Bellevue Avenue in Toronto on October 6, 1942, was initially a provincial project and only later brought under the terms of the Dominion-Provincial Agreement.[98] A second day nursery in Ontario, the first under the Agreement, opened in Brantford on January 4, 1943. February brought the opening of Ontario's third, fourth and fifth day nursery units in St. Catharines, Oshawa, and Toronto; March, the sixth and seventh, also in Toronto.[99] To accommodate the increasing numbers of married women entering the labour force in the spring and summer of 1943, six more day nurseries were opened in Ontario between April and September.[100]

In addition to day nursery care, the Agreement also provided for foster home care for children under two and school day care for children between six and sixteen. The latter included supervision of school-age children during vacations as well as provision at school of a hot noon meal and supervision before and after school hours during the regular term.[101]

By September 1945, there were 28 day nurseries in operation in Ontario, 19 in Toronto, 3 in Hamilton, 2 in Brantford, and one each in St. Catharines, Oshawa, Galt, and Sarnia, caring for about 900 children in all. There were also 44 school units, 39 in the Greater Toronto area; Hamilton had two, and Windsor, Oshawa, and Sarnia each had one. The Wartime Day Care Programme for School Children accommodated about 2,500 children.[102]

*Mothers were charged fees under the Agreement. For Day Nursery care, mothers paid 35c per day for the first child, and 15c in Ontario, 20c in Quebec for additional children. Where both parents were working, the fee was 50c per child. For Day Care of School Children, mothers in Ontario were charged 25c per day for the first child, 10c for additional children.[93]

The child care programme was even slower starting in Quebec, and never developed there as much as in Ontario. The first wartime day nursery in Quebec opened on March 1, 1943, in Montreal. In 1943 five others opened in Montreal, four on May 1, and one on October 1. As the latter closed on December 31, 1944, there were in September 1945 only five wartime day nurseries operating in Quebec, all in Montreal, and accommodating on the average only between 115 and 120 children.[103] There was no development in Quebec of the day care programme for school-age children.[104]

From the outset, the federal agencies involved viewed child care facilities as a war emergency measure designed "to secure the labour of women with young children" for "war industry."[105] One of the principles drawn up to govern Federal aid for day nurseries was: "That any such service should be strictly limited to provision for the children of women employees in war industries."[106]

The actual Dominion-Provincial Day Nurseries Agreement departed somewhat from that original intention.[107] Clause 11 provided that up to 25% of any facility could be opened to children of mothers in other than war industrial occupations. Furthermore Clause 1 (d) defined "war industries" liberally.[108] In practice, however, only firms with an A (very high) or B (high) labour priority rating were considered to be "war industries."[109] The Federal Government took the position that child care was "normally the responsibility of the Province, in cooperation with its local groups." Only the additional burden on the Provinces "caused by war conditions" justified the Federal Government's sharing that responsibility. Therefore the programme should "relate *chiefly* to war industries."[110]

In 1943 strong objection arose to Clause II of the Day Nurseries Agreement, particularly from the Toronto Board of Education and the Toronto Welfare Council. An officer of the former made representation to Labour Minister Humphrey Mitchell in February and the Chairman wrote directly to Prime Minister Mackenzie King in May.[111] They asked that "war work" be broadly defined as "anything essential to the community at war" so that the children of all working mothers would be eligible. The quota, they pointed out, put the principals administering the school day care programme in the difficult position of having to refuse some children while accepting others. Limiting eligibility discriminated against mothers working in firms with a low labour priority rating. This was unfair, they argued, as all working mothers were contributing to the war effort, if only indirectly. In many cases, the woman doing the "non essential" job was freeing a man or another woman for work in war industry.

On June 10, 1943, Mrs. Eaton chaired a meeting in Ottawa of NSS, Labour Department and Quebec and Ontario officials to assess the Day Nurseries programme. Heading the agenda was criticism of Clause II. The meeting agreed that "the ratio of 75 and 25 for mothers employed in war industry" should continue and that the interpretation of "war industry" as firms with A and B labour priority ratings should still hold. Labour Minister Mitchell approved this decision.[112] To Mrs. Eaton's mind, "If the Agreement is extended to include the children of all mothers who work, there is a further case that could be made out quite logically for the children of the woman who is ill or who is doing essential voluntary work."[113]

But objection to Clause II persisted. Newspaper editorials took up the criticism.

We are now into the fifth year of war. For at least three years the pressure has been heavy to get more women into industry. In the last year Government agencies have urged women with children to fill the gaps so that the nation's economy could continue to function.

If mothers are to follow the advice of those agencies, then surely this division of children of working mothers into two classes is beyond common reason.[114]

Mrs. Eaton observed that "a sort of crusade [has been] taken up by the papers, churches and women's organizations to get the children admitted regardless of any other consideration." By December 1, 1943, she concluded that: "It is now apparent the 25 percent [quota] does not altogether suffice."[115] Negotiations with Ontario and Quebec to revise Clause II were begun.

By Order-in-Council, on April 6, 1944, for Ontario, and on May 18, 1944, for Quebec, Clause II was amended to extend the Wartime Day Nurseries Agreement to include children of all working mothers. Nonetheless the amendment stipulated that "children of mothers working in war industry shall have priority at all times in admission" to any facility established under the Agreement.[116]

Despite the flexibility indicated here, the Dominion-Provincial Day Nurseries Agreement came to an end once the war was over. On August 23, 1945, J. A. Paquette, Quebec's Minister of Health and Social Welfare, wrote to Mitchell in Ottawa that he would close the day nurseries in Quebec on October 1. His argument read:

Article 23 of the Agreement, signed by the Federal Government and the Province of Quebec on the 3rd of August 1942, provides that the Agreement shall continue in force for the duration of the war.

Now that the war is over, I would be inclined to close these Day Nurseries immediately, but I feel that a month's notice to the parents would only be fair.[117]

Although W. S. Boyd of National Registration argued that Canada was still legally at war since no peace treaty had been signed and neither His Majesty nor the Governor in Council had proclaimed that the war had ended (as Section 2 of the War Measures Act required),[118] yet on September 1, 1945 Mitchell wrote Paquette that he, "as chief administrator of the scheme," had the right to close the nurseries when he chose and "upon such notice as is deemed advisable."[119]

Despite appeals from the Montreal Council of Social Agencies,[120] the Welfare Federation, the Federation of Catholic Charities, the Montreal Association of Protestant Women Teachers,[121] and mothers of children attending the first wartime day nursery in Montreal, the Quebec Government's position remained firm. The Dominion-Provincial Day Nurseries programme had been a war measure; the war was now over, and therefore the Agreement came to an end. The Day Nurseries closed on October 15, 1945.[122]

The situation was different in Ontario where more wartime child care facilities had been established and there was correspondingly greater pressure to keep them open after the war. It was the Federal Government which opened discussions to end the Dominion-Provincial Wartime Day Nurseries Agreement in Ontario.

On September 11, 1945, Fraudena Eaton reported to Arthur MacNamara that applications for day care in Toronto had "increased rather than diminished during the past two months." She was having Miss Grier investigate "this seemingly unreasonable situation."[123] Although the Wartime Day Nursery and School Day Care Centre in Oshawa were closed on October 31, 1945, owing to decreasing enrolment,[124] elsewhere in Ontario reports from local employment offices showed in November "a continuing high demand for day care of children of working mothers."[125]

Mrs. Eaton's reaction was to give a gentle nudge to Mr. MacNamara:

The time will come fairly shortly when the employment of mothers will not necessarily be related to production for war purposes or for highly essential civilian goods. It brings the matter of providing day care for children back to the point where it may be reasonably looked upon as a responsibility of the Provincial Government.[126]

MacNamara took the hint and instructed Mrs. Eaton to draft a letter to the appropriate Ontario Minister asking his views on when to end the Agreement on Day Care of Children.[127] The letter stated:

You understand that the financing of these and similar plans by the Dominion Government has been done as a war measure and our Treasury Board naturally takes the position "now that the war is over why do you need money?"

Then came the suggestion they terminate the Agreement at "the end of the Dominion Government fiscal year or soon thereafter."[128]

Hope grew in Ontario that, after the Dominion Government pulled out of the Agreement, the Provincial Government might pick up the whole tab. Margaret Grier informed Arthur MacNamara on February 15, 1946, that Deputy Minister of Public Welfare B. M. Heise himself had told her "he now had every hope that the Province would continue to maintain the day nurseries."[129]

Meanwhile four months had elapsed since the Dominion Government's proposal to end Federal participation in the Day Nursery project. On February 19, 1946, Mrs. Eaton wrote to Mr. MacNamara suggesting that, as Ontario might continue to operate day nurseries, provincial authorities were in no hurry to see Federal funds cut off. The time, however, had come.

No suggestion could be made now or even four months ago, that the employment of those women whose children are in day care centres is essential for work of national importance.[130]

Humphrey Mitchell took up this argument in his letter of February 26, 1946, to W. A. Goodfellow, Ontario Minister of Public Welfare. "As you know," Mitchell wrote, "the Dominion share in financing this project was undertaken as *a war measure* for the reason that women whose children were in day care centres were engaged in *work of national importance.*" Implying that the employed mothers of Ontario were no longer doing work of national importance, he announced his Department's decision to stop Dominion participation on April 1.[131]

Now a three-way passing of the buck began. W. A. Goodfellow informed the Federal Minister that enabling legislation was before the Ontario legislature to make day nurseries a municipal concern, with the Provincial Government sharing costs. The end of Federal contributions on April 1st together with the planned transfer of day nurseries from the Department of Public Welfare to municipalities, threatened to disrupt the existing child care programme before the end of the school year. In view of that, the Ontario Minister requested the Federal Minister to consider extension of the Dominion-Provincial Wartime Day Nurseries Agreement to June 30, 1946.[132]

Humphrey Mitchell approved an extension to June 30th, although this information got lost in the shuffle of intradepartmental memoranda and did not reach the Ontario Welfare Minister until after April 2, 1946.[133] In the interim, the Ontario Legislature had given first and second reading to Bill 124 allowing cities to "provide for the establishment of day nurseries for the care and feeding of young children" with the Provincial Government to contribute one-half of the costs of their operation. The Bill passed third reading on April 4th and became law as the Day Nurseries Act, 1946.[134] The day care programme for school-age children was to be dropped altogether.

On May 17, 1946, Goodfellow wrote the Federal Minister of Labour with a new request. Some of the cities had indicated that, as their budgets for 1946 had already been passed, they had no funds to pay fifty percent of the costs of operating day nurseries for the last half of 1946. Therefore:

> For those municipalities which indicate a desire to have the [day nursery] programme continued and which are prepared to assume the administrative responsibilities from July 1, would you consider continuing the 50 per cent net cost of operation until December 31, 1946?[135]

When consulted, Brooke Claxton, Minister of National Health and Welfare could "see no reason why the Dominion Government should continue in peace-time to share in the costs of a program, the interest in which is apparently centered almost entirely within one province, and indeed largely within one large city in that province." Claxton had learned from his Deputy that Hamilton had agreed to pay its share of the day nursery costs from its 1946 budget. In Claxton's opinion, if Hamilton could do that, "even after the municipal tax rate has been struck and the budget set for the year," certainly other cities, such as Toronto and London, should have been able to do so.[136]

On June 12, 1946, Mitchell conveyed to W. A. Goodfellow the Dominion Government's decision not to grant Ontario a further extension.[137] On June 30, 1946, the Dominion-Provincial Wartime Day Nurseries Agreement with Ontario came to an end. The day care programme for school children ended in Ontario on that date. By the end of November 1946, nine out of the 28 day nurseries were closed.[138] How long the rest lasted will require further research.

IV

The post war abrogation of government-supported day nurseries in Quebec and day care for school children in Ontario, the post-war reduction of government support to day nurseries in Ontario, as well as the post-war cancellation of the tax concessions to employed married women, were all in keeping with the official attitudes towards working women during the war. As labour shortages developed in 1942, women were regarded as a large labour reserve that Canadian industry could draw on in the war emergency. But women's place was in the home, and so initial recruitment aimed at young unmarried women and then married women without children. To meet increased labour demands in 1943, recruitment had to dip more deeply into the female labour pool, down to women with home responsibilities, even to mothers of young children. In deference to "majority opinion" which tended "to favour mothers remaining in the home, rather than working, where at all possible," NSS and Labour Department officials invoked abnormal times, war conditions, to justify their having to encourage mothers with young children "to accept industrial employment, as an aid to our national effort." Even after the establishment of child care facilities in Ontario and Quebec, the Federal Department of Labour insisted that its policy was "to put emphasis on single or married women without children accepting employment in the first instance."[139] As only war service justified a mother's leaving home for the public work place, the Dominion-Provincial Wartime Day Nurseries Agreement was to provide day care primarily for the children of mothers working in war industries. According to Mrs. Eaton, the Women's Division of NSS had "found that women with children were unwisely deciding to look for employment," and had therefore in October 1943 advised the Counselling Service of local Employment and Service offices "to hold back from employment those who seem to be neglecting their home and family."[140] Where there was opposition to the employment of women in industry, as there strongly was from certain quarters in Quebec,[141] the Women's Division of NSS did not adduce women's equal right to work, but instead invoked the necessity of sacrifice for the nation at war and stressed the temporary nature of the sacrifice. If women took jobs previously held only by men, they were generally regarded as replacing men temporarily. The large-scale part-time employment of women was not supposed to last. The very increase in numbers of women in the labour force, from about 638,000 in 1939 to an estimated 1,077,000 by October 1, 1944,[142] was regarded as a temporary phenomenon. Therefore, it is not surprising that, faced with problems of women's unemployment and economic dislocation in the post-war period, the Women's Division of NSS sought to return married women to the home and to channel young unmarried women into traditionally female occupations: domestic service, nursing and teaching. A "feminine mystique" did not have to be manufactured in Canada after the war had ended; it had been there all along.

Bibliographical Essay

ABBREVIATIONS USED IN THE ESSAY

CHM   Canada: An Historical Magazine
CNRW Canadian Newsletter of Research on Women
CRSA   Canadian Review of Sociology and Anthropology
OH   Ontario History
SS   Sociologie et Sociétés

The footnotes in these essays alone should convince the reader of the scope and variety of sources for the history of women. Anyone still doubting should consult any of the teachers of women's history in a Canadian university; all of us have mammoth files. Unfortunately no effort has yet been made to co-ordinate these separate files; perhaps that could be one of the initial tasks of the Canadian Research Institute for the Advancement of Women or for the Canadian Committee on Women's History. In any case, this essay will not attempt such a gargantuan task. Rather it will indicate to the newly converted where to begin in the field; for those already initiated it will point out some of the more recent studies; and it will end, as much in women's history does, with a plea for an interdisciplinary approach.

STATE OF THE ART

Beginners should start with the "state of the art", the approaches and methods and questions that historians of women have asked and are asking. For the Canadian scene two introductions are useful: that of Ramsay Cook to the new edition of Catherine Cleverdon, *The Woman Suffrage Movement in Canada* (1974); and that of Veronica Strong-Boag to the new edition of Nellie McClung, *In Times Like These* (1972). Quantitative approaches may be one of the ways to crack the silence which the past imposed on women and E. Shorter, *The Historian and the Computer* (1971) and S. Kleinberg, "The Systematic Study of Urban Women", *Historical Methods Newsletter* 9 (1975) are readable introductions to these methods. Some of the results of the methods can be seen in M. Katz, *The People of Hamilton, Canada West: Family and Class in the Mid-Nineteenth Century* (1975). The problems and questions raised by the very writing of women's history can be seen in three recent articles: N.Z. Davis "Women's History in Transition: the European Case", *Feminist Studies* 3 (1976); J. Kelly-Gadol, "The Social Relations of the Sexes: Methodological Implications of Women's History", *Signs* (Summer, 1976); G. Lerner, "Placing Women in History: Definitions and Challenges", *Feminist Studies* 3 (1975).

BIBLIOGRAPHIES

From there the beginner should head for bibliographies. The most extensive one is by Veronica Strong-Boag, "Cousin Cinderella" in Marylee Stephenson, ed., *Women in Canada* (1973). Except for P. Atnikov *et al, Out from the Shadows: a Bibliography of the History of Women in Manitoba* (1975) and R. Hamel, *Bibliographie sommaire sur l'histoire de l'écriture féminine au Canada 1769-1961* (1974) the others are less historically oriented. See, for example, E. Bayefsky, "Women and Work: a Selection of Books and Articles", *Ontario Library Review* 56 (1972); G. Houle, *La femme au Québec* (1975); M. Eichler and L. Primrose, "A Bibliography of Materials on Canadian Women" in M. Stephenson, ed., *Women in Canada* (1973); and Sandra Gwyn, "Women", in R. Fulford *et al., Read Canadian* (1972). A very useful bibliography has just appeared as special publication #3 of CNRW: *Women; a Bibliography of Special Periodical Issues* 1960-75 (1976).

For the beginner too there are some recently published guides to archival material. H. Reilly and H. Hindmarch have compiled an annotated guide to holdings in the Public Archives: *Some Sources for Women's History in the Public Archives of Canada* (1974). V. Strong-Boag and J. Dryden have made a preliminary study of Ontario Libraries: "Archival Holdings on Canadian Women's History: Ontario" in CNRW (Feb. 1976) and M. Lavigne and J. Stoddart have done the same for Quebec: "Rapport sur les archives au Québec", CNRW (Oct. 1976). Some universities are beginning to make their holdings known. An example is the listing available from the Douglas Library at Queen's compiled by A. MacDermaid, "General Listing of Sources Relating to Women's History in the Queen's University Archives."

GENERAL ACCOUNTS

As the dates of most of the articles in this volume indicate, studies in the history of Canadian women have recently begun to appear in great number. The references which follow are necessarily a selection and for the most part have been published since 1972, the terminal date of the Strong-Boag bibliography. Not surprisingly International Women's Year produced a spate of articles and many periodicals put out special issues on women in and around that year. The CNRW bibliography mentioned above lists both the names of the periodicals and the articles contained in them. Those containing historical material on Canadian women are the following: *Alberta Historical Review* (autumn, 1967); CHM (December, 1975); *Canada Manpower and Immigration Review* (1975); *Canadian Dimension* (June, 1975); CRSA (November, 1975); SS (mai, 1974). At least a dozen other Canadian periodicals and more than one hundred non-Canadian ones are in the bibliography; perusing is a must. Recent general accounts in book form include the reflective essay by N. Griffiths, *Penelope's Web* (1976) and the collections of essays in G. Matheson, ed., *Women in the Canadian Mosaic* (1976) and J. Acton *et al.*, eds., *Women at Work, Ontario 1850-1930* (1974).

PRIMARY SOURCES

The current interest in women's history has resulted as well in the publishing of primary source material on women in Canada's past. Documents from the times include B.G. Jeffries, *The Household Guide or Domestic Cyclopedia* [1894] (1972); N. McClung, *In Times Like These* [1915] (1972); and the National Council of Women, *Women of Canada, Their Life and Work* [1900] (1975). Collections of contemporary documents are R. Cook and W. Mitchinson, eds., *The Proper Sphere: Women's Place in Canadian Society* (1976); M. Jean, ed., *Québécoises du 20e siècle* (1974) and A.L. Prentice and S.E. Houston, eds., *Family, School and Society in 19th Century Canada* (1975). Diaries and recollections include C.A. Carter, ed., *The Diary of Sophia MacNab* (1974); J. Duncan, ed. *Red Serge Wives* (1974); P. Godsell, ed., *The Diary of Jane Ellice* (1975); A.S. Miller, ed., *The Journals of Mary O'Brien* (1968) and M.A. Ormsby, ed., *A Pioneer Gentlewoman in British Columbia: the Recollections of Susan Allison* (1976). Collections of letters are M. Jordan, ed., *To Louis from your sister who loves you, Sara Riel* (1974); H. Robertson, *Salt of the Earth* (1974) and L. Tivy, ed., *Your loving Anna: Letters from the Ontario Frontier* (1972). Autobiographies include D.

Anderson, *Ways Harsh and Wild* (1973); S. Burnford, *One Woman's Arctic* (1973); H.R. Campbell, *From Chalkdust to Hayseed* (1975); T. Casgrain, *Une femme chez les hommes* (1971) and its English translation, *A Woman in a Man's World* (1973); T. Davidson, *The Golden Strings* (1973); Anne Francis, *An Autobiography* (1975); E. Goudie, *Woman of Labrador* (1973); R. Knight, ed., *A Very Ordinary Life;* M. Peate, *Girl in a Red River Coat* (1973); and J. Willis, *Geniesh: an Indian Girlhood* (1973).

SECONDARY SOURCES

Secondary sources – studies of aspects of women's history – have also begun pouring from the presses in the last few years. These include monographs and theses and articles. To keep abreast of monographs and theses a student should comb regularly *Canadiana*, the monthly publication of the acquisitions of the National Library of Canada; the bibliography is tedious to use but usually rewarding. For articles in periodicals, the Canadian Periodical Index, an annual publication listing articles by subject and author, is essential. See also the "Recent Publications" section of the *Canadian Historical Review* and the "Bibliographie" section in the *Revue d'histoire de l'Amérique française.* The following notations of all three types of secondary material are divided chronologically: the 17th and 18th centuries; the 19th century; and the 20th century. Again the material listed is chiefly that published since 1972 and is necessarily selective.

17th AND 18th CENTURIES

For the seventeenth and eighteenth centuries, three recent studies deal in part with women: L. Dechêne, *Habitants et Marchands de Montréal au XVIIe siècle* (1974) and M. Trudel, *La Population du Canada en 1663* (1973) and *Les débuts du régime seigneurial* (1974). More directly concerned with women are M. D'Allaire, *L'Hôpital général du Québec* (1971) and "Conditions matérielles requises pour devenir religieuse au XVIIIe siècle," in M. Allard *et al., L'Hôtel-Dieu de Montréal* (1973); and S. Dumas, *Les filles du roi en Nouvelle France* (1972). An article from the late 60s but perhaps worth noting is L.F. Bouvier "The Spacing of Births among French Canadian Families: an Historical Approach" in CRSA 5 (1968) and the latest demographic study is H. Charbonneau, *Vie et mort de nos ancêtres* (1976). A more popular account which in fact begins with a Viking woman and continues into the twentieth century but includes two women from New France is J. Johnston, *Wilderness Women* (1973). And there are two recent religious biographies by G. Oury: *Marie de l'Incarnation* (1974) and *Madame de la Peltrie et ses fondations canadiennes* (1974).

19th CENTURY

Aspects of nineteenth century women's history are contained in the following recent studies: R. Ball, "A Perfect Farmer's Wife: women in 19th century Ontario," CHM 3 (1975); H.P. Bammon, "The Ladies Benevolent Society of Hamilton," *Canadian Social History Project,* Interim Report No. 4 (1972); L. S. Bohnen, "Women Workers in Ontario; a socio-legal history," *University of Toronto Faculty of Law Review* 31 (1973); W.E. Bryans, "Virtuous Women at Half the Price: the Feminization of Teaching and Women Teachers' Organizations", (M.A. thesis, University of Toronto, 1974); J. Cooper, "Red Lights in Winnipeg", *Transactions of the Manitoba Historical and Scientific Society* 27 (1971); J.S. Crosbie, *The Incredible Mrs. Chadwick* (1975); I.E. Davey, "Trends in Female School Attendance in Mid-Nineteenth Century Ontario", *Histoire Sociale/Social History* 8 (1975); M.E. Fowler, "Susan Sibbald: Writer and Pioneer", OH 56 (1974); M. Gillen, *The Wheel of Things; a Biography of L.M. Montgomery* (1975); C. Hacker, *The Indomitable Lady Doctors* (1974); M. Katz, *The People of Hamilton, Canada West: Family and Class in a mid-nineteenth century city* (1975); L. Kernaghan, "M.J.K.L. [Mary Jane Katzman Lawson] – a Victorian Contradiction", *Nova Scotia Historical Quarterly* 5 (1975); R. Matthews, "Susanna Moodie, Pink Toryism and Nineteenth century Ideas of Canadian Identity", *Journal of Canadian Studies* 10 (1975); T. Morrison, "Their Proper Spheres: Feminism, the Family and Child-centered Social Reform in Ontario, 1875-1900," Pt. I, OH 68 (1976); A. Prentice, "Education and the Metaphor of the Family: an Upper Canadian Example", *History of Education Quarterly* 12 (1972); D. Ronish, "The Montreal Ladies' Educational Association, 1871-1885", *McGill Journal of Education* 6 (1971); M.V. Royce, "Arguments over the education of Girls", OH 67 (1975); R. Stamp, "Adelaide Hoodless, champion of Women's Rights", in R.S. Patterson, *et al., Profiles of Canadian Educators* (1974); J. Stoddart and V. Strong-Boag, " ... And Things were going wrong at home", *Atlantis* 1 (1975); V. Strong-Boag, *The Parliament of Women: the National Council of Women of Canada* (1976); N. Thompson, "The Controversy over the admission of women to University College", (M.A. thesis, University of Toronto, 1974); L. Tepperman, "Ethnic variations in Marriage and Fertility: Canada 1871", CRSA 11 (1974); W.L. Thorpe, "Lady Aberdeen and the National Council of Women of Canada", (M.A. thesis, Queen's University, 1973); W. Turner, "Eighty Stout and Healthy looking Girls", CHM 3 (1975).

20th CENTURY

Women in the twentieth century are the subject of the following studies: H. and P. Armstrong, "The Segregated Participation of women in the Canadian labour force", CRSA 12 (1975); G.H. Harvey, *Canadian Hospitals, 1920 to 1970* (1974); B. Brigden, "One Woman's Campaign for Social Purity and Social Reform," in R. Allen, ed., *The Social Gospel in Canada* (1975); C. Bacchi, "Liberation Deferred: the Ideas of the English Canadian Suffragists", (Ph.D. thesis, McGill University, 1976); R.M. Buck, *The Doctor Rode Side-Saddle* (1974); C. Carisse and J. Dumazedier, *Les Femmes innovatrices* (1975); E.N. Conklin, "Women's Voluntary Associations in French Montreal: a study of changing institutions and attitudes", (Ph.D. thesis, University of Illinois at Urbana, 1972); M. Dolment and M. Barthe, *La femme au Québec* (1973); A. Dupont, "Le suffrage féminin," in his *Les relations entre l'église et l'état sous L.-A. Taschereau* (1973); E. Forbes, *With Enthusiasm and Faith: a history of the Canadian Federation of Business and Professional Women's Clubs 1930-1972* (1974); M.-J. Gagnon, "Les femmes dans le mouvement syndical québécois", ss 6 (1974); three articles by D. Gorham: "The Canadian Suffragists", in G. Matheson, ed., *Women in the Canadian Mosaic* (1976); "English Militancy and the Canadian Suffrage Movement," *Atlantis* 1 (1975); "Singing up the Hill", *Canadian Dimension* 10 (1975); L.M. Grayson and M. Bliss, eds., *The Wretched of Canada* (1972); C.M. Hill, "Women in the Canadian Economy", in R.M. Laxer, ed., *(Canada) Ltd.* (1973); M. Lavigne, Y. Pinard and J. Stoddart, "La Fédération nationale St Jean Baptiste et les revendications féministes au début du XXe siècle", *Revue d'histoire de l'Amérique française* 29 (1975); Y. Laurencelle, "La promotion de la femme dans l'église catholique depuis 1939," (thèse de Ph.D., Université d'Ottawa, 1972) P. Marchak, "Les femmes, le travail et le syndicalisme au Canada", ss 6 (1974); I. McKenna, "Women in Canadian Literature", *Canadian Literature* 62 (1974); H.E.L. Murray, "The Traditional Role of Women in a Newfoundland Fishing Community," (M.A. thesis, Memorial University, 1972); C.W.L. Nicholson, *Canada's Nursing Sisters* (1976); J.E. Oster, "The Image of the Teacher in Canadian Prairie Fiction, 1921-1971", (Ph.D. thesis, University of Alberta, 1972); J. Rouillard, *Les travailleurs du coton au Québec 1900-1915* (1974); R. Roy, "Positions et préoccupations de la Confédération des syndicats nationaux et de la Fédération des travailleurs du Québec sur le travail féminin", (thèse de M.A., Université Laval, 1974); J. Stoddart, "The Woman Suffrage Bill in Quebec", in M. Stephenson, ed., *Women in Canada* (1973); M. Street, *Watch-fires on the Mountains: the Life and Writings of Ethel Johns* (1973); P. Voisey, "The 'Votes for Women' Movement", *Alberta History* 23 (1975); "Women's Employment in Canada: a look at the past", *Canada Manpower and Immigration Review* 8 (1975); 1-8. For both the 19th and 20th centuries, see also the essays in *Women at Work: Ontario, 1850-1930,* cited above.

In spite of the fact that this book and this essay have stressed the *history* of women in Canada, anyone interested in such a field cannot be limited to history. The questions that historians of women's experience are asking can only be answered by selective borrowings from anthropology, sociology, economics, demography and psychology. Students of women in Canada's past should be aware of contemporary studies in other fields. Beyond the historical journals, which are only beginning to publish articles on women's history (the dates of most of the selections in this book are an indication), the best Canadian source to keep an eye on is CRSA. And the best way to keep abreast of on-going research and publications is through the CNRW. A new Canadian journal, *Atlantis*, is attempting to provide a national outlet for women's studies articles. The complexities and scope of women's studies – including the past of women – can be seen in the recently launched American journal *Signs: A Journal of Women in Culture and Society.*

Notes

INTRODUCTION

1. Barbara Roberts deals with this question in "They drove him to drink: Donald Creighton's Macdonald and his wives," *Canada: an Historical Magazine,* III (December, 1975), pp. 50-64.
2. C.L. Cleverdon, *The Woman Suffrage Movement in Canada* (Toronto, 1950; reprint edit., 1974).
3. Some of the best, the most recent and the most read texts in Canadian history treat women in this way. W.L. Morton, *The Critical Years* (Toronto, 1964) mentions women eleven times. P.B. Waite, *Arduous Destiny* (Toronto, 1971) finds more women – there are twenty-eight – but the additional ones are chiefly the subjects of cartoons or anecdotes. Although Ramsay Cook and Craig Brown, *Canada: A Nation Transformed* (Toronto, 1974) are more sensitive to current questions and current research, they too can only produce eleven items involving women. The importunate lady referred to here is Lady Tupper as described by W.S. MacNutt, "The 1880s," in J.M.S. Careless and R.C. Brown, eds., *The Canadians*, Part I (Toronto, 1968) p. 90.
4. The encapsulated style of much economic history often precludes reference to the roles played by either men or women, except in the most abstract terms. Thus an essay by Harold Innis on the history of the dairy industry refers to the people involved only as participants in settlement patterns or as producers and consumers of goods. We are told, for example, that the "release of labour by agricultural machinery in areas with large families . . . contributed to the development of the dairy industry," but nothing about the sexual division of labour within such families, which often gave to women the sole responsibility for the work of the dairy. "The Historical Development of the Dairy Industry in Canada," Mary Q. Innis, ed., *Essays in Economic History* (Toronto, 1956; reprint edit., 1965) pp. 211-20. Discussion of women in labour history seems to have been limited to the subject of protective legislation or the need for it.

5. Perhaps it would be appropriate here to enter a plea for the preservation of records. How many diaries and collections of letters are consigned to the garbage each year or lie forgotten in attics and basements because grandmother's old letters aren't thought important enough for the public record? These are precisely the records that are of great value to the social historian and in particular the historian of women.

WOMEN OF THREE RIVERS

1. [The documents and their locations are described in the original published version of this essay. See the *Canadian Historical Review,* XXI (June, 1940), pp 132-33. Eds.]
2. Armour Landry, *Bribes d'histoire* (Pages trifluviennes, série A, no. 1, Trois-Rivières, 1932), 25. Unfortunately, there is no explanation of these figures nor of the source from which they are taken.
3. Their marriage contract is in the Palais de Justice, Quebec, *Greffe Martial Piraube,* 23 août 1641, no. 33. The intention was apparently that Jacques Hertel should fetch her, and so they may have been married in Rouen.
4. Benjamin Sulte, *Histoire des Canadiens-fran*çais (Montréal, 1882-4), IV, 80.
5. [As Foulché-Delbosc points out in note 5 in the original version, population estimates are problematic. Readers interested in pursuing this subject are referred to the original, p. 134, and to the works by H. Charbonneau, L. Dechêne and M. Trudel cited in the bibliographic essay. Eds.]
6. It should be noted that this essay touches only incidentally upon the legal aspects of marriage during the period, which are interesting and complex enough to deserve special treatment.
7. For the names of the few young Canadians entering convents during this period, see, R.G. Thwaites (ed.), *The Jesuit Relations and Allied Documents,* (Cleveland, 1896-1901), XLIV, 121, Journal des Jésuites; P.-G. Roy, *La Famille Gelefroy de Tonnancour,* Lévis, 1904, 12; *Histoire de l'Hôtel-Dieu de Québec,* Montauban, 1751, 77, 94, 100, 106, 107, 129.
8. On October 29 of this year, Marie-Madeleine Hertel, elder daughter of Jacques Hertel and Marie Marguerie, who are considered to be the second family of colonists to settle in Three Rivers, was married to Louis Pinard at the age of thirteen (Parish register, marriages). It would seem highly probable that she is the first *Trifluvienne* to marry in the place of her birth.
9. Marguerite Sédillot who married Jean Aubuchon in 1654 was born in Quebec according to Tanguay *(Dictionnaire généalogique,* 1, 541) as were also her brothers and sisters, but the entry in the marriage register seems to indicate a Parisian origin. Louis Cloutier who married François Marguerie was born in Quebec or in Château-Richer.

10. The marriage contracts, unlike modern ones, do not give their ages, nor do the marriage registers. Mgr Tanguay, with indefatigable zeal, has discovered their ages in the register of burials when he has not pursued his researches to France itself.

11. These are Louise de Mousseau (contract of March 29, 1655); Marie Pomponnelle (contract of July 24, 1656); and Anne Boyer (contract of May 14, 1658).

12. Noelle or Nathalie Landeau (contract of June 24, 1660).

13. Musée de Québec. *Prévôté des Trois-Rivières,* 1, 8 janv., 1656, 5 fév., 1656, 9 fév., 1656, and 15 mai, 1656. They were married on January 16, 1656, "duobus factis denunciationibus" (parish register). Jean Desmarais and Anne Le Sont had no children. On January 27, 1661, they made a mutual donation of their possessions before the notary Ameau. According to Mgr Tanguay, she was born in 1619, he in 1626. If this is correct, the Sieur du Hérisson was more than exaggerating when he claimed to name her age. According to Tanguay, she was the widow of Jean Lafortune before marrying Desmarais. I have respected Mgr Tanguay's deciphering of her name, although to me it would seem to be Le Jonc.

14. The passage money to be paid to the captain or ship-owner must have been a fixed sum. But the *advance* given for this purpose by one of the contracting parties to the other seems to have been calculated according to the full amount of time to be remunerated. The later document is thus expressed: "condamnons ledict Le Maistre et ladicte Rigaud sa femme rembourser ladicte Damoiselle de la Potherie de la somme de 31 livres, 8 sols, 4 deniers pour ce que ladicte Rigaud doibt des dépenses de son passage, à raison de deux ans cinq mois restans des cinq années esquelles elle s'estoit obligée par son marché."

15. Three Rivers, Palais de Justice, judicial archives, June 9, 1654 and July 21, 1654.

16. There are many examples of this to be found in the notarial archives in the Palais de Justice at Quebec. See also Palais de Justice, Three Rivers, *Greffe Herlin,* 27 mars, 1663.

17. These examples are taken from Mgr Tanguay's *Dictionnaire généalogique,* I.

18. *Greffe Ameau.*

19. Parish register.

20. *Greffe Ameau,* contract of July 27, 1653.

21. On January 20, 1671 *(Greffe Ameau),* Jeanne Aunois (or Auneau), widow of Pierre Lefebvre, divides her property among her five sons to the absolute detriment of her two daughters. She refers to her husband's will which had also favoured the sons, practically disinheriting the daughters, although the latter, we are made to understand, have not done badly by the arrangement (probably waiving all claims for a definite sum or a piece of property). Like

the Napoleonic Code which followed it, the Custom of Paris was an egalitarian institution: except for land whose tenure was noble, property was inherited equally by the children, whether male or female. A parent could not disinherit any of his or her children beyond what was called the "légitime," amounting to half of what the inheritance would have been had the operation of the Custom been normal. This act of Jeanne Aunois (made without the consent of her daughters) may be an isolated case, but it is significant that the notary did not disallow it.

22. Madeleine Hertel, whose mother was illiterate and Marguerite Seigneuret, both of whose parents were illiterate.

23. There are, however, exceptions to this rule. Mme Louis d'Ailleboust (*née* Barbe de Boulogne) did not remarry although left a widow at an early age; neither did Mme Pierre Le Gardeur de Repentigny (*née* Marie Favery) whose husband died while she was still young. She is mentioned in 1668 as being guardian to the orphaned children of her daughter Madeleine and the latter's husband Paul Godefroy (*Papier terrier de la Compagnie des Indes Occidentales,* pub. par P.-G. Roy, Beauceville, 1931, 275), a duty which she could not have performed, had she remarried.

24. Given in facsimile and transcription by M. P.-G. Roy in *Rapport, 1921-1922,* before p. 1.

25. This is Eléonore de Grandmaison, who married successively: Antoine Boudier, Sieur de Beauregard; François de Chavigny, Sieur de Berchereau; Jacques Gourdeau, Sieur de Beaulieu; et Jacques Caillault, Sieur de la Tesseril (Godbout, *Les Pionniers de la région trifluvienne La Famille Chavigny de la Chevrotière,* Lévis, 1916).

26. It is printed in Moreau de St. Méry, *Loix et constitutions des colonies françoises de l'Amérique sous le vent* (Paris, n.d.), 6-7.

27. This practice apparently continued, at least until the disproportion in numbers between the sexes was not so acute, that is for a long period. In 1672, the Abbé Dollier de Casson uses an extreme example of rapid remarriage as an inducement to the women of France to come out to Canada. He tells of a woman who, having lost her husband, procured the publication of one bann, the dispensation of the two others, and her marriage to a new husband – all before her first husband had been buried! *(Histoire du Montréal,* published by the Société Historique de Montréal, 1868, 207).

28. Marriage contract between Mathieu Labat and Marie Denot, Jan. 26, 1653; marriage contract between Philippe Etienne and Marie Vien, Jan. 24, 1655; inventory of the widow Labat, May 19, 1655 *(Greffe Ameau,* parish register for the double marriage).

29. [On this subject, readers should consult the recent works on population in New France cited in the bibliographic essay. Eds.]

30. See Public Archives of Canada, *Correspondance officielle*, série 2, 134-42, "Articles accordés entre les directeurs et associés en la Compagnie de la Nouvelle France et les députés des habitans dudit pays (6 mars 1645)." By article 72 (p. 138) the settlers bound themselves to bring out only twenty people (men and women) a year. It does not seem that this condition was complied with any more than most of the others, as the Company of the Inhabitants became bankrupt.

31. *Greffe Ameau,* Jan. 24, 1658.

32. Three Rivers, judicial archives, July 14, 1655. The whole system of guardianship and division of property between mother and children can be seen in the same collection in the Hertel inventory, Aug. 21, 1651 to June 3, 1652; in the inventory Jeanne Jallaux, *veuve* Repentigny, Nov. 2, 1654, Aug. 4, 1655; in the inventory of Marguerite Hayet, *veuve* Véron, Jan. 14 and 21, 1654; in the inventory of the "mineure de Guillaume Isabel," Feb. 4, 1654, April 8, 1654, March 3 and 10, 1655, July 14, 1655; in the inventory of Marie Sédillot, *veuve* Bertrand Fafard, Dec. 28, 1660 to Feb. 12, 1661, Jan. 29, 1664.

33. "Tutelle de la mineure de Guillaume Isabel": Three Rivers, judicial archives, Feb. 4, 1654; "tutelle des enfants Véron," March 6, 1654.

34. Three Rivers, judicial archives, March 6, 1654.

35. Sulte, *Histoire des Canadiens-français,* 63.

36. Pierre Boucher, *Histoire véritable* (Paris, 1664), 155.

37. Published in *Bulletin des recherches historiques,* XXVII, 338.

38. *Relations des Jésuites* (Québec, 1858), II, 30-1.

39. Musée de Québec, *Archives des Trois-Rivières, Documents divers,* I no. 47, 14 juillet, 1665.

40. Montreal, judicial archives, copies in the Public Archives of Canada, I, 1653-1711, 18 janv., 1659; and I, 1651-1669, 8 fév., 1651, 17 juin, 1660, etc.

41. Laverdière et Casgrain (eds.), *Journal des Jésuites* (Québec, 1871), 120.

42. This was often a courageous stand, as it displeased the more influential type of colonists. *Journal des Jésuites,* oct., 1645, 11.

43. *Notes sur les registres de Notre Dame de Québec* (Québec, 1863), 39.

44. An inquiry was instituted in 1665 by Father Druillettes at the Cap de la Madeleine, on the seigniory of the Jesuits. See Musée de Québec, *Archives des Trois-Rivières,* I, 1665-6.

45. Musée de Québec, *Archives de Trois-Rivières, Documents divers,* I, 29 oct., 1662.

46. Parish register, 14 mai, 1657; Musée de Québec, *Prévôté des Trois-Rivières,* II, 28 août, 1660; *Greffe Ameau,* 16 nov., 1661. See also E. Z. Massicotte, "Les Chirurgiens de Montréal au XVIIE siècle" *(Bulletin des recherches historiques,* XXVII, 42).

47. Gérard Malchelosse (ed.), *Mélanges historiques: Etudes éparses et inédites de Benjamin Sulte* (Montreal, 1919), 7-27, "Histoire de la pomme de terre." Pierre Boucher, anxious to praise the quality of Canadian earth, mentioned several other grains, vegetables, and herbs, many of which grew wild. So far, he said, the colonists had concentrated upon the cultivation of wheat and neglected the other possibilities. He mentioned as having been tried; barley, rye, lentils, onions, melons, beets, carrots, beans, squash, parsnips, salsify, sorrel, chard, asparagus, spinach, parsley, chicory, leeks, garlic, chives, cucumbers, watermelons. He listed as already under cultivation by the Indians: Indian corn, beans, squash, sunflowers, and tobacco (Boucher, *Histoire véritable,* 82-5).

48. The Hertel inventory included "un manteau de drap garni de boutons d'or" selling for 54 *livres* and "un pourpoint, hault de chausses et bas de drap" for 40 *livres*, while a six weeks' old heifer cost only 24 *Livres* and even a house and lot in town was sold for 135 *livres*.

49. Testament of Christophe Crevier, Sieur de la Meslée, Dec. 1, 1652. (This date has been added by another hand.)

50. Palais de Justice, Québec, *Greffe Guillaume Audouart,* Sept. 6, 1658, no. 675, and Musée de Québec, *Prévôté des Trois-Rivières,* I, May 8, 1660.

FUR TRADE SOCIETY

1. Glyndwr Williams, ed., *Andrew Graham's Observations on Hudson's Bay 1767-91* (London: Hudson's Bay Record Society (hereafter referred to as HBRS), 1969), p. 248.

2. Hudson's Bay Company Archives (hereafter referred to as HBC), B22/a/6, Brandon House, f. 8d, Nov. 13, 1798: ". . . Jollycoeur the Canadian wanted an old Woman to keep ... he says every Frenchman has a woman & why should we stop him."

3. HBC, B239/b/79, York Factory, fos. 40d.-41, as quoted in Alice M. Johnson, ed., *Saskatchewan Journals and Correspondence, 1795-1802* (London: HBRS, 1967).

4. John Franklin, *Narrative of a Journey to the Shores of the Polar Sea in the Years 1819-20-21-22* (London: 1824). p. 101.

5. John West, *The Substance of a Journal during a residence at the Red River Colony. . . .* (London 1827), p. 16: "They do not admit them as their companions, nor do they allow them to eat at their tables, but degrade them *merely* as slaves to their arbitrary inclination . . ." See also pp. 53-54.

6. Franklin, *Narrative,* p. 106.

7. G. P. deT. Glazebrook, ed., *The Hargrave Correspondence, 1821-43* (Toronto: Champlain Society, 1938), p. 381, Jas. Douglas to Jas Hargrave, Fort Vancouver, 24 March 1842: "There is indeed no living with comfort in this country until a person has forgot the great world and has his tastes and character formed on the current

standard of the stage. . . . To any other being . . . the vapid monotony of an inland trading Post, would be perfectly unsufferable,
while habit makes it familiar to us, softened as it is by the many
tender ties, which find a way to the heart."

8. John Siveright in his letters to James Hargrave as published in the
Hargrave Corres. frequently observed that Indian traders who
retired with their families to farms in the Canadas were rarely successful. He cited the case of Alexander Stewart's wife who died
soon after her arrival in Montreal.

9. Margaret A. Macleod, ed., *The Letters of Letitia Hargrave*
(Toronto: Champlain Society, 1947), p. 72, To Mary Mactavish,
York, 1 Sept. 1840.

10. W. Kaye Lamb, ed., *Sixteen years in the Indian Country: The Jour-
nal of Daniel Williams Harmon* (Toronto: 1957), pp. 5-6. See also
W.S. Wallace, ed., *Documents relating to the North West Company*
(Toronto: Champlain Society, 1934), p. 211.

11. E.E. Rich, ed., *Minutes of Council of the Northern Department of
Rupert's Land, 1821-31* (London: HBRS, 1940) pp. 33-34.

12. Rich, *Minutes of Council,* pp. 33-34. See also HBC, B235/z/3, f. 545
for a circular outlining the proposals for the establishment of a
boarding school for female children, natives of the Indian Country. A similar institution for boys was not actually established until
the 1830's.

13. Rich, *Minutes of Council,* pp. 94-95. See also p. 382, Simpson to
Gov. & Committee, York, 1 Sept. 1822: "Messrs. Donald Suther-
land and James Kirkness have this season requested permission to
take their Families to Europe, which I was induced to comply with
being aware that they had the means of providing for them so as to
prevent their becoming a burden on the Company, and some
labourers are in like manner permitted to take their children
home."

14. Rich, *Minutes of Council,* pp. 358-59. See also HBC, A6/20, f. 74,
136d.

15. HBC, A6/62, f. 3-3d.

16. Rich, *Minutes of Council,* pp. 94-95. This rule eventually became
incorporated into the Standing Rules and Regulations. See also
HBC, A6/21, f. 32, 151d.

17. Quite a number of these contracts are to be found in the miscel-
laneous file (z) under the heading of the various posts, i.e.,
B239/z/1, f. 32d.

18. HBC, B49/z/1, B156/z/1, f. 96.

19. West, *Journal,* p. 26.

20. Nicholas Garry, *Diary of.* . . . (Ottawa: TRSC, Ser. 2, vol. 6, 1900), p.
137.

21. Rich, *Minutes of Council,* pp. 60-61. There is evidence that Chief
Factor James Keith drew up these rules during the winter of 1822-

23 at Severn. See HBC, B198/e/6, fos. 5d-6.

22. Frederick Merk, ed., *Fur Trade and Empire: George Simpson's Journal....* (Cambridge, Mass.: 1931), p. 108.

23. E.E. Rich, ed., *Simpson's Athabaska Journal and Report* (London: HBRS, 1938), p. 231.

24. HBC, B39/a/16, Ft. Chipewyan, Simpson to Wm. Brown, 17 Oct. 1820, et. al.

25. Rich, *Athabaska Journal,* p. 264, Simpson to Jn. Clarke, Isle a la Crosse, 9 Feb. 1821.

26. Rich, *Athabaska Journal,* pp. 392, 395-96.

27. HBC, D3/3, f. 35, 7 March 1822, Brandon House: "... no less than 87 people including women & children which is a very serious drawback." B239/c/1, f. 91, Simpson to McTavish, Isle à la Crosse, 12 Nov. 1822: "the Deptmt. is dreadfully overloaded with Families no less than 102 women & children & no less than three births since my arrival here ... "

28. Rich, *Athabaska Journal,* pp. 23-4.

29. Merk, *Fur Trade,* p. 131.

30. Merk, *Fur Trade,* pp. 11-12: "... they are nearly all *Family Men.*" See also p. 99.

31. HBC, D3/3, 1821-22, f. 52.

32. D3/3, f. 34.

33. Merk, *Fur Trade,* pp. 58, 131-32. These two Chief Traders were John McLeod, whose wife was a daughter of J.P. Pruden, and John Warren Dease. There is other evidence that jealousy often caused the men to shirk their duty, see B39/a/22, Ft. Chipewyan, f. 42.

34. HBC, Copy No. 160a, Selkirk Correspondence, f. 1157c, Simpson to Colvile, York, 11 Aug. 1824. These three men were Donald Ross, Clerk, who took Mary MacBeath, daughter of a Selkirk settler, in 1820; John Clarke, Chief Factor, who took a Swiss girl Mary Ann Traitley in 1822; and Robert McVicar, Chief Trader, who took Christy MacBeath at Norway House in 1824. Since there is no record of any of these marriages in the Red River Register of Marriages, it is likely that, initially at least, they were after the fashion of the country.

35. This is a good example of a lasting marriage " *la façon du pays".* William Sinclair, an Orkneyman who served in the Hudson's Bay Company from 1792-1818, spent most of his career at Oxford House which he built in 1798. Little is known about the origin of his wife Nahovway, by whom he had eleven children, but she may have been a daughter of Moses Norton. See Dennis Bayley, *A Londoner in Rupert's Land: Thomas Bunn of the Hudson's Bay Company* (Chichester, Eng.: 1969) and D. Geneva Lent, *West of the Mountains: James Sinclair and the Hudson's Bay Company* (Seattle: 1963) for details of the Sinclair family.

36. HBC, B239/c/1, York Inward Corres., f. 60, Geo. Simpson to J.G. McTavish, Rock Depot, 14 Dec. 1821; same to same, f. 71, 25 Jan 1822 and f. 83, 4 June 1822.

37. HBC, B239/a/130, York Factory, f. 38d. This is a curious entry for it has been crossed out by someone at a later date. However A.S. Morton in his biography of Simpson is wrong in stating that this child was born in October 1821 for he confused this Maria with another natural daughter also called Maria who was born in Britain before Simpson ever came to Rupert's Land. Simpson received the news that this daughter was to be married to one Donald McTavish of Inverness in 1833 (B135/c/2, f. 110, Simpson to McTavish, 1 July 1833) and if she was then sixteen, as Morton states, she must have been born in 1817. Furthermore, there is no evidence that Simpson ever sent Betsey Sinclair's child to Scotland to be educated; she appears to have been at Mrs. Cockran's school for girls in Red River in 1830 (b4/b/1. f. 5v, J, Stuart to Simpson, 1 Feb. 1830) and in the fall of 1837 she married the botanist Robert Wallace at Fort Edmonton (*Hargrave Corres.*, p. 274, J. Rowand to Hargrave, Edmonton, 31 Dec. 1838). That this daughter was not a child of Margaret Taylor's as Morton states is conclusively proved in a letter from Robert Miles to Edward Ermatinger dated 8 Aug. 1839 (HBC Copy No. 23, fos. 304-305) which tells of Betsey Sinclair's grief on learning that her first daughter Maria had been drowned at the Dalles on the Columbia River in the fall of 1838.

38. HBC, E4/la, Red River Register of Baptisms, f. 39.

39. B239/c/1, f. 92, Simpson to McTavish, Isle à la Crosse, 12 Nov. 1822.

40. HBC, B235/c/1, Winnipeg, fos. 3d-4, Geo. Barnston to Jas. Hargrave, York, 1 Feb. 1823. This country marriage was a long and happy one. Betsey bore Miles at least eight children and retired with him to Upper Canada. I have found no evidence to support the suggestion of two writers (Lent, pp. 30-31 and Bayley, p. 46) that Betsey Sinclair was left out of her father's will because of her loose behaviour. Whatever the reason, her actions seem no worse than that of other young ladies growing up in the Indian Country.

41. B239/c/1, Simpson to McTavish, Red River, 4 June 1822, f. 83.

42. Macleod, *Letitia's Letters*, p. 205, n. 1. The tombstone of James Keith Simpson records that he died on 28 Dec. 1901 at the age of 78. He is reputed to have had a very sickly childhood but eventually entered the company's service in the mid-1840's. He was definitely not a son by Margaret Taylor as Morton claims. Macleod suggests his mother may have been the "country wife" of Chief Factor James Keith; Keith does indeed seem to have had some interest in this child for he bequeathed him the sum of five pounds for the purchase of books in his will of 1836 (HBC, A36/8, f. 58).

During this period Simpson may also have had a liaison with Jane Klyne, who later became the wife of Chief Factor Archibald Mac-Donald. She was the half-breed daughter of a former Nor'Wester Michael Klyne who was stationed at Great Slave Lake in 1822-23. See *Letitia's Letters*, p. 213: " . . . poor Mrs. MacDonald was an Indian wife of the Govr's . . . "

43. B239/c/1, Simpson to McTavish, Red River, 7 Jan, 1824, f. 136. See also f. 127: Simpson refused to allow Capt. Matthey, one of the leaders of the de Meuron segment of the population, to introduce his wife to the English wife of the Colony's governor R. P. Pelly because Mrs. Matthey was not his legal wife and she had been guilty of some indiscreet amours.

44. HBC Copy No. 112, vol. 2, fos. 638-39, Simpson to A. Colvile, York, 16 Aug. 1822: " . . . I should certainly wish to get Home for a Season if my inclination continues to lead the same way . . . "

45. In his biography *Sir George Simpson*, A. S. Morton places much emphasis on a Miss Eleanor Pooler who is kindly remembered in Simpson's letters to her father Richard Pooler (see pp. 124, 161). One can only speculate, however; perhaps he intended to make an honest woman out of the mother of Maria, his Scottish-born daughter.

46. Merk, *Fur Trade*, pp. 104-05.

47. Merk, *Fur Trade*, p. 122.

48. HBC Copy No. 160a, f. 1112, Simpson to Colvile, York, 8 Sept. 1823.

49. B239/c/1, f. 283, S. to McT., Norway House, 28 Aug. 1826.

50. HBC, B239/a/136, York Factory, f. 111d. For the date 11 Feb. 1827, there has been added the tiny postscript /G.S. Born/ with a curious comment by Robert Miles "say 11th March". This may well establish the date of the birth of Margaret's son, christened George Stewart; Simpson's letter to McTavish of 15 Sept. 1827 confirms that a son had been born.

51. B239/c/1, f. 346, Memo. for J. G. McTavish.

52. Arthur S. Morton, *Sir George Simpson: Overseas Governor of the Hudson's Bay Company* (Toronto: 1944) p. 162. There may also have been another woman in Simpson's life at this time, maintained at his headquarters at Lachine established in 1826 – See HBC, D5/3, Aemileus Simpson to Geo. Simpson, Ft. Vancouver, 20 March 1828: " . . . I do not think it improves the arrangements of your domestic economy to have a mistress attached to your Establishment – rather have her Elsewhere."

53. B239/c/1, f. 366, Simpson to McTavish, Stuart's Lake, 22 Sept. 1828.

54. B239/c/2, F. 10, S. to McT., Saskatchewan River, 10 May 1829.

55. HBC, B4/b/1, fos. 2d-3, Jn. Stuart to Simpson, Bas de la Rivière, 1 Feb. 1830. This son was baptized by the Rev. Wm. Cockran at Red River on 26 Dec. 1830 (E4/la, f. 80).

56. B4/b/1, same to same, 1 Feb. 1830, fos. 2d-3.

57. B4/b/1, same to same, 20 March, f. 7.

58. B4/b/1, same to same, Norway House, 8 Aug. 1825, f. 18: " . . . permit me my heartfelt acknowledgements for the many Kindness [es] and marks of friendship manifested towards me on various occasions . . . before I can cease to be grateful I must cease to be myself. . . . " See also same to same, 1 Feb. 1830, fos. 2d, 6d.

59. D5/3. AEmileus Simpson to Geo. Simpson, Fort Vancouver, 20 March 1828.

60. B135/c/2, f. 76, Simpson to McTavish, Red River, 3 Jan. 1832: Simpson indulging in mutual congratulation on their choice of wives – "Now my good friend, we are in great measure indebted to each other for all this happiness, our mutual Friendship having been one of the "primitive" causes thereof . . . "

61. Macleod, *Letitia's Letters*, p. 83. This country wife of McTavish was reputed to have smothered two children, one while he was on his way to England. See also HBC, John Stuart Papers, Stuart to McTavish, Bas de la Rivière, 16 Aug. 1830 – Stuart reminds McTavish that it was at Moose "you abandoned the first of your Wives."

62. B135/c/2, f. 50, Simpson to McTavish, 10 July 1830. Donald McKenzie was the brother of Nancy's father Roderic McKenzie who had retired in the early 1800's to Terrebonne in Lower Canada.

63. Macleod, *Letitia's Letters*, p. 84, To Mrs. Dugald McTavish, York, 1 Dec. 1840.

64. B135/c/2, fos. 33d-34, Simpson to McTavish, London, 5 Dec. 1829.

65. B135/c/2, f. 35d, same to same, 26 Dec. 1829.

66. B135/c/2, f. 42, same to same, 26 Jan. 1830.

67. Morton, *Simpson*, p. 164.

68. HBC, D6/4, p. 2.

69. Macleod, *Letitia's Letters*, To Mrs. Dugald McTavish, Gravesend, 21 May 1840, pp. 34-36.

70. Macleod, *Letitia's Letters*, p. 36.

71. What little education his sons did receive was at various schools in the Indian Country (D5/9, f. 236) and this undoubtedly contributed to their lack of advancement in the Company's service. Simpson also demanded a standard of conduct, particularly from his son George, which made little allowance for the boy's background or the insecurity of his childhood (D5/10, f. 50). Although a small bequest was made to his sons George, John and James in a draft will of 1841 (D6/1, fos. 1-11), the Scottish-born Maria, now widowed and living in Upper Canada, was the only natural child to be remembered in his final will. Even she seems to have suffered his neglect, (see D5/9, fos. 260-61, Maria McTavish to Geo. Simpson, 22 Nov. 1843: " . . . Certain you must not be ashamed at counten-

ancing me a little everyone knows I am your acknowledged daughter...").

72. See G.L. Nute, "Journey for Frances", *The Beaver*, Dec. 1953, pp. 50-54; March 1954, pp. 12-17; Summer 1954, pp. 12-18.

73. Nute, "Journey for Frances", *The Beaver*, March 1954, p. 17.

74. B4/b/1, fos. 8d-9, Stuart to Nicholas Carry, Berens River, 8 Aug. 1830.

75. HBC, John Stuart Papers, John Stuart to Capt. Franklin, Lesser Slave Lake, 12 Dec. 1826. Stuart claimed that Dr. Richardson's contemptuous remarks about the morality of fur trade society were unjust, arising merely from ignorance and hearsay. See also B4/b/1, f. 14, Stuart to Jas. McKenzie, Lake Winnipeg, 7 Aug. 1831, f. 14: "... much of my present happiness is derived from the belief, that among the human race, are to be found ... women, that are equally chaste and virtuous, as they are acknowledged to be beautiful, not only among the children of nature, the savage race, but in civilized life also."

76. That the Governor seems to have been above reproach is corroborated by a comment of Richard Grant ... "I will use the saying of our Worthy friend J.G. McTavish many will bark at me, who dare not bark at those who have the power of doing them injury." *(Hargrave Corres.,* p. 277, R. Grant to Hargrave, Oxford House, 3 Jan. 1839)

77. PAC, MG19 A21(1), vol. 21, J. Hargrave to Donald McKenzie, York, 1 July 1830.

78. B135/c/2, fos. 50-51, Simpson to McTavish, York, 10 July 1830.

79. B135/c/2, f. 54d, same to same, 3 Jan. 1831.

80. Stuart Papers, Stuart to McTavish, Bas de la Rivière, 16 Aug. 1830.

81. B135/c/2, fos. 56-57, Simpson to McTavish, Red River, 10-11 Jan. 1831.

82. B135/c/2, f. 63d, same to same, 10 April 1831. For the actual marriage contract, see B235/z/3, f. 547a.

83. E4/1b., f. 230d.

84. HBC Copy No. 23, Ermatinger Papers, Wm. Sinclair to Ed. Ermatinger, Ft. Alexander, 15 Aug. 1831, f. 271: "... what a down fall is here ..."

85. B4/b/1, f. 13, Stuart to Simpson, Bas de la Rivière, 24 Aug. 1831.

86. A34/2, Simpson's Character Book, f. 4d-5, No. 14.

87. B135/c/2, Simpson to McTavish, Red River, 2 Dec. 1832, f. 95.

88. Glazebrook, *Hargrave Corres.*, Alexander Ross to Hargrave, Red River, 18 Dec. 1830, p. 59.

89. HBC Copy No. 23, Sinclair to Ermatinger, 15 Aug. 1831, f. 271. See also *Hargrave Corres.,* Jas. McMillan to Hargrave, Red River, 15 Dec. 1830, p. 58: ". . . Mrs. Simpson's presence here makes a change in us ..."

90. B135/c/2, Simpson to McTavish, Red River, 10 April 1831, f. 64d.

91. B135/c/2, f. 73, same to same, York, 15 Aug. 1831.

92. B135/c/2, f. 78, same to same, Red River, 3 Jan. 1832.

93. B135/c/2, f. 74, same to same, York, 15 Aug. 1831.

94. One of these women was Nancy Leblanc who nursed Mrs. Simpson's infant during her illness. Mrs. Simpson unflatteringly described her as "a complete savage, with a coarse blue sort of woolen gown without shape & a blanket fastened round her neck." *(Letitia's Letters,* To Mrs. Dugald McTavish, Gravesend, 20 May 1840, p. 36).

95. B135/c/2, f. 74d, Simpson to McTavish, York, 15 Aug. 1831.

96. B135/c/2, f. 70, same to same, York, 7 July 1831.

97. B135/c/2, f. 83, same to same, Red River, 1 May 1832.

98. B135/c/2, f. 85, same to same, York, 19 July 1832.

99. B135/c/2, f. 83, same to same, Red River, 1 May 1832.

100. Angus Cameron, for example, was happy to learn that the Governor intended to bring his family out to Lachine: "he will be more conveniently situated to superintend his various important duties than by going backwards and forwards to England every year." *(Hargrave Corres.,* Angus Cameron to Hargrave, Temiscamingue, 25 April 1843, p. 434.)

101. PAC, MG19 A21(1), vol. 3, p. 813, Ed. Smith to Hargrave, Norway House, 8 July 1834.

102. Macleod, *Letitia's Letters,* p. 84, To Mrs. Dugald McTavish, 1 Dec. 1840.

103. B135/c/2, f. 115, Simpson to McTavish, London, 10 Jan. 1834.

104. PAC, MG19 A21(1), vol. 21, Hargrave to Charles Ross, York, 1 Dec. 1830.

105. B135/c/2, f. 106, Simpson to McTavish, Michipicoten, 29 June 1833. Alexander Christie did eventually become the Governor of Red River. He appears to have been devoted to his country family, his wife being Anne, the daughter of Thomas Thomas.

106. Glazebrook, *Hargrave Corres.,* p. 66, Cuthbert Cumming to Hargrave, St. Maurice, 1 March 1831.

107. B135/c/2, f. 96, Simpson to McTavish, Red River, 2 Dec. 1832.

FEMINIZATION OF TEACHING

1. Report of the Superintendent of Education for New Brunswick for the Year 1856, p. 71.

2. Although parts of his thesis have been challenged, the most dramatic general account of this change remains that of Philippe Ariès, *Centuries of Childhood: A Social History of Family Life* (New York: Random House, Vintage Books, 1962) trans. by Robert Baldick.

3. For a Canadian example of a sudden increase in the average ages and number of children attending school in a particular locality, see Michael B. Katz, "Who Went to School?" *History of Education Quarterly 12 (Fall 1972);* reprinted in Paul H. Mattingly and

Michael B. Katz, eds., *Education and Social Change* (New York: New York University Press, 1975), pp. 271-93.

4. The variety of schooling in early Upper Canada is described in R.D. Gidney, "Elementary Education in Upper Canada: A Reassessment," *Ontario History* 65 (September 1973); reprinted in *Education and Social Change,* pp. 3-27.

5. In the absence of statistics it is impossible to estimate the number of women teaching in non-domestic schools before the mid 1840's. Early official encouragement to the idea of employing females may be found in Dr. Charles Duncombe's Report on Education to the Legislature of Upper Canada (1836) and in the Nova Scotia Board of Education's "Rules and Regulations for the guidance and government of the several Boards of Commissioners ..." (1841). J. Donald Wilson, "The Teacher in Early Ontario," in F. A. Armstrong, H. A. Stevenson and J. D. Wilson, eds., *Aspects of Nineteenth Century Ontario* (Toronto: University of Toronto Press, 1974) pp. 223 and 229; and School Papers, Halifax City 1808-1845, RG 14, No. 30, Public Archives of Nova Scotia.

6. This point is examined more fully in my doctoral dissertation, "The School Promoters: Education and Social Class in Mid-Nineteenth Century Upper Canada," (University of Toronto, 1974).

7. "The School Promoters," chapter 8.

8. Ibid, pp. 298-310.

9. In "Trends in Female School Attendance in Mid-Nineteeth Century Ontario," *Social History/Histoire sociale 8* (November, 1975) Ian Davey notes the extent to which the expansion of schooling was associated in that province with an increase in the enrollment of girls. But I have found no evidence of school authorities relating the hiring of more female teachers to this trend. On the other hand, the two factors were associated in early rural schools in the common practice of hiring women to replace the male teachers during the summer, when there were undoubtedly fewer male students at school, and in a reference to the need for female teachers if girls were to be educated in separate classrooms or separate schools from boys. On the latter point, see *Remarks on the State of Education in Canada by "L"* (Montreal, 1848) pp.129-30.

10. *Report of the Superintendent of Education for Upper Canada for the Year 1858,* Appendix A, p. 5; "The School Promoters," p. 299.

11. *Report of the Superintendent of Education for New Brunswick for the Year 1855,* p. 35.

12. Ibid.

13. *Report of the Superintendent of Education for Upper Canada for the Year 1860,* Appendix A, p. 160; *Report . . . for Ontario for the Year 1869,* Appendix D, p. 86.

14. Province of Canada, *Journals of the Legislative Assembly, 1851,* Volume 10, Appendix 2, K.K. "Report on Education in Lower Canada, 1849-50." In *Les Instituteurs Laïques au Canada Français,*

1836-1900 (Quebec: Les Presses de l'Université de Laval, 1965), André Labarrère-Paulé notes that the first Lower Canadian statistics giving the sex of teachers appeared in the annual education report for 1853-54, when there were already 1,404 female teachers compared to 808 males or a ratio of 63.5% to 36.5%. (p. 179.) *Les Instituteurs Laïques* traces the gradual increase in the number of women teaching in Quebec schools to the end of the nineteenth century, but, as the title suggests, is essentially concerned with the history of the French Canadian male lay teacher. In the context of the search of this group for professional status and better pay, the feminization of teaching is portrayed as no less than a disaster. For example, with respect to the mid-1850's, Labarrère-Paulé asks: "La profession d'instituteurs va-t-elle au Bas-Canada des sa naissance devenir la proie des infirmes, des incapables et des femmes? Va-t-elle tomber en quenouille?" (p. 181) The church, he states, favoured feminization: "Les jeunes filles sont plus maniables. Leur incompetance même est un gage de tranquilité." (p. 459.) Because of clerical influence and feminization, Labarrère-Paulé concludes, the early promise of a competent male teaching profession was virtually crushed by the end of the nineteenth century.

15. *Report of the Superintendent of Education for New Brunswick for the Year 1867*, p. 34.

16. *Report of the Superintendent of Education for Nova Scotia for the Year 1851*, p. 29; *Report . . . for Nova Scotia for the Year 1859*, p. 253.

17. *Report of the Superintendent of Education for Nova Scotia for the Year 1871*, p. xii. The evidence for a change in Forrester's attitude is to be found in his 1867 *Teacher's Text-Book* (Halifax: 1867) pp. 565-66. For another negative statement from the 1870's, see the *Journal of Education for the Province of Nova Scotia*, No. 48 (April 1873) p. 18.

18. Egerton Ryerson to Mr. Benjamin Jacobs, 1 February, 1848, Education Papers, (Record Group 2) C1, Letterbook D, p. 151, Public Archives of Ontario; "Proceedings of the Board of Education of Upper Canada, 29 February, 1848," J. G. Hodgins, ed., *Documentary History of Education in Upper Canada* (Toronto: Warwick Bros. & Ritter, 1894-1910) 7: 276.

19. *Report of the Superintendent of Education for Upper Canada for the Year 1865*, Part I, p. 7; *Report . . . for the Year 1866*, Part I, pp. 4-5.

20. *Report of the Superintendent of Education for New Brunswick for the Year 1867*, p. 8,

21. *Report of the Superintendent of Schools for British Columbia for the Year ending July 31st, 1873*, p. 7.

22. *Report of the Superintendent of Education for Ontario for the Year 1869*, Part II, Table K.

23. *Report of the Superintendent of Education for Lower Canada for the Year 1858*, Normal School Reports. On the interest of women in

the McGill Normal School, see Donna Ronish, "The Development of Higher Education for Women at McGill University from 1857 to 1899 with Special Reference to the Role of Sir John William Dawson," (M.A. Thesis, McGill University, 1972) pp. 15-19.

24. "The School Promoters," pp. 301 and 305.

25. Province of Canada, *Journals of the Legislative Assembly, 1852-53,* Volume 2 No. 4, Appendix J. J., "Report of the Superintendent of Education for Lower Canada for 1852."

26. *Report of the Superintendent of Education for New Brunswick for the year 1865,* p. 9.

27. *Report . . . for New Brunswick for the Year 1871.*

28. *Report of the Past History, and Present Condition, of the Common or Public Schools of the City of Toronto* (Toronto: 1859) pp. 108-25.

29. D. Legge to Egerton Ryerson, 31 October, 1850, Education Records, (RG2) C-6-C, Public Archives of Ontario.

30. "The School Promoters," pp. 304-05. This did not hold true for New Brunswick, however, where in 1855, at least, male teachers were paid an average, semi-annually of £26.16.2 without board; compared to the £20.19.18½ paid to women. Their salaries were thus closer, with women earning about 78% on the average of what was earned by men, than were the salaries of male and female teachers who boarded around, at £17.8.3½ and £10.13.5¼ respectively, for in the latter case women earned only 61% of what was earned by men. *Report of the Superintendent of Education for New Brunswick for the Year 1855.*

31. *Report of the Board of School Commissioners for the City of Halifax for the Year 1870,* p. 33.

32. W. H. Landon, *Report of the Superintendent of Schools for the Brock District* (Woodstock: 1848), pp. 3-4; The Colborne Memorial, 1848, RG 2 C-6-C, pp. 3-4, Public Archives of Ontario.

33. *The Teachers' Text-Book* (Halifax: 1867) pp. 565-66.

34. *Report of the Superintendent of Education for New Brunswick for the Year 1867,* pp. 8-9.

35. Elizabeth Ann Inglis to Egerton Ryerson, 29 December, 1849, RG 2 C-6-C, Public Archives of Ontario.

36. "Female Teaching," *Journal of Education for the Province of Nova Scotia* No. 36 (April 1871), p.559.

37. *Report of the Board of School Commissioners for the City of Halifax for the Year 1870.*

38. Miss E. Binmore, "The Financial Outlook of the Women Teachers of Montreal," *The Educational Record of the Province of Quebec* 13 (March, 1893) pp. 69-74.

THE NEGLECTED MAJORITY

1. Warren S. THOMPSON and P. K. WHELPTON, *Population Trends in the United States.* Demographic Monographs, vol. IX (New York: Gor-

don and Beach, 1969). p. 192.

2. *Census of Canada,* 1871, vol. ii, table 3.

3. Montreal *Herald,* 10.7.1871, 7.9.1871, 19.11.1872, 21.11.1872, 5.2.1873.

4. *Herald,* 7.9.1871.

5. *Post,* 4.3.1882.

6. Computed from the *Census of Canada,* 1861, vol. ii, table 16. 1881, vol. I, table 2.

7. *Herald,* 7.9.1871.

8. *Report of the 4th Annual Meeting of the Protestant House of Industry and Refuge,* p. 7.

9. Mary Quayle INNIS, *Unfold the Years* (Toronto: McClelland and Stewart, 1949). p. 21.

10. *Herald,* 22.11.1881.

11. *12th, Ann. Rep. of Home and School of Industry,* 1860. p. 3.

12. *21st Ann. Rep. of Home and School of Industry,* 1869. p. 4.

13. *Ann. Rep. of the Montreal Day Nursery,* 1889, p. 8.

14. *Montreal Illustrated, 1894: its Growth, Resources, Commerce, Manufacturing Interests, Financial Institutions, Educational Advantages, and Prospects; Also Sketches of the Leading Business Concerns which Contribute to the City's Progress and Prosperity* (Montreal: Consolidated Illustrating Co., 1894), p. 298.

15. *Montreal in 1856. A Sketch Prepared for the Celebration of the Opening of the Grand Trunk Railway in Canada* (Montreal: Lovell, 1865), p. 45.

16. The factories were: A. Z. Lapierre & Son, 1854 (Montreal Illustrated. . . . *op. cit.,* p. 146); Ames-Holden Co., 1853 *(ibid.,* p. 113); James Linton and Co., 1859 *(Industries of Canada. City of Montreal Historical and Descriptive Review,* Montreal: Gazette Printing Co., 1886, p. 114); J. I. Pellerin & Sons, 1859 *(Montreal Illustrated, . . . op. cit.,* p. 195); James Whithem & Co., exact date unknown (K. G. C. Huttermayer, *Les intérêts commerciaux de Montréal et Québec et leur manufactures,* Montreal: Gazette Printing Co., 1891, p. 169); G. Boivin & Co., 1859 *(Montreal Illustrated 1894, . . . op. cit.,* p. 204); George T. Slater & Sons, *circa 1864 (Montreal Illustrated 1894, . . . op. cit.,* p. 140); William McLaren & Co., *circa* 1860's (Chisholm & Dodd, *Commercial Sketch of Montreal and its Superiority as a Wholesale Market,* Montreal 1868, p. 50); B. J. Pettener, 1866 *(Montreal Illustrated 1894, . . . op. cit.,* p. 236); Robert & James McCready (Montreal *Post,* Jan. 3, 1885, *True Witness,* Oct. 15, 1890). Thirty boot and shoe manufacturers existed between 1845 and 1853 according to the Montreal Street Directories (1845-6, pp. 224-228, 1852, pp. 270-1) but most were probably very small concerns which did not employ women.

17. *Montreal in 1856, . . . op. cit.,* p. 46.

18. *Herald,* 6.9.1892.

19. *Montreal in 1856, . . . op. cit.,* p. 40.

20. John F. SNELL, *MacDonald College* (Montreal: McGill University Press, 1963), pp. 9-10.
21. *Montreal Illustrated 1894, . . . op. cit.,* pp. 138-139.
22. *Ibid.,* p. 292.
23. *Ibid.,* pp. 266, 294, 296.
24. *Herald,* 6.9.1892.
25. Dressmakers, milliners, seamstresses, furriers, hatters, corsetmakers, shirtmakers, glovers, tailors and tailoresses.
26. *Industries of Canada, . . . op. cit.,* p. 114; J. KANE, *Le Commerce de Montréal et de Québec et leurs industries en 1889,* p. 76; *Montreal Illustrated, 1894, . . . op. cit.,* pp. 146, 204.
27. *Census of Canada,* Industrial Schedules, 1871, 1891.
28. 19th century wage books, Molson's Archives.
29. *Le Diocèse de Montréal à la fin du 19° siècle* (Montréal: Eusebe Sénécal, 1900), p. 299.
30. *Salle d'asile* St. Joseph pour l'enfance, Registre d'Inscription 1859-1869, m.s.: *Salle d'asile* Sainte Cunégonde, Registre d'Inscription. 1889-1891, m.s. Archives des Soeurs Grises de Montréal.
31. *Salles d'Asile Tenues par les Soeurs de la Charité de Montréal,* Montréal: 1878, p. 2. Archives des Soeurs Grises.
32. 1747 *Souvenir 1897: Descriptions et Notes historiques sur la Maison des Soeurs Grises à Montréal,* 1897, N.P., p. 3.
33. *Salles d'Asile, . . . Montréal, op. cit.,* p.2.
34. *Herald,* 21.9.1874; S. LACHAPELLE, *La Santé Pour Tous,* Montréal: 1880. pp. 122-144; LACHAPELLE, *Femme et Nurse,* Montréal: 1901, p. 43.
35. Registre: Ecole St. Joseph, 309-700/11, archives de la Congrégation de Notre-Dame.
36. *11th Ann. Rep. of the Day Nursery,* 1899, p. 2.
37. *2nd Ann. Rep. of the Day Nursery,* 1890, p. 3.
38. *1st Ann. Rep. of the Day Nursery,* 1889, pp. 3-4.
39. Marie-Claire DAVELUY, *L'Orphelinat Catholique de Montréal* (Montreal, 1918), p. 14.
40. *Ibid.,* pp. 41-44.
41. J. J. CURRAN, *St. Patricks Orphan Asylum* (Montreal, 1902), p. 23.
42. *Le Diocèse, . . . op. cit.,* p. 281.
43. C. de LAROCHE-HÉRON, *Les Servantes de Dieu en Canada* (Montreal: Lovell, 1855), p. 78.
44. *Le Diocèse, . . . op. cit.,* pp. 261-262.
45. F.-J. AUCLAIR, *Histoire des Soeurs de Miséricorde de Montréal* (Montréal, 1928), pp. 14-16, 40, 46.
46. The most important included the Female Benevolent Society, the Hervey Institute, the House of Industry and Refuge, the Home, the Y.W.C.A., the Women's Protective Immigration Society, and the Women's Christian Temperance Union.
47. Adélard DESROSIERS, *Les Ecoles normales primaires de la Province de Québec* (Montréal: Arbour & Dupont, 1909), p. 182.

48. *Nos Ecoles laïques, 1846-1946. Album Souvenir d'un siècle d'apostolat* (Montréal: Imprimerie de Lamirande. 1947), pp. 57-58.
49. *An Account of the Schools Controlled by the Roman Catholic Board of School Commissioners,* 1893, pp. 12-13.
50. "Prospectus of the McGill Normal School, 1857." Dawson Papers, acc. 927-1-4. McGill Archives.
51. W. Brethone to J. W. Dawson, 26.2.57. Dawson Papers, acc. 927-4-26.
52. Dawson Papers, acc. 927-20-34A.
53. *Ibid., acc.* 927-3.
54. *Ibid., acc.* 927-19-8.
55. *Ibid., acc.* 927-20-8.
56. *Sess. Pap. Que.,* 63 Vict. 1899-1900, vol. 2. app. VIII, Table G, p. 308.
57. Dawson Papers, acc. 927-3, McGill Archives.
58. *Sess. Pap. Que.,* 63 Vict. 1899-1900, vol. 2, app. VI.
59. Gillian M. BURDELL, "The High School for Girls, Montreal, 1875-1914," (unpublished M. A. Thesis, McGill, 1963), p. 41.
60. *Sess. Pap. Que.,* 63 Vict. 1899-1900, vol. 2, app. VIII, Table 1.
61. *Herald,* 13.4.75.
62. Cleverdon pointed out that all eight graduates of the first class became "unwavering advocates of women's suffrage" at a later date. Catherine Lyle CLEVERDON, *The Woman Suffrage Movement in Canada* (Toronto: University of Toronto Press, 1950), p. 217.
63. Maude E. ABBOTT, *History of Medicine in the Province of Quebec* (Montreal: McGill University Press, 1931), p. 67.
64. H. E. MACDERMOT, *History of the School for Nurses of the Montreal General Hospital,* Alumnae Assoc. (Montreal, 1944), p. 17-18.
65. *Herald,* 6.4.1877.
66. MACDERMOT, *op. cit.,* pp. 28-30.
67. *Ibid.,* p. 32.
68. *Ibid.,* p. 43.
69. *Ibid.,* p. 53.
70. D. S. Cross "The Irish in Montreal, 1867-1896" (unpublished M.A. thesis, McGill University, 1969), pp. 261-2.
71. *Census of Canada,* Industrial Schedules, 1881 and 1891.

SETTING THE STAGE

1. Recognition of the importance of this "shift from small-scale, informal, locally or regionally oriented groups to large-scale, informal, organizations," is basic to the historical approach discussed by Louis Galambos: "The Emerging Organizational Synthesis in Modern American History", *Business History Review* 44 (1970): 280. The organizational life of North American feminists seems to portray many of the characteristics identified by Galambos. Certainly the development of women's voluntary associations

in Canada suggests that "bureaucratization" may be "as multi-faceted and omnipresent" (Galambos, p. 286) as scholars like Robert Wiebe, *The Search for Order 1877-1920* (N.Y.: Hill & Wang, 1967) have indicated. This theme, along with others referred to briefly in this paper, is considered in my doctoral thesis, *The Parliament of Women: The National Council of Women of Canada 1893-1929,* (Ottawa: National Museum of Man, Mercury Series, 1976).

2. In view of the close ties of the 'organizational synthesis' with the social sciences it is hardly surprising that one of the first Canadian scholars to experiment with this approach should be a sociologist. See, S. D. Clark, *The Canadian Manufacturers' Association. A Study in Collective Bargaining and Political Pressure* (Toronto: University of Toronto Press, 1939).

3. See, H. A. Logan, *Trade Unions in Canada. Their Development and Functioning* (Toronto: The Macmillan Co. of Canada, 1948): Ch. 2, "Expansion and Integration: 1880-1902."

4. See. Clark, "Religious Organization and the Rise of the Canadian Nation, 1850-85" in *The Developing Canadian Community* (Toronto: University of Toronto Press, 1968).

5. Wiebe's characterization of the United States in the late nineteenth century as the sum of its 'island communities' is equally valid for Canada well into the 1890s at least. See, *The Search for Order,* Ch. 1.

6. Clark, "Religious Organization and the Rise of the Canadian Nation, 1850-85", p. 116.

7. For a more detailed discussion of the forces prompting women to joint action see, *The Parliament of Women,* Ch. 1.

8. 'Club women' is a general term characterizing women involved in a great variety of feminine collectivities and was regularly used in the period under consideration. Female organizations dealt with educational, political, benevolent, cultural, reform, professional and religious matters. Although different in some respects, all such bodies were formally structured and female in membership.

9. For a more detailed treatment of the Victorians' faith in the morally superior woman see, Walter Houghton, *The Victorian Frame of Mind* (New Haven: Yale University Press, 1957): ch. 13 and Barbara Welter, "The Cult of True Womanhood: 1820-1860", *American Quarterly* 18 (Spring, 1966): 151-74. The great majority of Canadian feminists seem to have shared this faith. They did however, reject the emphasis on passivity which often accompanied this flattering portrayal. For a Canadian example of an activist and superior woman, see the character of Advena in Agnes M. Machar, *Roland Graeme Knight* (Montreal, 1892).

10. For an early instance of women's cooperation see the discussion of the work of Kingston's Female Benevolent Society in Patricia E. Malcolmson, "The Poor in Kingston c. 1815-1850", Paper presented at the meeting of the Canadian Historical Association,

Kingston, Ontario, June, 1973.

11. See, Dominion Woman's Association Council of the United Church of Canada, "A Brief History Relative to the Growth and Development of Woman's Associations from Local to Presbytery to Conference to Dominion's Courts 1913-1945", (n.d.); E. Willoughby Cummings, *Our Story ... Woman's Auxiliary to the Missionary Society of the Church of England in Canada 1885 to 1928.* (Toronto: Garden City Press, c. 1928); Women's Missionary Society, Presbyterian Church in Canada. "Our Jubilee Story", (n.d.); Women's Baptist Home Mission Board of Ontario West, "From Sea to Sea". (1940); Mrs. A. T. Spankie, "The Story of Baptist Women's Missionary Work and its Purpose in *Pioneering in Western Canada. A Story of the Baptists,* ed., Rev. C. C. McLaurin (Calgary: 1939); M. Allen Gibson, *Along the King's Highway, The Home Mission Board of the United Baptist Convention of the Atlantic Provinces* (Lunenberg: 1964); Union of the Woman's Missionary Societies of the Presbyterian, Methodist and Congregational Churches, "Diamond Jubilee of the Woman's Missionary Society in British Columbia 1887-1947", (n.d.)

12. For a short, but suggestive, treatment of the deaconess movement see, William Magney, "The Methodist Church and the National Gospel, 1884-1914", *Bulletin of the Archives of the United Church,* 1968, pp. 20, 40-2.

13. Prominent among these was the All Hallows Sisterhood which beginning in 1884 worked among the Indians of British Columbia.

14. There are many histories of nuns, usually hagiographic. Typical examples include, Sister Mary Electa, *The Sisters of Providence of St. Vincent de Paul* (Montreal: Palm Publishers, 1961); Rev. Sister St. Kevin, "The Early History of Notre Dame Convent in Kingston", *Historic Kingston* 9 (1959-60), pp. 5-20; John O'Gorman, "The Grey Nuns in Pembroke", (1928).

15. Public Archives of Canada (hereafter P.A.C.), National Council of Women Papers (hereafter NCWC Papers), v. 65, Lady Ishbel Aberdeen to Emily Willoughby Cummings, March 19, 1894.

16. For a description of these activities see, Mrs. S. G. McKee, *Jubilee History of the Ontario Christian Temperance Union 1877-1927* (Whitby, n.d.)

17. See, *Ibid.,* passim. In 1882 for instance 20 of 36 unions failed to send representatives to the annual meeting. (p. 14).

18. *Ibid.,* p. 28.

19. For WCTU efforts to gain the vote see, Catherine L. Cleverdon, *The Woman Suffrage Movement in Canada* (Toronto: University of Toronto Press, 1950), passim.

20. Mrs. Jacob Spence cited in Ruth Spence, *Prohibition in Canada, A Memorial to Francis Stephens Spence* (Toronto: Wm. Briggs, 1919), p. 69.

21. Graeme Decarie, "Something Old, Something New . . .: Aspects of

Prohibitionism in Ontario in the 1890s", in *Oliver Mowat's Ontario,* ed. Donald Swainson (Toronto: Macmillan, 1972), p. 169.

22. Both the negative and positive aspects of the temperance crusade are well illustrated in the life of the first president of the Ontario and Dominion WCTU, Mrs. Letitia Youmans. See, L. Youmans, *Campaign Echoes* (Toronto: Wm. Briggs, 1893).

23. Cited in Josephine P. Harshaw, *When Women Work Together. A History of the Young Women's Christian Association in Canada* (Toronto: the YWCA, 1966), p. 11.

24. See, *Ibid,* and Mary Q. Innis, *Unfold the Years* (Toronto: McClelland & Stewart, 1949).

25. This church also organized a Canadian branch of the Mothers' Union in 1888 with the object of upholding the sanctity of marriage and awakening a sense of maternal responsibility.

26. Brian Harrison, "For Church, Queen and Family: The Girls' Friendly Society 1874-1920", *Past and Present* 61 (Nov. 1973), p. 109.

27. "Report of the Girls' Friendly Society", *Report of the National Council of Women of Canada* (hereafter NCWC *Report)* (1894), p. 47.

28. For greater details on this organization see its annual reports in NCWC *Reports* beginning in 1894.

29. "Report of the Dominion Order of King's Daughters", *Yearbook of the National Council of Women of Canada* (hereafter NCWC *Yearbook:* the annual report of the NCWC changes its title from *Report* to *Yearbook* in 1912) (1927), p. 138.

30. For greater details on this organization see its annual reports in NCWC *Reports* beginning in 1894.

31. For greater details on this organization see its annual reports in NCWC *Reports* beginning in 1894.

32. Sympathetic appreciation was not always easy to discover in Canada as the life of Emily Carr illustrates. See, *Growing Pains* (Toronto: Oxford University Press, 1946).

33. For greater details on this organization see its annual reports in NCWC *Reports* beginning in 1894.

34. See, Cleverden, *The Woman Suffrage Movement in Canada,* passim.

35. For a short discussion of the role of this belief in the prohibition campaign in particular see, Decarie, "Something Old, Something New. . . .: Aspects of Prohibitionism in Ontario in the 1890s", pp. 169-71.

36. See, Joanne L. Thompson, "The Influence of Dr. Emily Howard Stowe on the Woman Suffrage Movement in Canada", *Ontario History* (Dec. 1962), pp. 253-66.

37. Special Collections, University of British Columbia, Papers of the Vancouver Local Council of Women, Folder "History and Memorabilia", clipping, Victoria *Times,* Nov. 7, 1895.

38. P.A.C., Aberdeen Papers, v. 14, clipping, Toronto *Mail,* Oct. 23, 1893.

39. Cited from *Council Idea* in *Women in a Changing World. The Dynamic Story of the International Council of Women Since 1888* (London: Routledge & Kegan Paul, 1966), p. 12.

40. At least one future member of the NCWC in addition to Lady Aberdeen took part in the early discussion organized by the British Unions. See, Mrs. Ashley Carus-Wilson, B.A., "Co-operation on a General Basis", *NCWC Report* (1894), pp. 51-5.

41. E. C. Stanton, *et al., History of Woman Suffrage* 6 vol. (N.Y.: Susan B. Anthony, 1902) 4: ch. VII; Rosa Shaw, *Proud Heritage. A History of the National Council of Women of Canada* (Toronto: Ryerson Press, 1957), pp. 2-4.

42. One leading historian of the American woman's movement finds that the NCWUS ". . . tended to strengthen the leadership of women with independent incomes or professional prestige." Eleanor Flexner, *Century of Struggle* (Cambridge: Belknap Press, 1959), p. 218. This description may also be appropriate for the NCWC although the first group was, generally speaking, more powerful in the Canadian organization.

43. Mildred White Wells, *Unity in Diversity, The History of the General Federation of Women's Clubs* (Washington: 1953) At least one Canadian club was formed as a member of the GFWC: the Montreal Woman's Club established in 1892. Like the American pioneers, initial ambitions were relatively modest: the promotion of useful relations between women of artistic, literary, scientific and philanthropic tastes. Soon, however, it went much wider afield into a variety of reform activities. See, Madge Macbeth, "The First Woman's Club in Canada", *Saturday Night,* March 15, 1913, p. 29. This organization, a founding member of the Montreal Local Council of Women, produced some of the leading women in both the Local and National Councils.

44. See, Ellen Key, *Renaissance of Motherhood* (1914) for an influential and not untypical assertion of maternal power by a leading international feminist.

45. See, Lord and Lady Aberdeen, *"We Twa",* 2 vol. (London: W. G . Collins Sons & Co., Ltd., 1926), 2: 295.

46. 'Lady Gay', "Between You and Me", *Saturday Night,* Jan. 8, 1898, p. 8.

47. *Ibid.,* May 26, 1894, p. 7.

48. See the account of the Aberdeens' trip to Canada in 1890 in *Through Canada with a Kodak* (Edinburgh: W. H. White & Co., 1893)

49. Aberdeens, *"We Twa",* 2:98.

50. For Aberdeen's activities in England see, Marjorie Pentland, *A Bonnie Fechter. The Life of Ishbel Marjoribanks Marchioness of Aberdeen & Temair, c.b.e., ll.d., j.p. 1857-1939* (London: B. T. Batsford Ltd., 1952).

51. Wendy Thorpe, "Lady Aberdeen and the National Council of

Women in Canada" (M.A. dissertation, Queen's University, 1973), p. 138.

52. *Report of the Toronto Local Council of Women* (hereafter *Toronto Report)* (1894).

53. "The Countess' Busy Day", *Montreal Gazette,* Dec. 1, 1893.

54. London Public Library and Art Gallery, Harriet Boomer Papers, "Verbatim Report of Proceedings to Organize a Local Council of Women of Canada for London", (typescript).

55. *Toronto Report* (1894).

56. Mrs. Curzon, "Women's Council", *Toronto Report* (1897).

57. "Report of the London Local Council", NCWC *Report* (1894), p. 90.

58. Mrs. Boomer, NCWC *Report* (1895), p. 187.

59. See Aberdeen's references to this problem in J. T. Saywell (ed.), *The Canadian Journal of Lady Aberdeen, 1893-1898* (Toronto: The Champlain Society), pp. 220-2.

60. Mrs. Hoodless, NCWC *Report* (1895), pp. 199-200.

61. "Constitution", NCWC *Report* (1894), p. 22.

62. For a discussion of Aberdeen's difficulties with the Conservative Party see, Saywell, "Introduction", *Lady Aberdeen's Journal.*

63. "Constitution", NCWC *Report* (1894), p. 22.

64. *Ibid.*

65. P.A.C., Aberdeen Papers, v. 24, clipping, Toronto *Globe,* April 2, 1896.

66. Ibid., v. 20, clipping. "Address to Women of Vernon", *Vernon News,* Oct. 3, 1895.

67. Aberdeen, "Presidential Address", NCWC *Report* (1894), p. 12.

68. P.A.C., NCWC Papers, v. 65, *First Annual Report of the West Algoma Local Council of Women* (1895), Mrs. Frank Gibbs.

69. Mrs. McDonnell, NCWC *Report* (1894), p. 16.

70. "Resolution", "Promotion of Patriotic Feeling", NCWC *Report* (1894), p. 103.

71. Dalhousie University, J.J. Stewart Collection, Mrs. Charles Archibald, ". . . Private Work of Women in Her Home and her Public Duty to the State" in "Inaugural Meeting of the Local Council of Women of Halifax".

72. Archives of the Montreal Local Council of Women, Lady Julia Drummond, "Practical Idealism", *Annual Report of the Montreal Local Council of Women* (1933-4), pp. 16-17.

THE WOMAN QUESTION

1. The *Gazette* gave the fullest coverage with almost daily, front-page reports of suffragette activities in London, during March and April of 1913. What little editorial comment there was condemned the militancy of the women. See also *Le Devoir,* 22 jan. 1913, 28 jan. 1913, 7 avril 1913, 7 mai 1913.

2. Mrs. Philip Snowden spoke in Montreal in Dec. 1909, Mrs. Emmeline Pankhurst in Dec. 1911, Mrs. Barbara Wylie in Nov. 1912, Mrs. Forbes-Robertson Hale in Dec. 1912. C. Cleverdon, *The Woman Suffrage Movement in Canada,* 2nd ed., Toronto, 1974, pp. 221-2.

3. Cited *ibid.,* p. 113 and also in *Canadian Annual Review,* 1912, p. 305.

4. Title of an editorial, April 5, 1913.

5. *CAR* 1913, p. 736.

6. Cleverdon, pp. 221-2. Ironically, the association was formed on the very day of Bourassa's last article in the series "Le suffrage féminin," *Le Devoir,* 24 avril 1913.

7. *CAR* 1913, pp. 471, 734.

8. Mrs. Minden Cole had remarked in a debate at the Montreal Women's Club that Quebec women were not sufficiently educated to make the best use of the vote. Despite her protest *(Le Devoir,* 5 avril 1913) that her remarks had been taken out of context, Bourassa used them to launch the first two of his four articles on the suffrage question: "Déplorable ignorance des Canadiennes-françaises," *Le Devoir,* 31 mars 1913; "Education et Instruction," *ibid,* 5 avril 1913; "Rôle social de la femme – concept français et tradition anglaise," *ibid.,* 23 avril 1913; "Le suffrage féminin – son efficacité, sa légitimité," *ibid.,* 24 avril 1913.

9. A contemporary euphemism for abortionists, it seems.

10. This notion, I suspect, stems from the way women were referred to at the time as "personnes du sexe." The implication of the epithet is that women represented the sexual side of life and since that side had been well and truly repressed, then to bring it out into the open would indeed be outrageous.

11. It is rather depressing to read those pages: the picture of women interested only in sewing, cooking, needlework, fashion, housedecorating and light reading is exactly the one presented to us today by women's sections of newspapers. Perhaps the notion of what *kind* of beings women are has changed, but only in degree; then they were frail creatures, given to nervous troubles and requiring the tonic of Lydia E. Pinkham's Composé Végétal; now they are smelly, ugly creatures needing all the potions and perfumes that the cosmetic industry can produce.

12. "Lettre de Fadette," *Le Devoir,* 2 jan. 1913.

13. *La Presse,* 8 mars 1913.

14. Joseph Moffatt of Verdun to *Gazette,* "Woman and the Vote," April 22, 1913.

15. L.-A. Pâquet, "Le féminisme," *Canada français,* I, 4 (Déc. 1918), p. 235.

16. *Canadian Woman's Annual and Social Service Directory,* Toronto, 1915, p. IX, I,

17. Something Bourassa thought should be better termed "Madtime elections act," in that it introduced a double error into Canadian society: the principle of woman suffrage, and the creation of a military caste. "Le dernier accès," *Le Devoir,* 11 sept. 1917.

18. Ernest Bilodeau, "Une délégation féminine," *Le Devoir,* 22 fév. 1918.

19. "A Week in Parliament," *Gazette,* March 25, 1918.

20. The federal suffrage bill had just passed second reading (March 22) and had not yet gone into clause-by-clause committee discussion where most of the debate occurred (April 11). Bourassa's articles were the following: "Désarroi des cerveaux – triomphe de la démocratie," *Le Devoir,* 28 mars 1918; "Le Droit de vote – La lutte des sexes – Laisserons-nous avilir nos femmes?", *ibid.,* 30 mars 1918; "Influence politique des femmes – pays avancés – femmes culottées," *ibid.,* 1 avril 1918.

21. Nellie McClung had a delightful response to that type of argument, beginning with "There seems to be considerable misapprehension on the subject of voting . . ." and ending with " . . . you are surprised at what a short time you have been away from home. You put the potatoes on when you left home, and now you are back in time to strain them." *In Times Like These,* 2nd ed., Toronto, 1972, pp. 50-1.

22. C.-A. Fournier, speaking on April 11, 1918. Canada, House of Commons *Debates,* 1918, pp. 637-8. Others repeating the same kind of arguments were H.-A. Fortier, pp. 634-5, J.-J. Denis, pp. 642-3; L.-T. Pacaud, p. 645; A. Trahan, pp. 648-9; R. Lemieux, p. 653; J.-E.-S. D'Anjou, p. 660; J.-E. Lesage, p. 672.

23. C.-A. Fournier, *ibid.,* p. 638.

24. J.-J. Denis, *ibid.,* p. 643.

25. *Gazette,* April 12, 1918, p. 10. The *Gazette* also picked up the *Toronto Daily News'* remark about "the old time Tory temperament which rules in Quebec province." *Ibid.,* April 19, 1918, p. 8.

26. E.g, J.-A. Albert Foisy, series of articles on "Le Suffrage féminin," *L'Action Catholique,* 7-15 fév. 1922; Arthur Sauvé's views on the question are referred to in two letters, Abel Vineberg, Conservative, M.L.A. to Arthur Meighen and Meighen to Vineberg, March 3, 1925, PAC, Meighen Papers; Mgr. Bégin (Archbishop of Quebec) to Mgr. Roy (Bishop of Montreal), 19 mars 1922, *Semaine Religieuse du Québec,* 20 avril 1922, p. 536. All of the opponents through the 1920s carefully avoided noting that the International Woman Suffrage Alliance had held its Ninth Congress in Rome in 1923 and that the Pope had sent his greetings and had granted audiences to many of the delegates. Broadside published by the Franchise Committee of the Montreal Women's Club in PAC, Meighen Papers, n.d.

27. A. R. McMaster suggested a vague awareness of what was going on when he contrasted the way MPs spoke of the woman as "queen of

the home" with what she was more often, "queen of the washtub." House of Commons *Debates,* April 11, 1918, p. 663.

28. The papers were full of reports of the quake. *La Presse* even reproduced pictures of the much more serious quake that had devastated Tokyo in Sept. 1923. *La Presse,* 2 mars 1925, p. 1.

29. The Western women could bring their cases to Ottawa, in order to receive "equal treatment" before the Federal Parliament but the expense of such a procedure was prohibitive.

30. On March 6, 1925, the very day that Bourassa was arguing the necessary inequality of men and women in the area of divorce, the Canadian Council of Agriculture, representing the organized farmers of Quebec, Ontario, Manitoba, Saskatchewan and Alberta, sent a series of resolutions to the Dominion government, one of which urged legal amendments to make grounds for divorce the same for women as for men. PAC, Meighen Papers, CCA to Dominion government, 6 March 1925.

31. "Divorce in Canada," *Gazette,* March 2, 1925, p. 12.

32. *Le Devoir,* 17-18 fév, 1921; 5-11 fév, 1925; 7 mars 1925. The *Canadian Annual Review* for the years in question provides details of the two cases.

33. Or, as Cardinal Roy put it in a pastoral letter in 1920 "Tout acte législatif instituant ou facilitant le divorce, est une oeuvre de perversion morale et de décadence sociale." *Semaine Religieuse du Québec,* 22 juillet 1920, p. 741.

34. The bill passed second reading by a vote of 109-68. Bourassa's articles were the following: "Divorce et Mariage – Quelques réflexions en marge d'un débat," *Le Devoir,* 5 mars 1925; "Imbroglio constitutionnel – où nous mène-t-on?" *ibid.,* 6 mars, 1925; "Préservatifs et remèdes – la plaie du mariage civil – poutre et paille," *ibid.,* 7 mars 1925.

35. Bourassa tried to do so in 1930, when he was an MP, with a bill to repeal all existing laws regarding divorce. The bill was rejected and Bourassa tried another tack: a resolution to do away with the hearing of divorce cases in Parliament. The resolution did not receive any discussion. *CAR* 1929-30, p. 58.

36. *Le Devoir,* 9 mars, 17 mars 1925.

37. House of Commons *Debates,* vol. 1, Feb. 26, 1925, p. 553.

38. In 1925 there were all of thirteen divorces in Quebec! *CAR,* 1926-7, p. 109.

39. Senators T. Chapais, L. Béique and N.-A. Belcourt. See Senate *Debates,* 1925, June 10, pp. 431-2, 434; June 11, pp. 456-9. Bourassa returned the favour by printing Senator Belcourt's entire speech in *Le Devoir* and calling it the strongest case yet made against divorce from the point of view of natural law and of the Canadian constitution. *Le Devoir,* 11 juillet 1925, p. 1.

40. "Colette" in *La Presse,* 1925; "La vie au foyer" in *La Presse,* 1925; "Fadette" in *Le Devoir,* 1925; *La Presse's* Saturday Magazine *La*

Presse revue illustrée always contained a few photographs of huge families with twelve or more children, with the caption, "Une belle famille canadienne-française."

41. Coubé spoke in Montreal on March 17 and 18, 1925. *La Presse* published full reports of both speeches, 18 mars 1925, p. 23; 20 mars 1925, p. 26 and commented upon them favourably in an editorial, 20 mars 1925, p. 6.

42. The pervasiveness of this double standard shows up much later in sociological studies where women themselves accept the notion that their sinning is much more serious than that of men. E.g. Colette Moreux, "The French Canadian Family", in K. Ishwaran, *The Canadian Family,* Toronto, 1971, particularly pp. 137-40. Bourassa of course belongs to a long and respectable tradition of writers about women, writers who stressed "the two spheres," separate, distinctive yet equivalent. Bourassa and Ashley Montagu would probably have enjoyed each other's company, although Bourassa might have disagreed with the title of Montagu's book, *The Natural Superiority of Women,* New York, 1952.

43. Forty-two lead articles provide constitutional, religious and legal precedents for his opposition. *Le Devoir,* 3 mars 1929 intermittently through 18 juillet 1929.

44. "Le divorce," *Le Devoir,* 11 juillet 1925, p. 1.

45. This too has been put into male/female categories, with men as the agents of change, women as the agents of preservation. Some studies of women have suggested that this latter is woman's place in civilization. Cf. Jessie Bernard, *Women and the Public Interest,* Chicago, 1971.

MASS CIRCULATION MAGAZINES

1. W. H. Chafe, *The American Woman: Her Changing Social, Economic, and Political Roles 1920-1970* (New York: Oxford University Press, 1972), p. 246.

2. C. Bacchi-Ferraro, "The Ideas of the Canadian Suffragists 1890-1920," Diss. McGill 1970, pp. 98f, 108.

3. Chafe makes similar comments about American women in the 1920s. *Ibid.,* pp. 51-2.

4. Only Canadian magazines are discussed in this article, but it must be remembered that Canadians read many more American magazines than they did their own in the 1920s. For example, *Ladies' Home Journal* had a circulation of 152,011 in Canada as of June 30, 1926, *Saturday Evening Post* 128,574, *Pictorial Review* 128,320 and *McCall's Magazine* 103,209. Meanwhile *MacLean's Magazine's* circulation was 82,013 as of December 31, 1925, *Canadian Home Journal's* 68,013, *Saturday Night's* 30,858 and *Canadian Magazine's* 12,604. See Public Archives of Canada, Canada, Advisory Board on Tariff and Taxation, Reference No. 9, Exhibit H.,

"A.B.C. figures from A.B.C. Blue Book to June 30, 1926"; A. W. Thomas and H. C. Corner, eds., *The Canadian Almanac,* 1926 (Toronto: 1926), pp. 404, 405. (Note that the figures in the *Canadian Almanac* were unofficial). Canadian publishers, in order to compete with imports from the United States, produced magazines which were as much like the American as possible in style and business practices, while emphasizing Canadian content. Canadian women did seem to have some desire for their own magazines – as shown by the fact that *Chatelaine* had a circulation of 70,000 within a year of its founding. Advertisement, *Chatelaine,* II (March, 1929), 62.

My principal concentration in this paper is on English language magazines, although a few from Quebec have been included as well. My general remarks apply to both, although the French Canadian magazines presented an even more conservative and traditional image of women than did the English publications.

5. A. Herbert, "What Shall We Do About Maids?", *MacLean's,* XXXIV (June 15, 1921), 61; Maude Petitt Hill, "What's the Matter with Housework?", *Chatelaine,* I (March, 1928), 13, 56-7.

6. Although some Canadian magazines, like *Chatelaine* and *Canadian Homes and Gardens,* had women as Associate Editors, a man's name always topped the masthead. A high proportion of the contributors to the magazines were women.

7. Canada. Department of Labour, *Women at Work in Canada* (Ottawa: Queen's Printer, 1959), p. 5, Table 3.

8. F. T. Denton and S. Ostry, "Historical Estimates of the Canadian Labour Force," 1961 Census Monograph (Ottawa: Queen's Printer, 1967), p. 23, Table 4.

9. Marjorie Middleton, "Lead-Strings That Bind," *MacLean's* XXXVIII (May 15, 1925), 74, 76.

10. Mable Crews Ringland, "The Family Purse: How the College Girl Can Make Money," *Chatelaine,* II (June, 1929), 34. See also Tomahawk, "Les Employés des Bureaux," *La Revue Moderne,* V (Octobre, 1924), 55-7; Ina Winifred Colwell, "A Business Girl's Assets," *MacLean's,* XXXVIII (December 1, 1925), 83-5.

11. Canada, Dominion Bureau of Statistics, Educational Statistics Branch, Biennial Survey of Education in Canada, 1938-40, *Higher Education in Canada, 1938-40* (Ottawa: King's Printer, 1941), pp. 36-41.

12. See Constance K. Seton, "Sending Claire to College," *Chatelaine,* II (September, 1929), 26, 61: A. E. Wilson, "Schools for the Homemaker," *MacLean's,* XL (November, 1927), 63; Katherine M. Caldwell, "College – and Then What?", *Canadian Home Journal,* XXVI (September, 1929), 44, 54, 72, 87; "Shall We Send Her to College?", *Canadian Home Journal,* XXVI (July, 1929), 80, 84.

13. *Women at Work in Canada,* p. 7.

14. Jean Graham, "The Event of the Month: Concerning a Career,"

Canadian Home Journal, xxv (May, 1928), 19.

15. Kathleen Archibald, *Sex and the Public Service* (Ottawa: Queen's Printer, 1970), p. 16.

16. See, for example, J. Herbert Hodgins, "Canadian Composer Has Two Selves – One for Her Music; One for Her Home," *MacLean's* xxxviii (June 1, 1925), 78-9; Gertrude E. S. Pringle, "Is A Business Career Possible to a Married Woman?" *Canadian Magazine,* xlvi (March, 1927), 30, 35; Virginia Coyne Knight, "Only a Super-Woman Can Juggle Both a Family and a Career," *Chatelaine,* i (July, 1928), 21, 56.

17. Jean Graham, "The Event of the Month: Concerning a Career," 19.

18. See, for example, Margaret Pennell, "The Woman's Point of View," *Canadian Magazine,* lxvi (March, 1927), 31; Arthur Somers Roche, "A Simple Equation," *Canadian Home Journal,* xxiv (April, 1928), 7; Dr. W. W. Chipman, "Preparing Women for the Greatest of Professions," *MacLean's,* xxxiv (October 15, 1921), 58; Odette Pannetier, "Une Question d'Avenir," *La Revue Moderne,* vi (Fevrier, 1925), 12; M. Bell, "Pamela Takes the Plunge," *Canadian Magazine,* lxiii (September, 1924), 282-7; J. Chatteris Livett, "The Gods Assist," *Canadian Magazine,* lviii (April, 1922), 539-48; A. U. Arland, "The Gates of St. John" *Canadian Magazine,* lix (July, 1922), 370-6. For comment on short stories in American magazines see W. H. Chafe, *op. cit.,* p. 99. For a British parallel see Cynthia L. White, *Women's Magazines 1693-1968* (London: Michael Joseph, 1970), pp. 112-3.

19. "Opportunities for a Career in Canada," *Canadian Magazine,* lxvi (December, 1926), 24; Dr. E. E. Braithwaite, "Canada's Educational Progress," *Canadian Magazine,* lx (April, 1923), 489.

20. Mabel Crews Ringland, "The Family Purse: How a College Girl Can Make Money," *Chatelaine,* ii (June, 1929), 34; F. C. Beckett, "Girls No Longer Wanted," *Canadian Home Journal,* xviii (March, 1922), 19.

21. Nellie McClung, "Shall We Reform Mothers' Day?", *MacLean's* xxxviii (May 1, 1925), 1-2; Joseph Lister Rutledge, "The 'Yes, Yes' Chorus," *MacLean's* xxxviii (January 1, 1925), 10-2, "Another Reply to 'Sister Jean'," *Saturday Night,* xxxv (June 19, 1920), 35; Mona E. Clark, "Are Brains a Handicap to a Woman?", *Canadian Magazine,* lxix (February, 1928), 27.

22. For British and American parallels, see C. L. White, *op. cit.,* p. 101, W. H. Chafe, *op. cit.,* p. 107 and Robert W. Smuts, *Women and Work in America* (New York: Columbia University Press, 1959), p. 154.

23. "The Housewife as Manager," *Saturday Night,* xxxv (January 17, 1920), 21. See also Ruth Davison Reid, "Bride's Progress," *Chatelaine,* i (June, 1928), 7, 68-9, 72-3; Mabel Crews Ringland, "The Family Purse," *Chatelaine,* i (June, 1928), 48; Ann Adam, "At the

Kitchen Cabinet or Work Table," *Canadian Home Journal,* xxv (March, 1929), 37; J. L. Love and L. Fillerbrown, "Kitchens and Wallpapers," *Canadian Magazines* LXV (February, 1926), 29.

24. Estelle M. Kerr, "The Little Servants of 1920," *Canadian Courier,* xxv (January 31, 1920), 17; "Electricity in Domestic Service," *Canadian Home Journal,* xix (July, 1922), 36; W. R. Carr, "The Emancipation of Household Slaves," *Canadian Magazine,* LXV (June, 1926), 27; "Pour Madame," *La Revue Moderne,* viii (Mars, 1927), 3; Series by Vera E. Welch, "The Domestic Workshop," *Chatelaine,* i (1928).

25. Advertisement for Fels Naphtha soap, *MacLean's,* xxxviii (February 1, 1925), 31.

26. W. B. Hurd, "The Decline in the Canadian Birth-rate," *Canadian Journal of Economics and Political Science,* iii (1937), 44, 51.

27. Hilda M. Ridley, "Canada's First Woman Inspector," *Canadian Magazine,* LXII (November, 1923), 50; Mabel Crews Ringland, "What About Father?", *MacLean's* xLi (August 1, 1928), 59. Although the main pressure in this matter was on women, there were also articles which called for more skill and training in fatherhood, a new emphasis in the 1920s. See also Frances Lily Johnson, "What of Your Child?", *Chatelaine,* i (April, 1928), 32; Stella E. Pines, "We Want Perfect Parents," *Chatelaine,* i (September, 1928), 12-3. For a similar comment on the United States in the 1920s see Anne Firor Scott, *The Southern Lady: From Pedestal to Politics 1830-1930* (Chicago: University of Chicago Press, 1970), p. 220.

28. For a full discussion of Taylor's scientific management movement see Samuel Haber. *Efficiency and Uplift: Scientific Management in the Progressive Era 1890-1920* (Chicago: University of Chicago Press, 1964).

29. "Le Système Nerveux de la Femme," *La Revue Populaire,* xx (Avril, 1927), 21; V. V. Murray, "Wives: Their Care and Management," *Canadian Magazine,* LXV (August, 1926), 12-3; Editorial, "Empty Clamor for Women Judges," *Saturday Night,* xxxv (March 27, 1920), 1; Muriel Wrinch, "Modern Eve and Harassed Adam," *Canadian Magazine,* LXV (July 1926), 19; N. de B. Lugrin, "L. Adams Beck – The Lady with the Mask," *MacLean's,* xxxviii (November 1, 1925), 72-3.

30. For example, see Myrtle Hayes Wright, "Blazing a Social Service Trail on the Prairies," *MacLean's,* xxxviii (December 15, 1925), 72, 74; Sister Jean, "Have We Like Sheep All Gone Astray?", *Saturday Night,* xxv (May 15, 1920), 21.

31. See S. Haber, *op. cit.,* p. ix; S. P. Hays, *Conservation and the Gospel of Efficiency: The Progressive Conservation Movement, 1890-1920* (Cambridge, Mass.: Havard University Press, 1959), p. 269.

32. Edward Moore, "Initiative – and – and – Nerve," *MacLean's,* xxxviii (March 15, 1925), 27, 48; "Questions and Answers for

Women Readers," *Canadian Magazine*, LXIX (January, 1928), 30; "Question Box," *MacLean's*, XXXVIII (June 15, 1925), 99; M. V. Speers, "Some 'Dont's' For a College-Trained Girl," *MacLean's*, XXXVIII (July 15, 1925), 59, 62.

33. Mona E. Clark, "A Woman in Business Is Still at Heart a Woman," *Canadian Magazine*, LXIX (January, 1928), 27; Editorial, *Canadian Magazine*, LXVI (February, 1927), 3.

34. Editorial, "Choses et Gens," *La Canadienne*, IV (Novembre, 1921), 1.

35. Grace Cowan, "What Do You Think?", *MacLean's*, XXXIX (December 15, 1926), 8, 61-2; I. W. Colwell, "A Business Girl's Assets," *MacLean's*, XXXVIII (December 1, 1925), 85.

36. See for example Dorothy Bowman Barker, "Vera Learns How to Keep a Husband," *MacLean's*, XXXIX (June 1, 1926), 71; Dorothy Bowman Barker, "Vera's Pickle Problem Promptly Capitalized as Canning Exchange," *MacLean's*, XXXVIII (January 15, 1925), 50-1. Especially interesting about this series was its encouragement to women to band together to help one another survive as housewives.

37. Indeed, the frequency of these stories hints at the prevalence of the feeling of frustration among housewives of the decade. See Victor Lauriston, "Her One Hour," *Canadian Magazine*, LXVIII (October, 1927), 26-7, 34; Anna Wolcott D'aeth, "The End of the Rainbow," *Canadian Magazine*, LXIII (October, 1927), 359-63; Arthur Somers Roche, "A Simple Equation," *Canadian Home Journal*, XXIV (April, 1928), 6-7, 29; Marjorie Bowen, "Fleur Ange," *MacLean's*, XXXIX (May 1, 1926), 19, 52-4, 56; Kathleen Blackburn, "Under the Wheels," *Canadian Magazine*, LVIII (November, 1921), 44-9. An interesting full-length study of this problem was Madge Macbeth's novel *Shackles* (Ottawa: Graphic Publishers, 1926), in which a woman who sought a career as a writer fought the tyranny of her husband and housework to the point of liberation, only in the end to succumb to her womanly instincts and stay.

38. "Questions and Answers for Women Readers," *Canadian Magazine*, LXIX (January, 1928), 30 and LXVIII (September, 1927), 28; M. MacMurchy, "Adam and Eve and the World God Made," *Canadian Magazine*, LVI (November, 1920), 4; "Canadian Women in the Public Eye," *Saturday Night*, XXXV (March 6, 1920), 26.

39. Anne Anderson Perry, "Is Woman's Suffrage a Fizzle?", *MacLean's* XLI (February 1, 1928), 7; Madge Macbeth, *Shackles*, [p. 8].

40. A recent survey of the historiography of American women in the 1920s which stresses that there was far less economic or social progress for women during the decade than has hitherto been assumed is Estelle B. Freedman, "The New Woman: Changing Views of Women in the 1920s," *Journal of American History*, LXI (September, 1974), 372-93.

THE LABOUR FORCE IN W.W. II

I owe the idea for this paper to Shirley Goundrey who audited the course I offered winter semester 1975 on the history of feminism. At the Public Archives of Canada, I have consistently received gracious assistance from Archivist John Smart, to whom I am truly grateful. For valuable help with revising the first draft, I should like to thank Charles Pye, Centre for Resource Studies, Queen's University, and my colleagues Ralph Pastore, James Tague, and Stuart Pierson in the History Department of Memorial University.

1. Barry Broadfoot, *Six War Years 1939-1945: Memories of Canadians at Home and Abroad* (Toronto: Doubleday Canada Ltd., 1974), p. 353. Work is beginning to be done on the relation of women's wartime employment to the long-term trends in women's participation in the labour force. See Hugh and Pat Armstrong, "The Segregated Participation of Women in the Canadian Labour Force, 1941-1971," *The Canadian Review of Sociology and Anthropology*, Vol. 12, no. 4 (Part 1), November 1975, pp. 370-384; Paul Phillips, "Women in the Manitoba Labour Market: A Study of the Changing Economic Role (or 'plus ça change, plus la même')," Paper given at the Western Canadian Studies Conference, University of Calgary, February 27-28, 1976; and, for the First World War, Ceta Ramkhalawansingh, "Women during the Great War," in *Women at Work: Ontario 1850-1930* (Toronto: Canadian Women's Educational Press, 1975), pp. 261-307.
2. Betty Friedan, *The Feminine Mystique* (New York: W. W. Norton & Company Inc., 1963); cf. the *Report of the Royal Commission on the Status of Women in Canada* (Ottawa: Information Canada, 1970), p. 2.
3. "Employment of Women and Day Care of Children" (completed sometime before August 24, 1950), Part 1, pp. 5-6, in the "History of the Wartime Activities of the Department of Labour," Public Archives of Canada [PAC], RG 35, Series 7, Vol. 20, File 10. Hereafter cited as "Wartime History of Employment of Women . . ." or "Wartime History of . . . Day Care of Children."
4. "The Development of the National Selective Service (Civilian) Organization in World War II to December 31, 1945," n.d., p. 7, PAC, RG 35, Series 7, Vol. 19, File 2; "History of the National Employment Service 1939-1945," n.d., p. 5, PAC, RG 35, Series 7, Vol. 19, File 3.
5. "Wartime History of Employment of Women . . . ," p. 6
6. Ten Points Enumerated in the Prime Minister's Speech of March 24, 1942, with a View to Bringing Women into Industry. PAC, RG 27, Vol. 605, File No. 6-24-1, Vol. 1.
7. Emphasis mine. "Wartime History of Employment of Women . . . ," p. 15.

8. Government Notice, September 8, 1942, Registration of Women, Department of Labour/NSS, PAC, RG 27, Vol. 605, File No. 6-24-1, Vol. 1. By Order-in-Council P.C. 1955 (March 13, 1942), every employer subject to the Unemployment Insurance Act (August 7, 1940) was required to register all employees on Unemployment Insurance Commission forms. "History of the National Employment Service 1939-1945," p. 6.

9. "Wartime History of Employment of Women . . . ," p. 16.

10. "Listing of Women Starts September 14, Says Mrs. Eaton," *Globe and Mail,* August 21, 1942, p. 12; "Mrs. Rex Eaton Announces Registration of Canadian Women," PAC, RG 27, Vol. 605, File No. 6-24-1, vol. 1.

11. *Ibid.*

12. A. Chapman, "Female Labour Supply Situation," December 12, 1942, PAC, RG 27, Vol. 605, File No. 6-24-1, vol. 1.

13. *Ibid.*

14. General Report on National Selective Service – Employment of Women, November 1, 1943, PAC, RG 27, Vol. 605, File No. 6-24-1, vol. 2.

15. See above, note 12.

16. See above, note 14.

17. "Wartime History of Employment of Women . . . ," p. 8.

18. See above, note 14.

19. A. Chapman's phraseology.

20. Letter of May 18, 1943, from Mary Eadie, Supervisor, Women's Division, Employment & Selective Service Office, Toronto, to Mrs. Norman C. Stephens, President, Local Council of Women, Toronto. PAC, RG 27, Vol. 605, File No. 6-24-1, vol. 1.

21. See above, note 14.

22. "Wartime History of Employment of women . . . ," p. 20.

23. Memo of May 7, 1943, from Mary Eadie to Mr. B. G. Sullivan, Ontario NSS Regional Superintendent. PAC, RG 27, Vol. 605, File No. 6-24-1, vol. 1.

24. "Wartime History of Employment of Women . . . ," p. 20.

25. Report on Recruitment of Part-Time Workers – Toronto, by Mrs. Rex Eaton to the NSS Advisory Board, July 28, 1943. PAC, RG 27, Vol. 605, File. No. 6-24-1, vol. 1.

26. Letter of May 22, 1943, from Mary Eadie to Mrs. Rex Eaton, PAC, RG 27, Vol. 605, File No. 6-24-1, vol. 1.

27. The National Council of Women of Canada is a federation of women's organizations, organized nationally, provincially and locally. For its early history, see Veronica Strong-Boag, *The Parliament of Women: The National Council of Women of Canada, 1893-1929* (Ottawa: The National Museum of Man/History Division, 1976).

28. See above, note 25.

29. "Wartime History of Employment of Women . . . ," p. 22.

30. See above, note 25.
31. NSS Circular No. 270-1, August 18, 1943, Employment of Women – Campaign for Part-time Women Workers. PAC, RG 27, Vol. 605, File No. 6-24-1, vol. 2.
32. Draft letter of August 31, 1943, signed by Mr. A. MacNamara and Mrs. Rex Eaton, to be sent to Local Councils of Women. PAC, RG 27, Vol. 605, File No. 6-24-1, vol. 2.
33. "Wartime History of Employment of Women . . . ," p. 23.
34. See above, note 32.
35. "Wartime History of Employment of Women . . . ," p. 24.
36. Mrs. Rex Eaton's Report to the NSS Advisory Board on Recruitment of Women for Work in War Industries, July 28, 1943. PAC, RG 27, Vol. 605, File No. 6-24-1, vol. 1.
37. Letter of August 16, 1943, from B. G. Sullivan to Mrs. Rex Eaton. PAC, RG 27, Vol. 605, File No. 6-24-1, vol. 2.
38. Minutes of July 26, 1943, Toronto, meeting of NSS with local Employers about the Campaign of War Plants. PAC, RG 27, Vol. 605, File No. 6-24-1, vol. 1.
39. Letter of September 1, 1943, from Mrs. Rex. Eaton to Mr. A. MacNamara, with copy to Humphrey Mitchell. PAC, RG 27, Vol. 605, File No. 6-24-1, vol. 2.
40. Memo. of September 22, 1943, from Mrs. Rex Eaton to Mr. A. MacNamara, PAC, RG 27, Vol. 605, File No. 6-24-1, vol. 2.
41. Letter of October 13, 1943, from Mrs. Eaton to Mme. Florence F. Martel, NSS Montreal, PAC, RG 27, Vol. 605, File No. 6-24-1, vol. 2; "Wartime History of Employment of Women . . . ," p. 23.
42. Minutes of Employers' Committee Meeting held on November 2, 1943, in Mr. Léonard Préfontaine's office, re Recruiting Campaign for Women War Workers. PAC, RG 27, Vol. 1508, File No. 40-5-1.
43. Letter of December 2, 1943, from V. C. Phelan, Director of Information, Department of Labour, to Mr. MacNamara. PAC, RG 27, Vol. 615, File No. 17-5-11, vol. 1.
44. "Wartime History of Employment of Women . . . ," p. 25.
45. Memo. of May 8, 1944, from Mrs. Rex Eaton to Mr. A. MacNamara. PAC, RG 27, Vol. 605, File No. 6-24-1, vol. 3.
46. "Wartime History of Employment of Women . . . ," p. 25.
47. Letter of August 8, 1944, from Gordon Anderson, Public Relations Officer, Department of Labour, to Mr. A. MacNamara. PAC, RG 27, Vol. 615, File No. 17-5-11, vol. 1.
48. "Wartime History of Employment of Women . . . ," p. 26.
49. *Ibid.*
50. NSS Report on Wartime Employment of Women in Canadian Agriculture, August 17, 1944. PAC, RG 27, Vol. 985, File No. 7.
51. See above, note 14.
52. "Wartime History of Employment of Women . . . ," p. 8.
53. "Comments re Wartime Programme," p. 5, Preface to "Wartime History of Employment of Women . . . "

54. See above, note 50.
55. See above, note 32.
56. See above, note 31.
57. December 1943 Design for Full-Page Newspaper Ad. to Recruit Women for War industry. PAC, RG 27, Vol. 615, File No. 17-5-11, vol. 1.
58. Memo of May 9, 1944, from Mrs. Rex Eaton to Mr. A. MacNamara, with Suggested Draft Circular re Tightening of NSS Regulations for Women. PAC, RG 27, Vol. 605, File No. 6-24-1, vol. 3.
59. Moffats "Help Wanted" Campaign Breaking July 20, 1944. PAC, RG 27, Vol. 615, File No. 17-5-11, vol. 1.
60. Memo, of March 5, 1943, from Renée Morin, NSS Montreal, to Mrs. Rex Eaton. PAC, RG 27, Vol. 605, File No. 6-24-1, vol. 1.
61. Letter of April 8, 1943, from B.G. Sullivan to Mrs. Rex Eaton. PAC, RG 27, Vol. 605, File No. 6-24-1, vol. 1. Unfortunately Sullivan's report of the questionnaire results does not give the number of women questioned.
62. Memo of May 11, 1943, from Percy A. Robert, Montreal, to Mrs. Rex Eaton and Mr. Goulet. PAC, RG 27, Vol. 605, File No. 6-24-1, vol. 1.
63. See above, note 57.
64. PAC, RG 27, Vol. 615, File No. 17-5-11, vol. 1.
65. Memorandum from J. L. Ilsley, Minister of Finance, "The Income Tax Change Applying to Married Employees in 1947," n.d. PAC, RG 27, Vol. 66, File No. 6-24-11.
66. Letter of November 7, 1946, from A. MacNamara to Mr. Fraser Elliott, Deputy Minister of National Revenue. PAC, RG 27. Vol. 606, File No. 6-24-11.
67. "Income Tax Change Benefits Employed Married Women/Aims to Keep Wives from Quitting Posts," *Globe and Mail*, July 16, 1942, p. 1.
68. Explanation received from the Minister of Finance by Douglas Hallam, Secretary of the Primary Textiles Institute, Toronto, and conveyed in his letter of November 4, 1946, to Humphrey Mitchell and in his letter of November 13, 1946, to A. MacNamara. PAC, RG 27, Vol. 606, File No. 6-24-11.
69. Minutes of the January 24, 1947, Meeting of the Vernon Local Employment Committee, a copy of which was sent to officials in the Departments of Labour and National Revenue. PAC, RG 27, Vol. 606, File No. 6-24-11.
70. J. R. Moodie Company, Hamilton. Information conveyed in memo. of April 17, 1947, from Margaret McIrvine, Acting Regional Employment Adviser, U.I.C., Toronto, to B. G. Sullivan. PAC, RG 27, Vol. 606, File No. 6-24-11.
71. Memo. of December 31, 1946, from George G. Greene, Private Secretary to the Minister of Labour, to A. MacNamara. PAC, RG 27, Vol. 606, File No. 6-24-11.

72. Memo. of January 30, 1947, from W. L. Forrester, Manager, Local Employment Office, Prince George, B.C., to William Horrobin, Pacific Regional Employment Officer. PAC, RG 27, Vol. 606, File No. 6-24-11.

73. School Board of Charlotte County, New Brunswick. Information communicated in a telegram of November 7, 1946, from A. N. McLean, Saint John, New Brunswick, to A. MacNamara. PAC, RG 27, Vol. 606, File No. 6-24-11.

74. T. Eaton Company, Ltd., Toronto, reported that 453 married women had left their employ since January 1, 1947. Information in a letter of April 26, 1947, from G. W. Ritchie, Chairman, Ontario Regional Advisory Board (Department of Labour), to A. MacNamara, PAC, RG 27, Vol. 606, File No. 6-24-11.

75. Letter of February 12, 1947, from A. MacNamara to F. Smelts, Chairman, Pacific Regional Advisory Board (Department of Labour). PAC, RG 27, Vol. 606, File No. 6-24-11.

76. Letter of November 13, 1946, from Douglas Hallam to A. MacNamara. PAC, RG 27, Vol. 606, File No. 6-24-11.

77. See above, note 65.

78. See above, note 6.

79. Memo. of June 13, 1942, from Mrs. Rex Eaton to Mr. George Greene. PAC, RG 27, Vol. 609, File No. 6-52-1, vol. 1.

80. Report on Day Care of Children, July 1, 1943, no authorship specified. PAC RG 27, Vol. 609, File No. 6-52-1, vol. 1

81. See above, note 79.

82. "Need for Day Nurseries," Editorial, *Globe and Mail,* July 16, 1942, p. 6.

83. See above, note 79.

84. Letter of April 30, 1942, from E. M. Little, NSS Director, to G. S. Tattle, Deputy Minister, Department of Public Welfare, Ontario. PAC, RG 27, Vol. 611, File No. 6-52-1, vol. 1.

85. Letter of May 14, 1942, from Fraudena Eaton to E. M. Little. PAC, RG 27, Vol. 609, File No. 6-52-1, vol. 1.

86. Letter of April 28, 1942, from George F. Davidson, Executive Director, The Canadian Welfare Council, to Mr. E. M. Little. PAC, RG 27, Vol. 609, File No. 6-52-1, vol. 1.

87. Memo. of April 30, 1942, to E. M. Little, and R. F. Thompson, Supervisor of Training, Department of Labour, subject: Conference with Dr. W. E. Blatz, Director of the Institute of Child Study of the University of Toronto. PAC, RG 27, Vol. 609, File No. 6-52-1, vol. 1.

88. See Above, note 80.

89. *Ibid.*

90. Memo. of November 10, 1943, from Mrs. Rex Eaton to Mr. V. C. Phelan. PAC, RG 27, Vol. 609, File No. 6-52-1, vol. 1.

91. Letter of April 27, 1944, from Mrs. E. C. (Marjorie) Pardee, NSS Representative on the Albertan Provincial Advisory Committee

on Day Nurseries, to Mrs. Rex Eaton. PAC, RG 27, Vol. 611, File No. 6-52-9.

92. PAC, RG 27, Vol. 611, File No. 6-52-9.
93. Memo. of May 27, 1943, from Mrs. Rex Eaton to Mr. George Greene. PAC, RG 27, Vol. 609, File No. 6-52-1, vol. 1.
94. Memo. of February 8, 1943, from Mrs. Rex Eaton to Mr. A. MacNamara, PAC, RG 27, Vol. 609, File No. 6-52-1, vol. 1.
95. Letter of March 17, 1943, from Mr. Grier to H. F. Caloren, Assistant Director of Administrative Services, Department of Labour. PAC, RG 27, Vol. 609, File No. 6-52-1, vol. 1.
96. Memo. of February 8, 1943, from Mrs. Rex Eaton to Mr. A. MacNamara, PAC, RG 27, Vol. 609, File No. 6-52-1, vol. 1; "Wartime History of . . . Day Care of Children," p. 3
97. Memo. of June 16, 1943, from Mrs. Eaton to Mr. Eric Strangroom, in response to request for information on Day Nurseries for the Minister of Labour, PAC, RG 27, Vol. 609, File No. 6-52-1, vol. 1; NSS Circular No. 291, October 15, 1943, on Women Workers – Day Care of Children, PAC, RG 27, Vol. 610, File No. 6-52-2, vol. 2.
98. Memo. of March 4, 1943, from Mrs. Rex Eaton to Mr. A. MacNamara. PAC, RG 27, Vol. 610, File No. 6-52-2, vol. 1.
99. July 1943 Monthly Summary of Dominion-Provincial Wartime Day Nurseries, Ontario. PAC, RG 27, Vol. 611, File No. 6-52-1, vol. 1.
100. September 1943 Monthly Summary of Dominion-Provincial Wartime Day Nurseries, Ontario. PAC, RG 27, Vol. 611, File No. 6-52-1, vol. 1.
101. Memo. of November 10, 1944, from Mrs. Rex Eaton to Mr. V. C. Phelan. PAC, RG 27, Vol. 609, File No. 6-52-1, vol. 1.
102. Survey of the Dominion-Provincial Wartime Day Nursery Programme in Ontario, submitted October 29, 1945, to Mr. B. Beaumont, Director of Child Welfare, Dept. of Public Welfare, Ontario, by Miss Dorothy A. Millichamp, Organizing Secretary, Wartime Day Nurseries, Dept. of Public Welfare, Ont. PAC, RG 27, Vol. 611, File No. 6-52-1, vol. 3.
103. Report of the Quebec Ministry of Health on the Dominion-Provincial Wartime Day Nurseries, November 15, 1946. PAC, RG 27, Vol. 611, File No. 6-52-2, vol. 2.
104. Memo. of July 7, 1945, from M. Grier to Miss Norris. PAC, RG 27, Vol. 609, File No. 6-52-1, vol. 2.
105. See above, note 84.
106. Memo of May 22, 1942, on Proposals for Day Nurseries for Mothers Working in War Industry, for file in Deputy Minister's Office, Department of Labour. PAC, RG 27, Vol. 609, File No. 6-52-1, vol. 1.
107. See above, note 79.
108. "Wartime History of . . . Day care of Children," Appendix, Part 2.
109. NSS Circular No. 291, October 15, 1943, on Women Workers – Day

Care of Children.

110. See above, note 80.

111. PAC, RG 27, Vol. 610, File No. 6-52-2, vol. 1.

112. Minutes of the Conference on the Day Care of Children, June 10, 1943, Ottawa. PAC, RG 27, Vol. 609, File No. 6-52-1, vol. 1.

113. Memo of May 19, 1943, from Mrs. Eaton to Mr. A. MacNamara. PAC, RG 27, Vol. 610, File No. 6-52-2, vol. 1, and RG 27, Vol. 1508, File No. 40-5-6.

114. "An Inequitable Division," Editorial, *Globe and Mail*, October 28, 1943, p. 6.

115. Memo. of December 1, 1943, from Mrs. Rex Eaton to Mr. A. Mac-Namara. PAC, RG 27, Vol. 10, File No. 6-52-2, vol. 3.

116. Order-in-Council P.C. 2503, April 6, 1944, PAC, RG 27, Vol. 610, File No. 6-52-2, vol. 4; Order-in-Council P.C. 3733, May 18, 1944, PAC, RG 27, Vol. 610, File No. 6-52-2, vol. 5.

117. PAC, RG 27, Vol. 609, File No. 6-52-1, vol. 2.

118. Memo. of August 30, 1945, from W. S. Boyd to Mrs. Rex Eaton. PAC, RG 27, Vol. 609, File No. 6-52-1, vol. 2.

119. PAC, RG 27, Vol. 609, File No. 6-52-1, vol. 2.

120. Letter of September 20, 1945, from Miss Gwyneth Howell, Assistant Executive Director, Montreal Council of Social Agencies, to M. Grier. PAC, RG 27, Vol. 611, File No. 6-52-2, vol. 2.

121. Letter of October 3, 1945, from Renée Morin to Miss M. Grier. PAC, RG 27, Vol. 611, File No. 6-52-2, vol. 2.

122. PAC, RG 27, Vol. 609, File No. 6-52-1, vol. 2.

123. Memo. of September 11, 1945, from Mrs. Rex Eaton to Mr. A. MacNamara. PAC, RG 27, Vol. 609, File No. 6-52-1, vol. 2.

124. Letter of October 22, 1945, from B. W. Heise, Deputy Minister, Department of Public Welfare, Ontario, to Mrs. Rex Eaton; letter of October 29, 1945, from A. MacNamara to Mr. B. W. Heise, PAC, RG 27, Vol. 609, File No. 6-52-1, vol. 2.

125. Memo of November 8, 1945, from Mrs. Rex Eaton to Mr. A. Mac-Namara. PAC, RG 27, Vol. 609, File No. 6-52-1, vol. 2.

126. *Ibid.*

127. Memo. of November 9, 1945, from A. MacNamara to Mrs. Rex Eaton. PAC, RG 27, Vol. 609, File No. 6-52-1, vol. 2.

128. Letter of November 22, 1945, from A. MacNamara to Mr. B. W. Heise. PAC, RG 27, Vol. 609, File No. 6-52-1, vol. 2.

129. Memo. of February 15, 1946, from M. Grier to Mr. A. MacNamara. PAC, RG 27, Vol. 609, File No. 6-52-1, vol. 2.

130. Letter of February 18, 1946, from Fraudena Eaton, Vancouver, to Mr. A. MacNamara. PAC, RG 27, Vol. 609, File No. 6-52-1, vol. 2.

131. Emphasis mine. Letter of February 26, 1946, from H. Mitchell to W. A. Goodfellow. PAC, RG 27, Vol. 609, File No. 6-52-1, vol. 2.

132. Letter of March 7, 1946, from W. A. Goodfellow to H. Mitchell. PAC, RG 27, Vol. 609, File No. 6-52-1, vol. 2.

133. Letter of April 2, 1946, from H. Mitchell to W. A. Goodfellow. PAC,

   RG 27, Vol. 609, File No. 6-52-1, vol. 2.

134. Bill No. 124, An Act respecting Day Nurseries, 1946. PAC, RG 27, Vol. 609, File No. 6-52-1, vol. 2.

135. Letter of May 17, 1946, from W. A. Goodfellow to H. Mitchell. PAC, RG 27, Vol. 611, File No. 6-52-1, vol. 3.

136 Letter of June 7, 1946, from Brooke Claxton to H. Mitchell. PAC, RG 27, Vol. 611, File No. 6-52-1, vol. 3.

137. Letter of June 13, 1946, from H. Mitchell to W. A. Goodfellow. PAC, RG 27, Vol. 611, File No. 6-52-1, vol. 3.

138. Memo. of November 28, 1946, from J. C. McK. to Mr. MacNamara. PAC, RG 27, Vol. 611, File No. 6-52-1, vol. 4.

139. See above, note 80.

140. Letter of April 4, 1946, from Mrs. Rex Eaton to Miss Grier. PAC, RG 27, Vol. 609, File No. 6-52-1, vol. 2.

141. Marie T. Wadden, "Newspaper Response to Female War Employment: *The Globe and Mail* and *Le Devoir* May-October 1942," History Honours Dissertation, Memorial University of Newfoundland, May 1976.

142. "Wartime History of Employment of Women . . . ," pp. 80-81. In February 1944, Mrs. Eaton estimated the number of women in the labour force at approximately 600,000 in 1939, rising to 1,200,000 by early 1944. Letter of February 2, 1944, from Mrs. Rex Eaton to Mrs. J. E. M. Bruce, Convenor, Trades and Professions Committee, Local Council of Women, Victoria, B.C. PAC, RG 27, Vol. 605, File No. 6-24-1, vol. 3.